PENG

ARKA

THE GOD BETWEEN

Born and educated in London, Freda Edis now lives in Glasgow. She trained as a teacher and completed her M.Sc. in Politics and Sociology at London University. She has worked as a lecturer and student counsellor in mainstream education and took further training in pastoral counselling and astrology. Currently she is a therapist and astrologer in private practice.

As well as organizing seminars and workshops in Glasgow, she teaches for the Faculty of Astrological Studies and continues to write and lecture.

CONTEMPORARY ASTROLOGY
Series Editor: Erin Sullivan

The God Between

A STUDY OF ASTROLOGICAL MERCURY

FREDA EDIS

ARKANA
PENGUIN BOOKS

ARKANA

Published by the Penguin Group
Penguin Books Ltd, 27 Wrights Lane, London w8 5TZ, England
Penguin Books USA Inc., 375 Hudson Street, New York, New York 10014, USA
Penguin Books Australia Ltd, Ringwood, Victoria, Australia
Penguin Books Canada Ltd, 10 Alcorn Avenue, Toronto, Ontario, Canada M4V 3B2
Penguin Books (NZ) Ltd, 182–190 Wairau Road, Auckland 10, New Zealand

Penguin Books Ltd, Registered Offices: Harmondsworth, Middlesex, England

First published 1995
1 3 5 7 9 10 8 6 4 2

Copyright © Freda Edis, 1995
All rights reserved

The moral right of the author has been asserted

Set in 10.5/12 pt Monophoto Bembo
Typeset by Datix International Limited, Bungay, Suffolk
Printed in England by Clays Ltd, St Ives plc

Except in the United States of America, this book is sold subject
to the condition that it shall not, by way of trade or otherwise, be lent,
re-sold, hired out, or otherwise circulated without the publisher's
prior consent in any form of binding or cover other than that in
which it is published and without a similar condition including this
condition being imposed on the subsequent purchaser

CONTENTS

ACKNOWLEDGEMENTS

My thanks to Anne Whitaker for her friendship and faith in me through the process of producing this book, and for her comments after reading the first draft of the manuscript; to Devam Hendry for her sound advice and many shared experiences.

Tom Schuller and Sheila Davey deserve a special mention for their friendship and support over many years, and, especially, when I moved away from a 'normal' career into the astrological one which provided the ideas for this book.

My thanks, too, to Warren Kenton for his advice and help, and for knowing where I needed to go before I did; to Steve Eddy, Robin Waterfield and Erin Sullivan, who all played a part in getting the text ready for publication.

The Spirit in the Bottle

Once there was a poor woodcutter who had an only son. He wished to send the boy to school, but he only had a small amount of money, so he said to his son, 'When you go to school, make sure that the money I give you lasts you until your studies are finished.'

The boy promised to do so and set off on foot to the town where the school was. He soon realized that however he scrimped and saved the money would not last until the end of his studies. By the time the examinations came, he had used up all his resources and had to return home, very disappointed, to help his father cut wood in the forest.

One day, while he was working in the forest, he stopped for a break at midday, for the sun was very hot. He put his axe over his shoulder and walked, looking for a shady tree beneath which he could rest. Soon he came to a huge oak tree whose branches spread out on all sides and which had a large trunk against which he could prop his back.

He sat down and took out his lunch packet, but before he could unwrap it and eat, he heard a small voice calling:

'Let me out, let me out!'

He looked around, but could see nobody, so he began to unwrap the packet.

'Let me out, let me out!'

This time he looked round and saw that the voice seemed to come from under the ground beside him. He started to dig among the roots of the tree and, as he dug, he uncovered a small glass bottle which had been well stoppered and sealed. Again, he heard the small cry:

'Let me out, let me out!'

Without thinking, he opened the bottle. Immediately, a small spirit flew out and, in the twinkling of an eye, grew and grew until he was half the size of the oak tree. The boy watched, his eyes growing wider and wider with amazement. The spirit loomed over him and cried out in a huge voice, 'Are you the one who freed me?'

The boy nodded.

'I am a great and mighty spirit and now you will have your reward,' the spirit boomed. 'I have been punished and will now have the revenge I promised. I shall kill the person who set me free.'

The boy became very afraid, but, thinking quickly, he said, 'But you're such a huge spirit. How could you fit into this small bottle?'

'I can easily show you how,' said the spirit, boastfully, and, making himself very small, he vanished back into the bottle.

The boy quickly pushed in the stopper and sealed the top. When the spirit realized he was trapped for the second time, he howled and raged but the boy would not free him. Then he cowered in a corner of the bottle and wept, but still the boy would not free him.

At last the spirit became quiet. He looked at the boy and said, 'If you free me, I will reward you richly.'

'I will not do that until you promise not to harm me or anyone else,' said the boy.

'Yes, yes, I promise!' replied the spirit and he gave the boy a small piece of cloth, saying, 'If you put this cloth over a wound it will heal it straight away. If you rub iron or steel with it the metal will turn to silver.'

Then he flew away as quickly as his wings would bear him.

The boy rubbed the piece of cloth over the head of his axe and, immediately, it turned into silver. He ran home to show his father and excitedly told him what had happened.

'Well, well,' said his father, 'perhaps we can turn this axe into money so that you can go to school again.'

They went into town and sold the axe to a rich merchant for a large sum of money. Soon the boy and his father were free of the poverty which had so beset them. While his father remained at home, he returned to school, completed his studies, and, later, thanks to his piece of cloth, became a rich and famous doctor.

After the Grimm Brothers

INTRODUCTION

When I first decided to write this book not much time or
writing space had been given to Mercury's place in psychological
astrology. Saturn and the transpersonal planets, Uranus, Neptune
and Pluto, were the ones regarded as having greater application
to depth psychology, while the personal planets were relatively
neglected for the purposes of special study. Some advances
have been made since then. Christine Valentine and Liz Greene
and Howard Sasportas have redressed the balance somewhat,
though there is still a need for a special study of Mercury. All
astrologers, as a matter of course, attempt to bring into synthesis the effects of all the planets, Mercury among them, as they
appear in the birthchart. Astrological textbooks, particularly
psychological ones, are beginning to reflect this because the
personal planets have as much correspondence with psychological development as do the outer planets and were, up until the
eighteenth century, the only ones available for the astrologer's
art of interpretation. We cannot assume that because, traditionally, the personal planets were only used for the interpretation
of life events they are now in some way deficient in providing us
with material with which to work at a deeper psychological
level.

Very often Mercury is not chosen for in-depth study and is
treated as a lightweight planet which overemphasizes the development of intelligence and intellectual abilities. The attributes of
the planet and the god are sometimes seen as tricky, cunning,
glib, superficial and facile – in other words, fairly childish. All of
this can be true, but only if the nature of the mature Mercury is
disregarded. The medieval alchemists and, later, Carl Jung had
some awareness of what this more hidden side of Mercury might
be; the mercurial child, the *puer*, had within him the seeds of the
alchemical *senex*, the wise old man. The essence of alchemy was

the transformation of a base substance into a rarefied and perfected one, using Mercury as a medium for change.

There is still much debate about whether the alchemical
transmutation was material, spiritual or psychological, but while
there is no doubt that some alchemists looked for a material
change, Carl Jung was more interested in seeing how the symbolism of alchemy corresponded to psychological development.
Alchemists themselves recognized that, as the work progressed,
some changes of a moral and perhaps spiritual nature also took
place within the people performing it. This indicated how much
the sphere of the material and the sphere of the unconscious
were intertwined, if not always fully understood, in medieval
times. Most alchemical writing noted both the quicksilver speed
at which the alchemical transformation took place and the
enormous length of time it took to complete the many stages of
the work. Symbolically, Mercury was the affective agent in this
process, changing the substance, changing the alchemist and
changing himself. Alchemists worked by correspondence and
noted that some of these transmutations bore a resemblance to
the characteristics of the god and planet. Many times they
invoked him in his transpersonal form of Hermes Trismegistos
to guard and guide the Great Work. Mercury as synthesizer,
spiritual guide and wonder-worker was central to any alchemical
development, as was the study of astrology itself.

In his alchemical form, Mercury shows a depth of awareness
of substances which are broken down and reformed, but his part
in this process needs to be more clearly defined in modern
astrological interpretation. Certainly he is not usually regarded as
a major agent of inner psychological change or of how these
changes are reflected in the external world. This is partly Mercury's fault: sometimes he is more content to gloss over quicker-
than-thought transformations than he is to explain carefully
what procedures are taking place; sometimes he himself may not
be certain just how those changes occur; occasionally he is
content to rest on his magical laurels and enjoy the adulation of
people who admire such wizardry.

Such attitudes may seem facile and childlike, if not childish, in
today's world. They were, though, acceptable to alchemists who

needed to clothe their work in obscure symbolism, perhaps because it was the only language of explanation, perhaps in order to protect the work, but also to cover up, in some cases, their own lack of understanding. Astrologers, and particularly psychological astrologers, do not accept such obscurantism today: the inability to understand the symbolism of alchemical and transpersonal Mercury would affect the quality of their work. For this reason, the superficially versatile and sometimes slippery Mercury needs to be encouraged to reveal his deeper and transformative secrets and grow up, however painfully.

As the maturity of Mercury in his aspect of soul-guide, transformer and internal miracle-worker needs now to be given greater attention in psychological astrology, so too does the power of his intellect. In our culture, rational thought is often overstressed, and therapists and astrologers often find themselves having to redress the balance between the rational and the irrational in ways that side-step the powers of the mind. Although the mind is worshipped most powerfully in patriarchal cultures, the intellect cannot remain neglected in psychological studies.

It is one of the central functions, according to Jungian theory, through which man makes sense of his world, and Mercury is the prime zodiacal carrier of the intellect, ruling as it does both Gemini and Virgo and the third and sixth houses in the natural zodiac. The alchemists themselves knew this, bringing their own intelligences to bear on work with the *prima materia*, the base material which was being acted upon. As with alchemical transmutation, psychological development is sometimes a painful process and Mercury too easily and airily uses his ability to rationalize and hide the pain of his inner wounds from himself and others. Quite often he has to go through his own transformative, alchemical and sometimes powerful emotional fires before he can reveal the depths of his own feelings and then contain them.

This is the essential struggle for astrological and alchemical Mercury: the growth process which leads to greater maturity, where intellect is consciously used in combination with deep feeling values. He is often designated in esoteric literature as the lower octave of Uranus and busy with the way in which intelligence works in the everyday world. But there is, as we shall see, enough substance in Mercury as diviner and magician, as alchemical worker and worked-upon, to indicate that he has much to offer in explorations of the personal and collective unconscious. To do so we need to inquire into his history, his myths and his development in some depth, and, in some cases, his pathology. Then, in addition to his childlike traits, his mature and transpersonal characteristics, as revealed in natal charts, may become more easily available for astrological interpretation.[1]

PART ONE

MERCURY: HISTORY, PSYCHOLOGY AND MYTHOLOGY

I

The Growth of a God

Mercury is a many-faceted god. His myths show us the complexity of his character and development from the deceitful child at odds with reality, but clever enough to manipulate it to his own advantage, to the wise old magus transformed by the power of experience and the pain of life and death. But the myths are from different cultures and different points of historical development and give us no consecutive picture of Mercury's growth in divine, let alone human terms. Many of his myths are fragmentary, but luckily for us are open to psychological as well as historical and cultural interpretation. As astrologers interested in the development of the psyche and the relevance of myth to inner growth, we are able to translate, as fully as we can, the god's experiences into a form which has close analogies with man's knowledge of his own existence and his own personal history. That way, hopefully, we can discuss with our clients material which indicates the close relationship between the human and the divine, the conscious and the unconscious, so that they may make more aware choices about the directions their lives can take.

We are in a position, also, to see more clearly how the function of Mercury enables people both to evade and to work on their own conflicts and pain. Here, too, our clients may receive fresh insights into the ways in which their own lives work. In addition, once the god's glibness has been transformed by the alchemical fire into a wise thoughtfulness based on a real understanding of his experiences and his path through life, an awareness of his ability to access the transpersonal dimensions of the psyche through the vehicles of speech, thought and learning can help us to help our clients further. The degree of the maturity of Mercury in our own charts is, perhaps, another aid in the process of allowing clients to move towards self-development. Before this can happen, however, we may require an understanding of how the god grows up, grows oland grows wiser.

DEVELOPMENTAL PSYCHOLOGY

We need, first of all, to see how contemporary astrologers interpret Mercury. They not only use the planet to show how the intellect and intelligence may develop; they are also interested in how both may be communicated. With mercurial activity in its pure form, this usually takes place verbally or just by thinking, but it can also happen through the written word, by teaching or lecturing, giving and receiving information, making connections of all kinds at a mental level. Astrologers are able, using their own mercurial and feeling processes, to interpret how a person thinks and communicates by studying where Mercury is active in a chart by aspect, sign and house. Quite often, though, people with an underdeveloped Mercury can be concerned with disseminating superficial factual knowledge and with compartmentalizing ideas, holding seemingly unopposable opinions and refusing to be influenced by human values and emotions because these are too subjective to be tested against external reality. So, for example, a person with Mercury in Capricorn square Saturn in Aries could, on some occasions, immovably opinionated, and, on others, silent when he should be speaking.

Such underdeveloped facets of the mercurial character pose a problem for psychological or counselling astrologers. People showing Mercury's more undeveloped characteristics may have difficulty in connecting with the hidden parts of their personalities. Even though astrologers know that astrological Mercury has the ability to make connections, to transport unconscious contents to the conscious mind, to bring about conscious awareness, it is often difficult for some clients to realize the importance of this process, or that they themselves can develop this potential. Approaching the difficulty in Mercury's own way, verbally and rationally, is not always the best way to do it. Sometimes, developing the courage to go through and endure life's more painful events, hopefully with some kind of understanding companionship, or counselling support where necessary, is the only way people discover the strength of their instincts, emotions and values. An insightful counselling astrologer can offer a range of non-verbal techniques, including dreamwork, active imagination, artwork and psychodrama, which may help a client over the threshold into new areas of personal knowledge and growth.

All of this presupposes a person's ability and willingness to learn new skills, to develop a flexible mind and to face the pain of growth, so astrologers look to Mercury to see where early learning experiences, both at home and at school, have been influential. How a child learns in its early years is likely to affect its future potential for learning. The child psychologist Jean Piaget indicates that growing conscious awareness increases with developing verbal skills and the manipulation of language. From early babyhood, the object-relations psychologists would say, among them Winnicott and Bowlby, a child becomes aware of the feeling tone of its surroundings and the people with whom it is most closely connected, primarily with the mother. Even at this early stage the child can pick up whether or not the world is a safe place to grow up in.

If the early environment is safe and the mother can allow a child growth at the essential developmental stages, then all is well. Where the environment is too safe and the child's growth is constricted due to maternal fears, then, according to Erich Neumann, the child finds it difficult to break away from those early bonds and develop as an individual later in life. If the early world is very unsafe, the child eventually develops various strategies to cope with it, among them lying, evasion, denial and repression. Psychological astrologers are aware that their clients can unconsciously and amorally use these negative characteristics of Mercury as ways of survival in a hostile world.

A child who has developed these traits has had the capacity to learn them; the same capacity may be tapped to help with the development of more positive mercurial qualities, and to make a conscious choice between traits to be encouraged and those to be managed, even if this doesn't take place until later in life. Where learning has been one-sided, sooner or later events will seemingly conspire to impel or compel people to redress the balance, or to

take the consequences of life-long resistance by arresting development. Quite often it is that feeling of *stuckness*, the inability to
rationalize their way out of ever-repeating patterns of behaviour,
which brings people to an astrologer or counsellor. Mercury
doesn't like the feeling of being pinned down and sometimes has
obscure ways, both appropriate and not, of communicating this.

As a child grows and its language skills develop, feelings also
begin to be communicated verbally. If there is no difference
between the mother's feelings, the way she communicates them
and the language she uses to express them, the child has a good
chance of growing up to trust his or her own feelings and
express them effectively. But this is a statement of perfection; no
parent is perfect and, at best, a parent can only be *good enough*,
according to Bruno Bettelheim, so all children react imperfectly,
in greater or lesser degrees, to imperfect parents. The quality of
communication between mother and baby, or the baby's interaction with other significant adults, provides the first learning
experience in life.

Astrologers are aware that Mercury's aspects to the Moon and
Venus can give indications of the quality of the communication
between mother and child. Similarly, the planet's aspects to the
Sun, Mars and Saturn tell us much about how a child experiences
and understands its father. The degree of success of the bond
between parents and child will reveal much about how the child
later reacts to the pressures of adult life, for good or ill. These
predispositions, whether they are learned or innate, conscious or
form part of the personal unconscious, or derive from the more
archaic collective unconscious, are further reinforced by other
childhood experiences.

The most significant early learning experiences take place in
the home, so, after the parents, relationships with brothers and
sisters and all communications with them are important for
future social development. Astrologers know that Mercury and
the third house show what interactions are likely to take place
between siblings, but it is less well known that these relationships
affect the way in which a child later makes initial approaches to
friends and peer groups.

Unlike the parent/child relationship, which, early on, is nearly always associated with dominance and authority, sibling interactions are among the child's first experiences of competing for survival and attention, and the first for making valued or difficult connections within a peer group. Play activities among siblings help children make concrete some of the lessons of co-operation and conflict they have learned from their parents, and issues of power and dominance within a group are often worked out initially in games between siblings. Mercury's aspects to fifth house planets or its ruler can indicate how the child learns through creative play and what strategies he or she uses for participating in groups or sharing among friends.

The family group is often the child's first experience of the collective as well as of individual relationships. Feelings about the safety or not of the collective at this level are soon reinforced with interactions with the extended family and with the world of early schooling. By this time, bearing in mind the tendency towards nuclear family formations in the West, a child needs to expand his consciousness and intellect by being exposed to other people, both adults and peers, who can provide a range of knowledge which is not available in the parental home.

One of Mercury's characteristics, well known to astrologers, is a feeling of curiosity which can draw a child into exploring new experiences without threatening him or inhibiting him from doing so. Planets in Gemini or Gemini's house position often show the way in which a child will approach new situations. Mercury can be naive as well as curious, and further scrutiny of the planet's relationships with Gemini planets and houses can indicate how a child might experience initially the collective and learning aspects of school. Fears of the great *They*, the world outside the safe and known world of home, are more likely to be revealed by Mercury's placement by house and sign and its aspects to Saturn and the outer planets, sometimes, also, in aspects it makes to planets in the eleventh and twelfth houses. Where there are fears, there are also the possibilities for co-operation and the positive aspects of the same placements and aspects may need to be encouraged by the psychological astrologer.

Early schooling in the West particularly has the disadvantage of splitting up the curriculum into different areas of study. In the main, subject differentiation is continued through secondary schooling and higher education and the prime accent is on intellectual achievement. A technological or vocational education is still not valued as highly. Human interaction and emotional understanding are of lesser importance still in this hierarchy of learning; if they are stressed at all it is usually only where behaviour has gone beyond the norm. While this traditional process may be necessary in order to discover where a child's talents are, it doesn't, for example, help the child to discover the relationship between music and mathematics, or between biology and poetry, or between a knowledge of his emotional self and the world of chemistry.

These kinds of imaginative connections, arrived at through exercising a flexibility of mind and feelings, the child usually discovers for himself randomly, if at all, or, if he or she is lucky, by meeting up with sympathetic teachers or other significant adults. Such discoveries are often made outside curriculum time. If the ability to make these connections is not consciously encouraged, either at home or at school, then the child may later have difficulty breaking away from a rigid, rule-bound existence, or may use underhand means to do so and, in some cases, may come to accept such splits in learning experience as the norm. The danger is that splitting can also affect the development of the psyche where emotions are separated from rational thought, intuition is devalued as womanish and unreliable, and the world of sensation is only for the artisan or the hedonist.

As a result, many therapists and astrologers have come across clients who are fearful of entering new psychological territory and have not developed the skills to combine different talents. Equally often we find that the child has been consciously taught to fit in with rules, usually by pressure and without any understanding of the human values and emotions involved. A powerfully aspected Mercury can often indicate how a child, and the later adult, either fits into or bends those rules. Where the social rules are evaded we may again see the negative characteristics of Mercury – thieving, lying, cheating, superficiality, amorality and glibness – and these can occur whether Mercury is poorly or well aspected.

The psychological astrologer's task is to assess how ready the client is to craft the materials he knows himself to possess, and those he is later able to access from the personal unconscious. He may benefit from developing such qualities and talents by an increase in self-confidence and an expansion of horizons. Greater personal insight, the acquisition of new skills, both concrete and abstract, and the exploration of an integrated system of values and consideration for other people, may help to underpin newly acquired knowledge. The abilities to craft and invent are two attributes of Mercury which the counselling astrologer may be able to encourage in clients who look for some understanding of their problems.

In order to do so, a person requires the capacity to sustain concentration for considerable periods of time. Children learn in short bursts and need a variety of activities to stimulate and interest them. Ideally, over time, they may deepen their interests and lengthen their concentration spans. Some adults, though, can still show signs of lack here, particularly where an undeveloped or childish Mercury occasionally wants to make connections quickly, to understand the task in hand now, immediately, and becomes bored and frustrated by complexities and time-consuming hard work. Patience and application often need to be developed and the role of the counselling astrologer may be to stress the positive side of deepening the thought processes so that the best possible connections are made. Mercury–Saturn links will often help here; so might Mercury's applications to the second, sixth and tenth houses, all of which can help ground the planet's sometimes flightier attributes.

The planet's quicksilver speed connects it with transport, travel and short journeys which are undertaken in the fastest possible time. While, in traditional astrology, this interpretation is taken literally and might have some relevance for those people whose Mercury operates in an unsophisticated way, psychological astrologers today might consider it to be inadequate. Mercury is about making connections between ideas, but the planet also has a part to play in linking thoughts with feeling values. In other words, it might help a person to develop the capacity to become his or her own mediator between conscious and the unconscious processes.

If people with Mercury very active in their charts eventually realize the importance of these last two attributes, then they may come to know that Mercury is as capable of making inner journeys as he is of making outer ones. The myths about the god and his relationship to psychological astrology, to be explored later in the book, show this very clearly. At the same time, they show Mercury at his most alchemical, able to deepen his experiences of life instead of gliding over them superficially. Mercury's aspects to the outer planets are important at this point because the functions of the outer planets, and the hidden houses, the fourth, eighth and twelfth, are more concerned with the less easily accessed parts of our personalities.

The planet's affinity with travelling, however short the journey, indicates that people with this characteristic strong in their birthcharts can make the connection between individual development and the needs of the collective. Again, Mercury's aspects to the outer planets will require investigation; so do any relationships the planet has with the seventh through to the twelfth houses. People whose mercurial qualities are immature often display a lack of awareness and regard for other people's feelings, as well as their own. So, sometimes, our clients can feel bewildered about who is feeling what, or whether they themselves really feel at all. Breaking through the conscious ego-barrier of constant rationality to the often undifferentiated feelings underneath is the first step to becoming sensitive to other people's feeling needs.

Sense has to be made of these raw feelings for personal development, for a recognition of collective requirements and to establish significant partnerships. Mercury is known for his friendliness and curiosity about people, but usually at a light-hearted, uninvolved level. Showing emotional commitment can be difficult for people who are overly rational. Lack of commitment usually means that the depths of the personal unconscious have to be fully plumbed before the inferior emotional function can be integrated. The myths which connect Mercury with Hades and the Underworld, and which show us how Mercury travels between the upper and the lower regions, indicate how mercurial people can begin that integration. Only when there is conscious awareness of the need to travel in this way can people begin a mature relationship with their deeper selves, the needs of the collective and, perhaps, their own transpersonal natures.

MYTHOLOGY AND HISTORY

All of Mercury's astrological attributes, both traditional and psychological, come to us through an interpretation of the myths, mainly those of Greece and Rome, but these may not be enough to explain Mercury's deeper functions. The archaic Mercury, Hermes of Arcadia, was a pastoral divinity, a shepherd, according to Charles Seltman. Fragments concerning his origins which survive indicate that he was a god who made much use of his instincts before he developed his well-known rationality. Astrologically and psychologically, if we are to broaden interpretation from its traditional base, we need to know as much about where Mercury came from as where he went to after the classical period.

The astrology and history of Greece and Rome were influenced by developments in Egypt, Babylonia and the Near East. The Greek myths of Hermes begin with the writings of Hesiod and Homer, *c.* 800 BC, and continue through the period of the conquest of Egypt by Alexander the Great, who died in 323 BC. His city of Alexandria, situated on the Nile Delta, became the seedbed in which the embryonic gnostic, cabbalistic and alchemical philosophies were nurtured. These philosophies, and the myths which developed from them, influenced the development of Hermes, the Greek Mercury, into Hermes Trismegistos, the patron of alchemy, with the help of Thoth, the ancient Egyptian god of truth.

His connections with Thoth, though, may have started long before the Alexandrian period, if Martin Bernal's thesis of 'Black Athena' is a valid one. Bernal indicates that there are earlier cultural links between the Greeks, Egyptians and the Phoenicians than have been accepted by Western scholars in the twentieth century. Robert Graves's explanatory comments in *The Greek Myths* also sound a similar note. If true, it means that Hermes started his cultural travelling and shape-shifting perhaps a millennium before the time when the main body of Greek myths was written. What we have traditionally received of Greek Hermes, then, may be very one-sided, curtailed and Eurocentric.

Even if the early history of Hermes is not clear or well preserved, the Alexandrine philosophies which surrounded the development of Hermes Trismegistos were, though they informed Islamic scholars for centuries before reaching Europe. In the main, these revived ideas reached Europe in the medieval period and had their great flowering during the Renaissance. Psychological astrology, then, may need to take account of the way Renaissance alchemists and philosophers viewed Hermes Trismegistos as a priest-like carrier of hermetic, gnostic and neoplatonic knowledge, though it was often hidden from the uninitiated, which, in this case, meant the uneducated. Medieval European culture did not have mass education on its agenda; ignorance was often a form of social control. This situation was not transformed until the alchemy of the Industrial Revolution was well under way in the nineteenth century. So the development of mass education, when viewed from this perspective, becomes very much an alchemical as well as a mercurial issue.

Though astrology and the hermetic philosophies faded from public consciousness somewhat after the split between rationality and belief in the seventeenth century, Mercury was still operative. His archetypal image may not have been recognized, but his functions were. They underlay the enormous growth in scientific development since Newton's time and the rise of public education systems. The shape of national systems of government, economics and ideologies is disseminated through the use of language and propaganda – all very mercurial. But the hermetic archetype itself went underground and was carried through the institutions of various esoteric and astrological schools of thought, though without much further development. The rise of psychological astrology has given us a new impetus to rediscover the roots of Mercury's archetype and assess its relevance to people's experience today.

In itself, this has been a further stage in the alchemical journey Mercury has made through history. Perhaps we now require more knowledge about the process of alchemical transformation itself, in order to understand how astrological Mercury can grow and develop beyond his sometimes childlike Graeco-Roman characteristics – the ones with which we are too familiar and which can give us a one-sided picture of mercurial qualities in our clients. The psychologically transformative and transpersonal potential of the alchemical process can, as Jung found in depth psychology and if applied to astrology, give us a further insight into the way depth of intellect can be married to true feeling, helping both us and our clients.

Another mythological system which may further our understanding of Mercury is the one which originated in northern Europe, beyond the conquering influence of the Roman Empire. The greater conscious and, in historical terms, élitist part of our collective inheritance derives from Graeco-Roman civilization. Celtic, Norse and Teutonic cultures are also part of our inheritance, though at a less conscious and, perhaps, less valued level. The research undertaken by Ellis Davidson and Turville-Petre into the gods of northern Europe goes some way towards redressing the balance.

The religions of these cultures offered to their people psychological and spiritual support in ways that have analogies with the Greek and Roman experience and are just as valid. Some of the gods of these pantheons show similar characteristics to Mercury and, occasionally, can offer an extension of them. Where they are relevant to a greater understanding of mercurial attributes, I shall use them. If the book is a study of how Mercury can be used to connect the conscious and the unconscious, perhaps he can also be used to help us resurrect some important cultural myths which have sunk, though not without some traces, into our collective unconscious.

We know that Hermes' Roman equivalent, Mercury, was worshipped in Roman Gaul and Britain, brought there by legionaries and merchants after the Roman conquest. A shrine dedicated to Mercury was found at Uley Bury in Gloucestershire. We also know that Mercury had some similarities with the Celtic gods, noted by Caesar and Tacitus. The Celtic Mercury, often identified with Lug or Lugh, the shining god, was a patron of merchants and travellers, according to Caesar. Cernunnos, the horned god, appears by Mercury's side on a stone fountain at Reims dating from the second century AD.

More importantly, Lugh, and so, Mercury, had many of the characteristics of Woden, Odin and Loki, all gods associated with the Teutonic and, later, the Norse cultures which the Romans never conquered. The worship of Woden in the German lands and Odin and Loki in Scandinavia lasted throughout the Dark Ages until the development of Christianity in northern Europe. Pagan worship did not finally die out there until the eleventh century AD, and remnants of it were then retained in northern Christian festivals and hagiography. We can see its development in the Prose and Poetic Eddas and sagas as well as in the underculture of folklore, fairy-tale and custom. But the ancient Germans kept no written records of their legends of Woden, so it is to the Scandinavian legends, sagas and myths that we must turn to see the similarities between Mercury, Odin and Loki.

Loki was the great trickster god of the Norse pantheon, while Odin had more shamanic qualities. The development of both parallels rather than replicates that of Mercury, and this may be because his cult did not penetrate the Teutonic lands to any great extent. Some of Odin's and Loki's achievements are reminiscent of shamanic/trickster practices found in Slavic Eastern Europe and beyond, from the Russo-Mongolian region. There is little hard evidence as yet that these cultures and practices penetrated the archaic and early Greek cultures, but Mercury does have some of the characteristics of the shaman, especially when he dons the helmet of invisibility, uses knucklebones for divination and can descend into the realms of the dead.

Mostly all that can be said, at present, is that there seem to be common characteristics between the Celtic and Norse shape-shifters and Mercury in the years of the Roman Empire and during the Dark Ages. The rise of Christianity ensured that, in the mainstream, there was little development of the powers of the pagan gods; these were either suppressed or assimilated. This happened even within Christian gnosticism itself, according to Elaine Pagels, in the first four centuries of the Christian era.

Only in the underground streams of 'paganized' and heretical gnosticism, hermeticism and alchemy, outside the purview of Christian orthodoxy, did Hermes retain some of his power. Shape-shifting became his particular prowess through the Christian centuries, and we begin to see some of his powers of survival in the current, if partial, renaissance of the arts of astrology, alchemy and natural magic.

PATRIARCHY AND CULTURAL CHANGE

We also need to look at what the myths mean in terms of the cultural development of the human psyche as personified by Mercury. In the classical Greek world, Charles Seltman indicates in *Women in Antiquity*, male dominance became the norm in all areas of life, political, cultural and social. Gerda Lerner argues that it may have happened earlier, in the Mesopotamian societies which also produced the first recorded instances of astronomy and astrology. Some writers and scholars, among them Graves in this century and Bachofen in the nineteenth, have argued that throughout the Aegean and the Near East mother-right was superseded by patriarchal forces in the centuries preceding the classical era, and certainly many of the myths which come down to us from the classical period are open to this interpretation. By Roman times, male dominance, at least among the ruling élites, was almost fully in place as a cultural phenomenon in the empire.

Although academic opinions still differ on the extent to which this took place, psychological astrologers may ponder on the way in which male dominance can be reflected in the personal and collective unconscious, develops and is then projected into, or is mirrored in, the myths and legends of a particular culture. We may also inquire into the extent to which Mercury remains a patriarchal force in astrology today. Certainly the myths from the classical Graeco-Roman civilization which concern Mercury, and which we mainly use, show the considerable extent to which he developed into a patriarchal god.

Gnosticism and alchemy, which show the influence of Greek, Semitic and Egyptian cultures, attempted some correction of this distortion, though in a piecemeal and sporadic fashion. The various gnostic cults and early alchemy itself reflected the diversity of religious, spiritual and cultural experience which informed the Mediterranean world in the four centuries that spanned the beginning of the Christian era. Within gnosticism and alchemy we see some attempts to incorporate the feminine; attempts which, after the Council of Nicaea in AD 325, were rendered even more heretical and suppressed by the patriarchal and victorious Christian church. Indeed, the Nicaean Council was called as part of the movement towards universalism within the developing church itself; heresy was to be eradicated within and without the church.

Gnostic philosophies, however, continued in the unconscious psyche of the collective for many centuries and made occasional reappearances, as Steven Runciman attests in *The Medieval Manichees*. That they never really died can be shown by the rise of, among others, the Bogomil and Cathar sects of medieval Europe and the revival of alchemy and neo-platonism in Europe in the twelfth to sixteenth centuries. Alchemical Mercury only went underground for a while, and it is time now to revive him so that he can give service to psychological astrology. We will explore this issue further at a later point in the book.

The value attached to rationality and logical thought increased during the classical period. Much emphasis was placed by Greek and Roman philosophers on deductive discourse and the methods by which to conduct it. The politics of Plato, the ethics of Aristotle and the mathematical precision of Euclid, among others, arose from the patriarchal need to impose order on an increasingly complex society, to underpin its mechanics with a rational system of explanation which was informed, in part, by the seeming regularity of the known universe, according to H. D. F. Kitto. But men had other, more irrational collective needs, E. R. Dodds states, and were still too close to their projected archetypes, their gods, to dismiss them completely, preferring to amalgamate emerging knowledge with the characteristics of the old gods. So mythological Mercury developed from an archaic pastoral and divinatory god into a divinity associated with rational thought, the invention of the alphabet, the development of musical scales (known by classical times to have a mathematical basis) and astronomy. These and others of his classical attributes were carried over into the curriculum of the education systems within the church in Europe from the fourth century onwards.

Psychological astrologers are aware that the importance given to the type of intellectual knowledge ascribed to astrological Mercury is now a function of Western male-orientated societies and has become rooted in our collective psychology, to the detriment of the more feminine-honouring modes of thought and expression indicted by his gnostic and alchemical past. Mythological Mercury's relationships with women were elusive and patriarchal (with some important exceptions); he attempted, in the main, to subdue women, to deny not only the power of their femininity but also the feminine part of his own psychological make-up. In this, Mercury came to resemble the other classical gods, projecting the repressed feminine on to women, goddesses and nymphs and on to mythology itself.

It is not until we study alchemical Mercury that we begin to see an additional way to raise unconscious contents to awareness, or how the masculine and the feminine might begin to integrate and what part the volatile human intellect plays in this process. Such integration has to take place initially at a very conscious personal level before collective norms and values can be influenced, if at all. Mercury, traditionally, has affinities with healing and, astrologically, we might encourage his potential to heal the splits between the conscious and the unconscious, the personal and the collective, the mundane and the transpersonal. The implications of myth, alchemy and depth psychology for the astrological interpretation of Mercury and his attributes are wide-reaching.

Together with its relevance to personal needs and development, the mythology of any culture represents the more conscious manifestations of social and collective control through systems of religious organization. It also indicates what has been lost to the collective, leaving the researcher, historian or astrologer to read between the lines of available material. The mercurial archetype is plain enough from the study of classical mythology and traditional astrology. Mercury is the extrovert boy-god who was seemingly never the object of any of the classical mystery cults which existed in the ancient world alongside the city-state worship of members of the Olympian pantheon. Yet the myths which connect him with Hades, Persephone and Hecate indicate that there may have been a cultural role for Infernal Hermes, one which might have connected him to the death cults, if not to the mystery cults.

By the time of the early alchemists, it is obvious that Mercury had developed a mystical and transpersonal nature, more inward-looking. It seems as though he had undergone a profound change from the quick-thinking, youthful archetype permeating classical mythology, through one which was more contained, to one which then withdrew from personal and collective projections, concentrated on inner development, and went underground. It was a reflection, perhaps, of the more disparate and sect-ridden Alexandrian culture in which hermetic literature made its first appearance and which it needed to survive. As psychological astrologers, we might inquire how such a figure can undergo such a change, what the processes were that led to the transmutation, and if such a study has any relevance to an astrological investigation into the nature of human intellect and consciousness.

So the book is to be an examination of the function of the archetype of mythological and astrological Mercury, combined with his travels and transmutations down the centuries. It will be an attempt to examine both his damaging and his healing aspects through his most prominent sub-personalities, the Eternal Child, the Rapist, the Trickster, the Traveller, the Healer and the Alchemist − all of which are relevant to the development of psychological astrology.

2

The Eternal Child

INFLUENCE OF A DIVINE MOTHER

Astrologers often see childlike, inquisitive and quick-thinking characteristics most clearly in people who either have a strongly active Mercury or have their Suns in Gemini. Virgoans, too, are seen to have these qualities, though they tend to be more discriminating, with the ability to craft their thoughts into some kind of action. How these people use or misuse their mercurial abilities reflects the position Mercury holds in the chart and the way in which the planet is aspected. Quite often we meet people whose charts show the capacity for using their intellects to reflect on life's events, to seek for a deeper understanding of themselves and to make connections between the two. Somehow, despite their abilities, they seem lost, or incapable of resolving the conflicts which beset them, though they may be able to talk and think endlessly about their difficulties. This quality of woundedness and irresolution can have its roots in the early interactions between the parents and the mercurial child. An understanding of not only the astrological qualities of Mercury, but also the Graeco-Roman myths about him and his Greek counterpart, Hermes, can be used to deepen our knowledge about the intensity of the relationship which affects, perhaps damages, the future development of the child.

Hermes gives us a role-model. He was the son of the chief god of Olympus, Zeus, and Maia, whose divine status, by the time of the classical writers, had degenerated into that of a nymph. She was the daughter of Atlas, the Titan who held up the heavens on his shoulders, and Pleione, who gave birth to Maia and her six star-sisters, the Pleiades. They appear in the night sky in mid-May, heralding by a week or so the movement of the Sun into Mercury-ruled Gemini.

Mythologically, we know little more about her than this, but the presentation of her offered by the classical writers indicates that, long before Hermes was born, Greek patriarchal culture had superseded a culture in which she may have had some importance as a goddess in her own right. That Zeus felt compelled to mate with her may reflect the classical Greek need to subordinate all women, divine or not, to the dominance of the male. If so, then we can understand the split in Hermes' psyche between what he experiences as the male intellect and female emotions, especially when he is in circumstances which seem to compel him to drive his emotions underground. Sometimes we can see products of a similar split in our more mercurial clients.

There are indications in mythology that Maia, when resident on Mount Kyllene, may have been an aspect of the Great Goddess. Whether she resolved the tensions between her mountain-rooted and star-fixed states we do not know, but, if her existence was as earth-bound as her now very compressed myth suggests, she may have had difficulty living out, under patriarchy, the more freedom-loving, quick-acting and intellectual side of her character. She was, after all, a star-child, typically airy by nature and birthright, though access to the side of her nature which could connect heaven and earth appeared in mythology to be curtailed after her illicit and perhaps forced union with Zeus resulted in Hermes' birth. In the 'Homeric Hymn to Hermes', she has no other function than to be a nymph and Hermes' mother.

She was not to know, then, that, as an outcome of the restricting ties of motherhood under patriarchy, her relationship with Zeus was to bind her closely to an earth-rooted existence. Feeling values about restrictions placed on her star-directed pursuits seem not to have been taken into account by the mythographers. So the stories we have of Hermes' birth may signify both the splits and the bonds forged between two cultures at a collective level, and between male and female at an individual level. The tragedy was that the masculine emphasis on the importance of the intellectual component of the Greek psyche won out, as far as we can discern from Hermes' myths. It grew from the establishment of patriarchal culture and authority and the suppression of the feminine, a legacy which is still with us today, and which helps to fill the consulting-rooms of astrologers and therapists alike. As now, there was not too much freedom for Maia or other women when Zeus, the law-giver, was around. Hermes was to reflect the seeming freedom which comes from clever, and male-orientated, intellectual development.

No doubt Maia, shut up as she was in the cave on Mount Kyllene, initially projected her need for freedom on to Zeus, that roving and rarely present god, who needed to establish his patriarchal rule over all women, human and divine. It certainly seems that, later, she projected that need on to Hermes. With his winged helmet and sandals, performing as messenger and mouthpiece of the Olympians, Hermes was not a god to stay at home, or feel happy with an existence which was circumscribed by domesticity and responsibilities. In his Graeco-Roman form, he always remained something of a *puer aeternus*, always childlike, many times avoiding facing up to the need for conscious self-restraint, or to ground himself, as much reflecting his mother's inner need to escape as his father's need to absent himself from responsibility.

This quality astrologers often note in their mercurial clients, and a psychologically needy mother with repressed escapist tendencies may, in part, account for its appearance. It also may reflect a characteristic already present in the child, and, in a sense, the *puer* child has the very parents who are likely to enhance that trait, consciously or not, just as Hermes' parents did.

All children, even divine ones, have imperfect parents and Hermes was no exception. As well as a mother who may have wished to absent herself, but could not, from earthy and earthly responsibilities, Hermes also had a physically absent father, at least during the early stages of his development. Zeus, it seems, in his role of invading sky-god, had shown interest only in Maia's availability and fecundity, perhaps to ensure the survival of patriarchal superiority on earth as in the Olympian heaven, and not in establishing any stable partnership with her. But, whatever his reasons, he was not at Mount Kyllene to provide

his son with a strong model of responsibility and male qualities
in his early life.

What Maia felt about having to assume sole responsibility for
Hermes' early upbringing we can only deduce from Zeus'
attitude towards her. He mated with her, if not raped her,
despite being married to Hera, possibly to lay claim to the earth
goddess's shrine on Mount Kyllene. Maia was a territorial acquisition in divine form and the myths do not tell us if Zeus was
concerned about her subsequent feelings and pregnancy. He
seemed as uncaring about her and Hermes as he was about many
of his other illicit liaisons and illegitimate children; the absent
father and mate is a recurrent theme in Zeus' relationships. We
can partly deduce from myth that Maia repressed a great deal of
bitterness, anger and resentment at the constraints put on her
freedom by his continuing absence and by Hermes' birth. So, as
well as having no effective father, Hermes was left to internalize
the image of a weak but angry woman. His lasting childhood
image, stemming from early babyhood, was that of an escapist
father and a mother who repressed her longing for freedom. The
split for Hermes was difficult to resolve, and, as long as he
didn't, he, too, often escaped and repressed his feelings, as we
shall examine later in other myths.

In psychological terms, the child who cannot grow up to
resolve this particular split in his nature is reflected in the god
who was known for his youthful, sometimes childlike qualities.
For Hermes, as for many mercurial clients who come for an
astrological reading, these qualities are a cut-off aspect of his
own personality, because he identifies so closely, though unconsciously, with his emotionally unreliable parents. The pain of
inconsistent and seemingly uncaring parents would be too difficult to carry at a conscious level – and so he cut off from it,
becoming seemingly unfeeling and amoral himself. Similarly,
with no true guidelines for consistent and reliable parenting, or
until life's patterns bring them face to face with the problems of
repressed feelings and lack of commitment, some of our more
mercurial clients may seem incapable of growing up and accepting responsibility for the results of their own non-feeling actions.
This may happen for some children who are born into house-

holds where patriarchal norms unconsciously apply; where the father may be psychologically absent and withdrawn from any child-rearing. It might also apply to some children who, for whatever reason, are brought up in one-parent families.

As astrologers and as counsellors, we occasionally see clients who cover up the wounds caused by early emotional deprivation, finding it difficult to make the links between present conflicts and past pain. One client, with Mercury in the tenth house square Jupiter in the seventh, herself a very chatty person and given to writing long screeds of self-revelatory material on which she found it difficult to act, could not understand why she always seemed to involve herself in relationships with men who were pompous and overbearing, quick to put down her prolific thoughts and ideas, which she increasingly came to resent.

As a child, she had experienced her father as a man who constantly 'laid down the law' at home, allowing no deviation from family rules which he established, and who belittled her early attempts at writing and experimenting with language and ideas. In any real family crisis, though, it was her mother who took charge and acted, her father absenting himself behind dramatic scenes which eventually fizzled into inaction. Her reaction to this was to become quieter and quieter throughout her childhood, avoiding by silence and submission what must have seemed like the wrath of the gods, a protective trick unconsciously designed to get her off many a family hook. Having given up her powers of expression so early, she was unaware that she attracted men who initially lived out these very characteristics for her, whom she later treated with silent contempt when they showed signs of being 'more concerned with words than people', as she put it. She had not come to any realization of her hidden contempt for men, nor to an understanding of her own inability to act. Not until the connection was made with her image of her father was she able to live her own pain, alter her choice of men and begin to express her need to be understood in a more coherent and less exaggerated form.

The manner in which this particular client was tricked by her unconscious into less obvious forms of expression reflects one of Hermes' chief characteristics – the slipperiness he showed in deceiving others as well as himself as he grew up. The seeds of such behaviour were sown very early in his life, as they were in my client, and a child is powerless in any obvious and rational way to ask for the form of loving recognition he or she needs. So we see children, and Hermes, begin to act out their needs in a distorted fashion.

SIBLING RIVALRY

Within a day of his birth, we are told, Hermes grew into a small boy capable of stealing and herding his half-brother Apollo's cattle into a cave. Maia recognized that her son was capable of trickery and theft, but when Apollo complained to her, she contradicted him, pointing to the child asleep in his cradle. In doing so, she was quite consciously colluding with her son's childish irresponsibility. Hermes was learning early how to outwit women by playing the eternal child. It shows some lack of personal power and a degree of ineffectualness on Maia's part that she could not adequately and lovingly direct her lively and quick-moving child into a moral and feeling concern for the needs of others, ignoring the fact that children need to be helped, consciously or by example, with their moral development if they are to grow into mature and loving adults. She was unaware that her weakness here was to stunt her son's inner growth for some considerable time.

Maia's lack of power in directing Hermes' development may have been a reflection of the denigration of the feminine in both women and goddesses in patriarchal and classical Greece. If so, the implications for men and gods were enormous. With no real value given to the feminine characteristics of nurturance, let alone self-determination, all gods and all men were at risk of denying the power of the feminine within themselves and treating women, and the softer components of their own psyches, with contempt. Women and goddesses would learn, or be forced to learn, to repress their own power and project it on to men – and boy children.

Hermes' inheritance was not an easy one. Left to himself, a

child and without the resources to resist these psychological pressures, he externalized this conflict by stealing some of the power of his half-brother, the Sun god, in an attempt to win recognition for his cleverness. It was also a childish cry for attention from his emotionally neglectful parents. Unable to trust that his parents would give him the emotional support he needed, he learned early to act in an untrustworthy way himself, to grab from the world, the collective, some of the sustenance he could not get in any other way.

Many parents know that one way in which children gain their attention is to squabble among themselves. Often the younger children feel that they are unable to compete fairly against bigger and older brothers and sisters. The result may be that they either feel squashed, or overcompensate, or manipulate for extra attention. Ways of inducing attention vary from being the comic of a family to doing something so outrageous, or outside the family norm, that it cannot pass without notice. Even if the subsequent attention is negatively expressed, at least it is attention of a kind. Hermes certainly succeeds in his myths. He is witty, a thief, outrageous in his own defence, and keeps his goal in mind.

Interestingly, he goes about it by stealing some of the life-sustaining power of the Sun, in the form of Apollo's cattle. It seems that Hermes' psychological need to survive was very great and many astrologers and counsellors have met with clients whose needs to be 'fed' are just as urgent and just as demanding. Hermes' use of alchemy at this stage was unconscious and very crude, but he was certainly going to try and transform those circumstances which were within his power, and survive by an introjection of primitive Apollonian vitality and healing. In so doing, however amoral he was at this point, he was sowing the seeds for the great work he was to carry out at a later period of development. Many mercurial clients, too, show the ability to transform their attitudes in simpler, sometimes devious ways before tackling and understanding their deep inner needs and values.

One man, with Mercury in Cancer square Neptune in Libra, was known in his childhood as a liar and a thief. His child-hood had been problematic, with a father who was silent and uncommunicative, whose elusive behaviour was difficult for him to understand, until he became aware of the way in which his mother seemed to misinterpret and devalue his father's every word. While she could not talk about her own emotional needs, she was ever ready to go into a huffy and martyred silence at his father's more obvious withdrawal from family life and to emphasize how like him his son was. Family life consisted in continuous and insidious attempts of each member to subtly undermine the others. His only way out, as a young child, was to construct a fantasy world in which he was the most important person, the details of which he remembers to this day.

It was only when his fantasies died, some time after starting school, that the lying and thieving began. Unable to share any of his emotional life with his withdrawn father, he was reluctant to trust his equally uncommunicative mother. He outgrew both these traits, but not the identification with his parents, and he was left with the unrealized feeling that people were basically as untrustworthy as he knew himself to be. It took him some years, when adult and in an increasingly unhappy partnership, to become aware of the feelings of his own worthlessness, confusion and depression. Though he has some way to go in exploring the depths of these, he can now deliberately use his once slippery communication skills and good sense of humour to begin the work of understanding his own sometimes destructive behaviour. He began to do this by spending more time with his own children, using his story-telling skills to make up tales for them which, when analysed, have profound archetypal significance for his own inner searching.

CULTIVATING PHYSICAL SKILLS

Easy, sometimes slippery communication skills are often characteristic of people with a strong mercurial cast to their birthcharts and astrologers occasionally note in their clients a correspondence between the psychological and the physical qualities of Mercury. Again, mythology helps us here. Hermes' *puer* image was reflected in his bodily characteristics as well as in his psychological make-up. His slight build, and need for winged helmet and sandals to sustain the fleetness of thought and actions, suggests a low vitality and quick rate of burn-out, often a characteristic of mercurial people with a fast flow of mental energy and little bodily strength.

It takes a good deal of energy to set up strategies to transform circumstances and to escape from them. Similarly, Hermes, as a child, could not keep up physically with the speed of his own mental processes and quick reactions. Retiring to bed after his escapade with Apollo's cattle indicates both the need to hide from the consequences of his own actions and the need to recoup some overstretched strength. Mentally overactive and highly stimulated children often need to relax, otherwise nervous tension results, and Hermes must have been feeling rather strung-out as he lay in bed hoping to escape notice. Either he was a good actor and could disguise the quick breathing and physical twitchiness which comes with overstimulation, or Maia was particularly unobservant of her son's usual sleeping rhythms, knowing little about the reality of this day-old divine child, or about what he had already put in motion.

Astrologers often notice that people with Mercury strong in their charts have a quality of physical wiriness, but some frailty, as if their mental capacities far outstrip their physical capabilities. Frequently, periods of rest or enforced rest are an essential. One client with a Gemini Ascendant and a Sun/Mercury conjunction which was opposed by Mars felt that he had to excel both mentally and physically. Ambitiously carving out a medical career for himself, he also took up running, squash and cross-country walking and wondered why he periodically collapsed with colds and bouts of flu, damaged joints. He needed to sleep more during the daytime than most people, though he was rarely in a position to allow himself to do so. He came to recognize that perhaps he needed these short periods of rest to recuperate from the strains of an overextended mental and physical life, but he would not have considered changing his lifestyle to include them on a regular basis. Like Hermes, he both does and does not escape the consequences of his own actions; he continues to collapse occasionally and retires to bed, most often at times least convenient for his work and plans. The mercurial body often has ways of enforcing times of relaxation and essential rest, whether these are welcomed or not.

None the less, mercurial people are often drawn to physical activities and sports which display agility and quick-footedness. While they may not have much physical stamina over the long haul, sports which rely on fast responses and an awareness of bodily control are the ones which they may prefer. Gymnastics and boxing represent the kinds of all-engaging physical activities which offset and channel the sometimes overactive mercurial mind that may have, on occasions, an impulse to an angry and aggressive outlet. This interrelation between the body, the mind and the emotions was consciously encouraged by the Greeks and the Romans and gymnastics and sports were a recognized part of the classical curriculum; one went to the *gymnasium* to be educated and Hermes was the patron of both gymnastics and boxing. 'Mens sana in corpore sano', a sound mind in a sound body, was as much part of the classical education process as it is today.

It also indicates where classical culture is still part of our contemporary thinking, though, at a conscious level, we may not always be aware of our inheritance, just as Hermes, initially and in his youth, seemed not to be aware of his. Body and mind are well taken care of; emotional development may not be given quite so much importance. Anger and aggression are contained and displaced in appropriate physical activities. That those activities are not necessarily appropriate for all circumstances is never discussed. Anger between people cannot always be displaced and there is no recognition that other strategies might need to be learned. The unquestioned ideology behind channelling aggression into sport does not allow, very often, for a flexible mercurial response.

A JUDGEMENTAL FATHER

Whatever his inheritance and his patterns of early learning, Hermes was forced to face, if only partly, the results of his thievery. Apollo was not taken in by his feigned sleep, even if his mother was, and hauled him before Zeus and the Olympians for a reckoning. He cunningly managed to charm his way back into his father's favour, using his glib tongue and skilful means of expression to get himself out of serious trouble. Just as Hermes found a way of being accepted by others without having his lying and amorality fundamentally challenged, so, too, did Zeus. Zeus always managed to cajole the enraged Hera into forgiving his extramarital affairs, and afterwards went on to have more.

Little wonder, then, that Hermes had more than a tinge of amorality about his actions and took to theft so readily. The patterns in both the father's and the son's lives at this point seem strangely familiar. But Zeus could still play the judgemental father-god who knew when to take over from a weak and ineffectual mother and how to channel his son's more notorious abilities. Hermes, for the first time in his life, knew when to defer to powerful authority; because he was a child and in a less powerful position than the King of the Gods, he had little choice. Zeus, while chiding his son for stealing the cattle, was amused by the child's bright and eloquent wit and put it to what he thought was good use by making Hermes his messenger and herald.

In this incident Hermes learned both to defer to and to manipulate his father, even though his more outrageous behaviour had been challenged by Apollo. Similarly, counsellors, more often, perhaps, than astrologers, find themselves in Apollo's confrontational role with some mercurial clients. It takes constancy and compassion to discover the depth of emotional pain beneath such bright logic and facile humour. By not accepting the surface explanations and by constantly referring to feeling values, counsellors and therapists can sometimes support a growing awareness in their clients of the need 'to please father' in this way. For some mercurial people, pleasing father is a game they learn to play at an early age. Mother's part in early childhood development is seemingly superseded because the child unconsciously recognizes where power under patriarchy really lies.

This was exactly the way in which Hermes regained a father with whom he took service and to whom he remained eternally and uncritically loyal, identifying with Zeus' orders to an extent no other god did. Maia fades from the myth at this point. She had fixed Hermes' image of women as unchallenging and deceivable and had left him the legacy of forever needing to escape from the realities of an earth-bound existence. Hermes, without knowing it, was bound by damaging ties to both parents, themselves split off from taking responsibility for deceiving themselves and others. Hermes, the arch-deceiver, had, it seems, role-models from whom he could not break away.

For a god who needed his freedom, Hermes was surprisingly contained by acting as Zeus' mouthpiece; the pay-off in terms of reflected power must have been worth it. Only under Zeus' command could he use his eloquent tongue and quick thinking to persuade men and gods to do his father's will. Even then, he was more at ease with using his subtle mind to outwit others than he was with exercising emotionally empathic behaviour; his own emotional life seemed buried beneath his bright and capable exterior. Neither Maia nor Zeus seemed to have taught him that emotions were to be valued, mainly because neither was aware of the depth or meaning of their own. Yet only under Zeus' command could some of his more obvious irresponsibility be contained; he was not at a point in growth where he could contain himself. That was to come at a more alchemical stage of development, as it does for most mercurial people.

Rejecting his own dark irrationality and illogical behaviour, he was content to see it reflected in Zeus, at the same time accepting without question the strictures his father put on him. Though this was a sign that he may have been looking for containment, there are very few myths from the classical period which suggest that Hermes grew away from his father's control, acting on his own behalf with conscious responsibility for his own behaviour; there are no stories of his youth which suggest that he openly acknowledged or resolved the conflict between freedom and containment. That, too, had to wait for the development of alchemy and gnostic thought. It seems there were good reasons why the Hermes of classical and patriarchal times was known as the youthful god: in many ways he failed to grow up; in many ways he was prevented from doing so.

Mercurial people, too, can have this quality of youthfulness
and irresponsibility about them. Used to rationalizing their own
behaviour, they are often detached from the emotional complexities of a situation, perhaps having to learn the hard way to value
their emotional lives and contain their behaviour, before it can
be said that they have matured. My own chart is a case in point.
I have a Mars/Uranus conjunction in Gemini which is trined by
Mercury in Libra. It corresponds to an eternally inquisitive and
restless cast of mind which always wants to know at the beginning of a process the reasons why events happen as they do,
ignoring the impact of associated emotions, even if they are
disturbing and sometimes disruptive. It is sometimes not helped
by my tendency to overemphasize the part logic and order play
in life, reflected in my Virgo Sun's square to Mars/Uranus. I
occasionally forget that other people don't always have the same
need to know, and push them for more answers than they can be
expected to give. The results are not always the ones I would
choose and can be explosive. I am still in the process of learning
how to contain my own impatience and the lack of awareness of
this trait, which I now see as a form of mercurial and childlike
irresponsibility which has to be contained, yet given constructive
outlet.

EARLY WOUNDEDNESS

It seems, too, that Hermes' parents were not conscious of their
own irresponsibility. Neither Maia nor Zeus was aware of the
internal dynamics they helped to set up in their son, and only
Apollo had the wit to confront him openly. Even so, Hermes
was astute enough, and in control of enough of the situation, to
bargain for some rewards. It shows that a certain steadiness of
purpose and a seemingly cool nerve underlay his sharp-witted
and shameless intelligence, and he was not above portraying
himself as something of a prankster and being playful in order to
get what he wanted. Hermes was, it seems, a clever and dangerously manipulative child who could cajole his father into grant-
ing him divinity and recognition. Zeus fell into the trap, which

reinforced Hermes' tendency to material gain by trickery and theft.

It is no surprise that he later became the patron of merchants and thieves, having few scruples when he found he could have the best in any bargaining. Morality and reliability of intentions were never his strong point and what he gave with the one hand he very often took with the other – certainly the mark of a dualistic turn of mind noted by astrologers in some of their more unhappy mercurial clients. A god to be watched, then, even in his more dependable moments; there was a certain fluidity in Hermes's intentions which, as a child, he could allow to get frighteningly out of control. Hermes needed to learn some very deep ethical lessons before he could enter the world as an adult.

The myths reveal that Maia was incapable of teaching him these and Zeus seemed unaware that, by his actions, he was giving his son a double message – to reform and use his gifts profitably in his father's favour, but not to use them to break away from his father's control. So he was conditioned by his early learning experiences under patriarchy to be a *puer aeternus*, a classical Peter Pan, irresponsible, a thief and crafty. Unable to make mature relationships with gods and humans, he was in thrall to an equally irresponsible father, and to a mother who repressed her anger and resentment at the curtailment of her freedom. He would not have known, early on, how he internalized, buried within his psyche, the split between his father's assertive amorality and his mother's closeted anger, for amorality and hidden resentment can both be ways of denying deeper feelings of loss and pain. Unconsciously denying his own emotions in favour of an all-too-easy rationality was patriarchal Hermes' way of papering over the cracks of his world and his woundedness.

Quite often we see clients who have suffered from the split brought about by a childhood conducted according to the laws of patriarchy, where feminine feeling values are cut off from what is seen as masculine assertion, if not aggression. As often, we come to realize that our clients' parents are as wounded as their children and have inherited similar wounds from their own parents. Where it is possible, looking at the generational charts of families can often indicate the types of psychological wounds, sometimes intertwined with ill-health, which are handed on from parents to children.

Issues of health are often the province of Mercury-ruled Virgo, and the affinity between Mercury and the lungs is well known to medical astrologers. Three generations of women in a particular family have aspects between Mercury and Jupiter. The grandmother's chart shows a sextile between the two planets and her Sun is in Sagittarius. She was known to be very talkative and overbearing in manner, strong-minded, always right, and a person whose husband left her early in her daughter's childhood. There was always some mystery attached to the grandfather's disappearance. This was resented by their daughter, whose own Jupiter in Sagittarius is in a T-square formation with Mercury and Saturn, Mercury being at the apex and in Virgo. She often complained that she felt dismissed and unwanted by both her mother and her father. Not only did the daughter eventually show signs of behaving like the grandmother, but she also developed asthma in early middle age when her second marriage broke up. She seems to have inherited this from her father, whose birth-chart is not available. Both her marriages had ended in separation, and both, eventually, in the death of the husband. Both husbands were experienced as dominating, powerful and escapist.

Unfortunately, the birth times of both women are unavailable, though the birth time of the granddaughter is. This shows her Sun/Mercury/Jupiter conjunction to be on the IC and in the same sign as her mother's Mercury–Virgo. At the age of fourteen, on returning from evacuation during the Second World War, she found her mother remarried and with a young family. Her own father had been killed early in the war and she never really knew him because her parents had separated when she was only two years old. Within six months of returning to her mother, and during considerable readjustment problems that were never satisfactorily resolved, she, too, developed asthma. She, too, complained of feeling unwanted by her mother and continued to resent the attention given to her second family. Although she married and stayed married, so in some ways breaking the family pattern, in times of crisis and stress her asthma severely restricts her activities, causing more anxiety in the family. Although she is superficially quiet and reserved, like her grandmother and mother she also has a tendency to dominate people within her immediate family with her opinions.

All of the women show aspects of the needy child which has not had its feeling values nurtured and they all found it difficult to show and receive love. All were known as dutiful mothers who were disgruntled and would rather have been doing something else than raising children, though it was never clearly defined what that 'something else' was. Though the grandmother and mother broke away from poor marriages, escape from the duties of rearing children never seemed an option to any of these women, and constriction for two of them meant breathing problems. The asthma was real and distressing for both women, but always seemed to occur at a point in family life when other family members were in need or crisis. It seems a cruel and tragic way to gain attention. Freedom-loving but damaged Hermes, who was bound to his escapist parents, does not seem very far away from these women's experiences.

IN LOVE WITH LEARNING

Difficult as it sometimes is for mercurial people to understand and come to terms with their early woundedness, there is often the capacity to compensate partially for this by developing other skills and the love of learning known to be associated with astrological Mercury. Most often people acquire these skills through their interaction with others, though they may not consciously acknowledge this. The danger for those who have little understanding of their psychological make-up is that they may concentrate too fully on their skill-building life while ignoring the importance of their emotional lives and interactions with others – and so a further split develops.

At the same time, the very woundedness which causes personal difficulties and pain, and splits off into less threatening intellectual and practical activities, can add something of great worth to the collective; it can also induce a love of learning for its own sake, and which goes nowhere. The mercurial inheritance is sometimes a double-edged sword, perhaps fitting for a god who was known for his ambivalence and ambiguity. But in a patriarchal society worldly skills are useful and encouraged; people who fit in with that world view, or who learn to manipulate it, are more acceptable than those who value their emotional lives. It was a lesson Hermes also learned early; although his essence is to connect the intellect and the feelings, under patriarchal Zeus he learned to devalue both women and his own emotional life. But he had another teacher; one who was to encourage his learning potential and, indirectly, to sow more seeds for his own later self-healing.

By stealing from Apollo, Hermes had met up with the one god who could confront him and channel some of his potential into fruitful activities, though he always had a tendency to become stuck in the mode of operation which made him misuse his own knowledge, but brought him most immediate gain. Astrologers and counsellors often see the versatility and quick-mindedness with which their mercurial or *puer* clients may tackle new learning skills, but it is more difficult to see the impatience and lack of depth which may lie behind this. Even the forthright Apollo had been deceived initially by Hermes' cleverness. Not only had he stolen the cattle, he had made them walk backwards to their hiding-place so that their tracks seemed to come from the cave where they were hidden. Apollo could only discover the thief by divination. This aroused Hermes' curiosity and one of the bargains he wrung from Apollo was permission for the Triae, three archaic goddesses who lived on Mount Parnassus, to teach him augury using pebbles. Divination might have been a destructive weapon in the hands of an untrustworthy and manipulative boy who was always impatient to develop his skills, but we are not told whether Hermes used it for good or ill.

What we can be sure about is that forms of psychological divination are used by both therapists and astrologers in their work with clients. If mercurial clients are to heal themselves, they often need to learn these same skills of divination for themselves, to read damaging patterns and life-enhancing forms in order to make the best possible choices in their future lives within the limits which their characters allow. This is much the same pathway that Hermes took later, though when young he was unaware of where it might lead him.

It may have been, for a time, that Hermes, the magical god and eventual god of magicians, was content to have men project on to him any clarity or confusion which resulted from a reading of the stones. Divination was another act which reflected his constant duality of purpose, dishonestly shifting power from other people to himself. It also had another meaning. By taking power to himself, he put himself in a position to teach himself and mankind the need to confront their own actions, and to work in harmony with a conscious sense of destiny. While the youthful Hermes' motives may have been hidden from him, he was driven enough and curious enough to want to learn the art of augury. So, too, with mercurial people who come for counselling or an astrological reading. Psychological skills, based on divining correspondences between their own development, chart symbolism and the world around them, may help in self-discovery, provided they grow alongside a system of ethics which is protective of themselves and other people.

One woman, who has Mercury conjunct the Sun and Pluto in Leo at the apex of a T-square with Mars and Jupiter, throughout her life has been involved with developing her writing skills in some form. She has worked as a typist and a secretary, in advertising and journalism, and has written short stories as a way of improving her writing skills. What she could not do early in her life was find work which combined her need to discover more about her own life-path with her sometimes very deep perception of other people's needs and motives and with her writing abilities. Then she found herself drawn to graphology, became interested in the psychological interpretations which could be drawn from it and took a training to develop her skills. Now she teaches and practises graphology and is interested in psychosynthesis, which may help to underpin her already considerable knowledge. Quite a lot of this process involved personal pain and many difficulties to be overcome, but she feels she has found a way of synthesizing the many skills she is serving such a long apprenticeship to acquire.

Divination and the written arts are similar in some respects in Hermes' realm; his invention of the alphabet and its association with augury in early cultures helped men and gods to become aware of the dualistic and vacillating workings of the human mind. Language and the use of elegant speech could be used to obscure or clarify issues; the young god was intent on gaining mastery here. Egyptian, Greek, Roman and Norse myths all have counterparts to Hermes, who invented alphabets. Roman Mercury, it is told, invented an alphabet based on the wedge-shaped formations made by cranes as they flew on migratory flights. He also supposedly took the alphabet to Egypt and there is certainly a close historical association between him and the Egyptian scribe-god, Thoth. Norse Odin, too, invented the runic alphabet and used it for divination purposes.

Though the association between divination and formal learning is lost to the Western world, it comes as no surprise that Hermes and his counterparts grew to be the patrons of learning in their own cultures. The association of magic, religious worship and learning in Bronze Age and Iron Age cultures was very close, and may have been an indication of man's attempt to come to terms with the developing intellectual component of the psyche. Divisions between areas of knowledge were not so marked as they are now; the gods associated with divination and forms of intellectual expression, Hermes among them, are also shown to have an interest in many arts and sciences. Similarly, a need to gain knowledge in a variety of ways, though not necessarily to synthesize them all, is typical of many Virgoans and Geminians and those with an active Mercury in their birthcharts.

Many astrologers note a capacity for learning and literary work in some of their more mercurial clients, but we need to consider its psychological implications, too. Any form of speech, writing, publishing and use of the media is an attempt at communication, to establish meaningful connections with other people, to divine how they really think and feel, and to share in the spread of that knowledge. Hermes, we have seen, was impelled to do so; it is one of his divine functions. Even as a child, he made sure that some communication was established with his previously absent father, though it was limited and gained by trickery. Hermes was not a god to exist in a communication vacuum. So, too, with mercurial clients. The inability to communicate with other people in a meaningful way can bring them great unhappiness. Where they are able to communicate meaningfully and to connect the world of learning with an understanding of true human emotions and values is where they are able to contain the more outrageous side of mercurial behaviour within the alchemical development process. For this to take place, mercurial people need deep understanding of other forms of knowledge about the development of the personality.

The myths of Hermes do not fail us here, either, and they show us that both Apollo and Maia were associated with other aspects of Hermes' early education. The mastery of augury led him to acquire skills in music and astronomy. Before his confrontation with Apollo, he had demonstrated his versatility and dexterity by inventing the lyre and a set of shepherd's pipes. Apollo desired these and, in a bargaining session with Hermes held before Zeus, parted with his cattle and a golden staff in exchange for the instruments. So, before maturity, Hermes had demonstrated considerable bartering skills and inventiveness. The pursuit and gain of any kind of knowledge, material, emotional, received education, implies an exchange with others; it does not necessarily have to be a theft. His relationship with Apollo after the theft changes into one in which he consciously recognizes his brother's talents and needs. This recognition of others as people in their own right is a step forward from the childish, more self-serving aspect of the theft of the cattle.

Apollo, it seems, had some civilizing influence on Hermes, having the ability to bring out the best in him. The myths suggest that there was, after the theft, always great friendliness and cooperation between the two gods. What he also learned from this meeting were formal musical skills, the ability to make sense of a collection of random notes, bringing musical order out of primitive chaos, and that he had a talent for crafting musical instruments. The organizing ability this entails is a theme in many mercurial birthcharts; it is also emphasized in the signs of Virgo and Gemini. The capacity to bring together seemingly unconnected materials which are then used as components in a new composition is a necessary one in mercurial and psychological work. The meaning of music and instrument making was important for Hermes' future development. We see further echoes of these and other developing capacities in the myths about Hermes' involvement with astronomy.

AN ESCAPIST MOTHER

Hermes' interest in astronomy can be traced back to Maia's influence. Herself a child of earth and sky Titans, torn between her terrestrial and heavenly origins, it would have been unusual if she had not passed on some of her knowledge about the formations of stars in the night sky. As a child, Hermes would have noted, perhaps unconsciously, how ethereal his star-aunts and grandmother were as they seasonally changed their positions in the night sky and were sometimes obscured from human view. On the occasions that his mother disappeared into the sky with her kin, we are not told how Hermes might have reacted.

For knowledge of that we have to return to the human world. Children of about a year old can react badly to being left by their mothers, perhaps afraid that she might never return. Later they learn to bury their fears or seek to ward them off by magical means initially, or by projected activities as rationality develops. So Hermes gradually learned to impose order and rationality on the night sky by learning astronomy, trying to come to terms with his early experiences in the only way he knew would act as a charm against emotional turbulence. For mercurial people, as for Hermes, learning and education can be a way of attempting to control a sometimes alien and frightening world. Mercurial insistence on rationality and order can cover up great insecurity at the same time as it inclines those same people to realize, control and direct some of their learning potential into publicly recognized and useful channels. What is offered to the collective is often of great use, but what can remain blocked in them is an easy and integrated emotional release in satisfactory interactions with other people.

A silent and uncommunicative man whose Sun/Mercury/ Pluto/Venus conjunction in Gemini sextiled his Moon in Virgo, buried his powerful and emotional communication needs in his work, which was tailoring, denoted by the Moon's square with Saturn in Taurus and Jupiter in Sagittarius. Whenever the atmosphere at home became unbearable, which was frequently, he would disappear into his workshop and stitch away, producing, on occasions, some inspired designs, but he would not talk about his emotional life, nor was he aware of the deeply buried rage which caused him to act in this manner and which he projected on to his obviously angry and disappointed wife. In collective terms he was a successful man, able to gain from a reputation for well-finished work, but his emotional life was impoverished. He was seen within his family as weak and ineffectual and he warded off any intrusion by stitching away a good part of his life. He died in late middle age from a heart attack when Pluto squared the Stellium by transit. Hermetic magic and woundedness indeed, which could keep away the conscious knowledge of the horrors of personal involvement, self-destruction and self-discovery while offering, at the same time, something of worth and value to the collective and, had they realized it at the time, to members of his family.

TWO SIDES OF SKILL-BUILDING

The diversity of mercurial skills, interests and learning can serve two purposes: it keeps a lively, inquiring mind active and concentrated while also disguising a deep psychic wound – the incapacity for emotionally close and meaningful relationships. But there is a further price to pay for such diversity of interests. Mercurial people are sometimes accused of being dilettante and superficial, acquiring knowledge in many fields for the sake of outmanoeuvring others, not because of any need to understand life's experiences to the fullest and relate them to people's deepest emotions and fears in a compassionate way. If they are deprived of the variety of their interests, they can become bored, restless and, occasionally, verbally aggressive. There is often a need for constant mental and physical stimulation to offset the pain of facing their own inner turmoil – a confrontation which astrologers and therapists cannot guarantee, or, where the process of self-discovery is in motion, cannot deny.

Neither can we deny that some mercurial clients may be split and full of ambivalence which holds them in the *puer* role. Quite often they may be born to parents who themselves are unaware of their own potential for destructive behaviour. This trait may be passed on, unconsciously, to their own children. Mercurial people may not become aware, until much later in life, how to use consciously their considerable abilities and potential to free themselves from the enormous shadows cast on them at birth by both parents. But as often as they react unknowingly to their parents' psychologically unexplored inner life, they are laying down foundations, as we have seen, for their own eventual emancipation and redemption.

Their very strong learning capacities and the areas of knowledge in which they become involved can help them to understand and transform, to a large extent, the damaging inheritance which compels them into equally damaging activities and behaviour. First, however, they may need to become emotionally and consciously aware of the harm they are inflicting on themselves and others when they avoid confrontations with the conflicting components in their own psyches. Usually and sadly, only repeated frustrating patterns of negative behaviour and a sense of deep meaninglessness will bring them to that point. Though it is a painful process, the major task is willingly to step across the threshold between childhood and adulthood, consciously taking the road towards maturity. On the way, they may offer great gifts of communication to the collective and help to heal the split between male and female, intellect and emotions, brought about by patriarchal dominance.

3

The Itinerant Rapist

ESCAPE FROM THE FEMININE

Mercurial people who have suffered early wounding may turn to intellectual development as a way of compensating for, and covering up, their inability to relate at a human and emotional level. They may also find that their later relationships are painful and difficult, so difficult that their only way to stop the pain is to come out of them. Astrologers and therapists often see clients, both men and women, who are irresponsible and escapist, full of buried anger, who suppress the development within themselves of a wise intelligence which interacts with and values feminine feeling and nurturance. They fear and deny both the feminine and mature masculine principles. Often this is projected on to women, and on to the children who arrive as a result of incomplete and unsatisfying unions. In this way, people with Mercury strong in their charts often seem to echo in their own lives the little-known myths of Hermes and his relationships with women and his children.

Mercury-ruled Gemini and Virgo people are sometimes unaware of the defences they use against women or the feminine parts of their own natures in order to ward off the pain of involvement and commitment. So, too, with Hermes. In this he was very like his father, but perhaps more wounded: Hermes never married, while Zeus did. For the most part, Hermes' *affaires* were casual; often he was brutally insensitive to women's fears and emotions, certainly without any depth of feeling, but there was always a meaning behind the external act. The real content of his fears was hidden from Hermes himself. He both needed and despised women, as Zeus did.

The myths about his childhood show how this ambivalence was partly the result of his mother's lack of real engagement with her son. Unconsciously angry with herself because of her disempowerment, angry with Zeus because of their enforced union, angry with her son because care for him restricted her star-directed activities, Maia ensured Hermes imbibed these feelings with his mother's milk. As a child, he would not have felt powerful enough to bring so much anger out into the open. The result was that he repressed his own, turning himself into a cheerful, witty and evasive god. This can be a characteristic of mercurial people. It seems that the values established in Greece two and a half thousand years ago under patriarchy are still with us today. Collectively, we are likely to find cheerful people initially more acceptable than those whose woundedness is apparent, although constant cheerfulness in all situations is likely to be felt by others as false and a way of avoiding reality.

As it can also be where Mercury is active in the natal chart, slipperiness was Hermes' chosen mode of being to stave off facing the pain behind his emotional detachment. It characterized his rape of Apemosyne, a princess of Crete, a virgin and, perhaps, a moon goddess. She set him a challenge by refusing his advances. Never a god to be outwitted, and certainly not by a woman under encroaching patriarchy, Hermes set wet hides on the ground. When Apemosyne walked over them, she slipped and fell and so Hermes was able to rape her. Hermes, as with the other male Olympians, seems, in this myth, out to destroy the power of the feminine in the ancient world with as much spite and humiliation as possible. This mercurial shadow, often noted by astrologers and therapists as a killer when it ignores feminine feeling values, first made its presence felt in this tale of sorry conquest.

That his act of rape led directly to Apemosyne's murder by her brother seems not to have concerned him; at least, the mythographers tell us nothing about his reactions to it. This fact in itself reveals the depth with which the mercurial ability to cut off from the feminine had entered classical culture. Men's, or gods', reactions to a woman's death, particularly one in which they may have been implicated, are not worth commenting on, so the real tale is cut short, consciously or unconsciously censored, suppressed by its narrators, the mythographers. Though the conquest of women in the real world was conscious, the repression of the inner feminine is one legacy left to us by the classical world which was not, perhaps, intended. It is none the less as destructive of the collective and individual psyche as the punishment and rape of women, real and mythological.

Spite and the humiliation of women, together with a refusal to accept the consequences of actions, can sometimes be noted in the birthchart. One woman had Mercury and Venus in sextile, both in a Yod formation with Saturn in Gemini which was square her Virgo Ascendant. She came for counselling about whether or not to leave her husband and, on leaving him, to start up a new business abroad. During the course of her sessions, and after much initial resistance, she realized that her tendency not to speak to her husband for days after an argument was both punishing and spiteful, as well as making it difficult for her to express consciously her own vulnerable feelings. She came to know that she would lay verbal traps for her husband so that he would explode with anger and appear controlling and vindictive.

Before she recognized this pattern in herself, she had blamed her husband for her subsequent cut-off behaviour, denying and devaluing her own feeling nature by emphasizing the factual and apparent base of the arguments. Her wish to work abroad was the flight from a reality she felt was not her fault. Recognizing her projections left her feeling emotionally shaken and unsure of her future direction, and she terminated counselling. At that point in her life she was unable to put her new insights into action and, rather than that, risked destroying the marriage and devaluing her husband. More than that, she risked devaluing herself even further by accepting yet another manifestation of a recurring problem. Internally she was in despair, defeated and desperately sad, but could only work in the world if she turned away from the pressures that might have forced her to change.

This woman, though, had moved further than Hermes had at the time of his rape of Apemosyne. At least she had had a glimpse of the destructiveness of her own behaviour; from what we are told, Hermes had none. The psychological dimension of her relationship with her husband was clear. Unable to realize

her own inner feminine potential, she was compelled to external-
ize the act of union she so desperately needed for herself, but in
such a way that she set up its dissolution. Like Hermes, she could
not resolve the tensions between male and female. She had no
way of banking those internal, alchemical and sexual fires within
herself because she had no understanding of the strength and
diversity of her own feelings, let alone those of other people.
The integration of these opposites would have allowed her to
balance her own needs against those of her husband, something
she felt unable to do at the time she left counselling, preferring
to return to the old, known Saturnian situation. Her act of
volition at this time was to choose the known but unhappily
destructive aspects of her marriage, rather than to work towards
true relatedness with a human and imperfect husband.

Hermes, too, could not integrate his own and other people's
needs at this stage of his development. He had lived on his wits
since childhood, picking easy female prey like Apemosyne, 'the
unknowing one' and innocent, then ensuring the women he
picked were not of the type who would emotionally entangle
him. Unable to face his own feelings, Hermes was incapable of
recognizing the worth and depth of other people's lives, or the
need for a continually growing and developing union. To take
on the position of conqueror and rapist meant that the gods, and
the culture which engendered them, had to deny to themselves
and their subject-peoples those values which could not be assimilated and contained without causing internal conflict. To allow
feelings for the women to rise into consciousness would have
meant the eventual dissolution of their own power.

UNCONSCIOUS ALLIES

As it was at the collective level, so similar controls filtered down
to the individual level, and those in positions of power often find
allies among the repressed. Those men or gods who deny the
feminine, but are obsessed by the need to conquer women, often
unconsciously recruit other women to help them achieve their
aims. The pattern is clear in Hermes' myths. He seems to have

had a penchant for moon goddesses, as well as for youngest daughters, as his rape of Herse, princess of Athens, indicates.

He bribed her sister to arrange access to Herse's bedchamber, ravished her and subsequently had two sons by her. She later committed suicide by leaping from the walls of Athens after illicitly penetrating Athene's mysteries. Athene was a true daughter of patriarchy, born by springing fully armed from her father's, Zeus', head. By the time the classical pantheon was established on Olympus and in recorded mythology, she was unlikely to defend any woman taken by force, particularly if she was about to discover her own feminine roots of being, as Herse seems to have done. Herse's sister and Athene here appear as the guardians of patriarchy, rather than defending the feminine principle for its own worth. Hermes, as far as we know, did not use his famed eloquence and persuasiveness to defend her, showing no concern for her or for the fate of their motherless children. The amorality of his actions here parallels the amorality sometimes noted in mercurial clients. Occasionally, as with Hermes, it is difficult to know where amorality stops and immorality begins.

Herse's myth, though, does indicate that Hermes, indirectly and unconsciously, was about to begin his alchemical journey. People, and gods, have a habit of picking mates who reflect their own, unlived needs and unrecognized characteristics. If Herse represented the feminine part of his nature which Hermes denied, then she was willing to risk her life in order to discover who she really was and what the feminine principle in her life really meant. To transcend opposing principles means that they have to be understood for what they are; Herse was willing to take the risk to make the first move. She failed in the attempt. Any life can contain false starts and failures, and people with an actively mercurial chart are sometimes too impatient to stay and find out why they failed. But Hermes was repeatedly brought back to similar starting-points in his relationships with women and goddesses, as if to make the point that here was a life situation which needed to be transformed.

The myth of Herse takes the story of Hermes' transformation one step nearer completion. We are told that he was able to have children by her. So he did not escape his connection with the world of the feminine as easily as he had done with Apemosyne, though he still refused responsibility for his actions. Even under patriarchy in the classical period there had to be some connection with the feminine, if only to ensure that society continued, and continued to propagate, as far as it could, patriarchal norms and values. But where women exist, there is always the danger that feminine power will resurface. Astrologers often see this push-pull pattern at work in the birthchart.

A man whose Mercury in the twelfth house was square Neptune in the fourth and quincunx the Moon in the fifth refused to acknowledge that the child of the woman with whom he had been living for some years was his, preferring to return home and live with his mother, who supported his story. There was no evidence that his partner had had a relationship with another man, and she did not form one for some years after the break-up. Nevertheless this was the reason he gave for refusing to see the child or its mother subsequently. He seems to have been unwilling to distinguish fact from fantasy, and rather than take some emotional and financial responsibility for the family he had created, he preferred to escape from a difficult situation in the only way he could – by going home to mother. So, because he could not reach and act upon a morality acceptable to himself and others, he both did and did not escape the pull of the feminine. Ultimately he neither controlled feminine power nor did he avoid its deeper and damaging implications.

SHORT-TERM RELATIONSHIPS

As we have seen above, women, too, particularly as part of their patriarchal inheritance, can show something of the same emotionally irresponsible and cut-off aspects of behaviour when they deny their own feminine natures. Another woman with a Gemini Ascendant, and whose Mercury in Libra in the fourth house squared Mars in Capricorn in the seventh, was continually disturbed by rows in the parental home. She was the focal point of them. Having a fierce tongue herself, she was often on the receiving end of tongue-lashings from her father. When that happened, rather than resolve issues between herself and her father, she left home for a short time, in reality punishing him, but saying that she was attempting to establish an independent life for herself. Each time she met and set up a relationship with a man, which would end in mutual recriminations and shouting matches. When that happened, she would return to her parents' home, shattered but unable to see her part in the process. Once home, the cycle would repeat itself and she would find herself in yet another flat with another man. She began to see that these cycles repeated themselves and, defeated by the constant emotional turbulence, returned to her parents' home and stayed there, giving as her reason that her parents were now old and depended on her. She has not been able to take responsibility for her own emotional life, nor confront her internal parental images, nor has she been able to forgive the men who disappointed her.

An unconscious trait underlying this woman's behaviour was the belief in quantity rather than quality in order to test out her ability to relate. This can also be a mercurial trait, often encouraged in male-dominated cultures which support unrelatedness in the pursuit of individual satisfaction. Hermes, too, shared this characteristic. He acquired women as he initially acquired his skills, easily and separately, pinning them up like so many beautiful butterflies, unable to see the connection between them or the patterns he was repeating. The more women he had and the farther apart they were the better. Sicily, Crete, Thessalia and Athens were all sites for his amorous adventures, but at home on Olympus he took no goddess permanently to himself. While Hermes had many women, he never married; neither did his Roman and Egyptian counterparts, Mercury and Anubis, nor his Celtic counterpart, Cernunnos.

At that stage in his development, capable only of short-term liaisons with nymphs or virgin priestesses, he hadn't the maturity to take on a full relationship with either goddess or woman. That would have meant living out a degree of thoughtful responsibility which he did not, at that time, possess. He would have had to accept the occasional boredom and limitation that comes with even Olympian domesticity, and Hermes, like some mercurial people, could cope with nothing that threatened to trap him in body, mind or spirit.

Where Mercury is strong and poorly placed in the birthchart, emotional relationships can be short-lived and casual, but at some point lack of commitment needs to be faced, otherwise there is a danger of a continual and ineffectual search for the ideal beloved. When this happens we see the person who either repeats the same patterns in every relationship or is disappointed and bitter however much it is hidden behind a mask of carefree detachment. But deepening emotional partnerships and living through the sometimes painful alchemy of relatedness are the ways in which the mercurial person can redeem and ground him- or herself. Hermes' myth indicates that this was a possibility in his mating with Aphrodite, though for a long time it remained only a possibility.

Even that relationship was short-lived, but Hermes needed his women, much as he misused them, and his liaison with the goddess of love had in it the seeds of much of his future development. For a start, it was Aphrodite, not Hermes, who initiated the affair, and neither was there a rape. It was a new experience for him to realize that love could come to him freely, just because he appreciated it for itself. Aphrodite was grateful for Hermes' defence of her after Hephaistos, her husband, had publicly exposed and humiliated her for her sexual exploits with Ares. Women and goddesses in the classical period were not to be allowed the same sexual freedom as their men, but Aphrodite was not to be wholly contained by a morality her husband might wish to impose upon her. As a reward, she granted Hermes a full night of lovemaking. This was the one of the two times that the goddess gave herself to him of her own free will and because both honoured the act of love itself. Hermes had not tricked her into submission, nor did he refuse the offer, transient as the relationship had to be because Aphrodite was still married. It seems he had the potential to appreciate love freely given and, in so doing, realized something of the value of love for himself.

UNCERTAIN BEGINNINGS

Therapists, as well as astrologers, sometimes see in the transference/countertransference process the beginnings of self- recognition and self-love. A client who came for therapy because of severe depressions had a history of poor work and personal relationships stemming from an early, emotionally deprived childhood in which he felt he received no love or attention from either of his professionally busy parents. The emphasis in the home was on presenting a capable and acceptable face to the world, whatever private emotional strains there were. My client was the carrier of the family image to the extent that he had little ego-strength of his own. His need was to explore his own negative, raging mother image and the negative, withdrawn father image in the safe, alchemical retort of the consultation process. He needed a supportive, trustworthy environment in which to do so, even though he found it difficult initially to trust both me and the process itself. Therapy proved something of a burning ground for him, and many times he was on the point of giving up. What sustained him was that he slowly and uncertainly learned to recognize that he was, even during the pain of the transformation, beginning to love and trust himself.

Hermes had to go further than his affair with Aphrodite before he reached the same point as this man. At this time in his history Hermes was hoist by his own petard of involvement in casual relationships; Aphrodite was not available for a more permanent partnership, whatever his feelings might have been — and, as ever, the mythographers give us no indication of his feelings. He also succeeded in protecting his most vulnerable emotions by the lack of commitment implicit in a one-night stand. Hermes was not about to trust even the goddess of love very far, any more than she showed a fixity of trust in him, but for the first time he was with a woman who showed him something of female emotions and revealed to him a little of the marriage of male intellect with female feeling. Male dominance in any relationship with Aphrodite was out of the question: she knew only too well that the power of sexual attraction and love could gradually, if it were given expression, undermine the rational intellect so often found in Hermes and mercurial clients. But, at this stage, Hermes was still resisting the implications of full relationship, as was she.

One client who went further than Hermes decided to work on herself and her current relationship by coming for therapy and seeing what her birthchart revealed during the process. The chart showed a split between her images of men and women.

Her father had been a powerful man with a questing intellect, though in reality, and psychologically, often absent. His work took him away from home and he was unfaithful to his wife. Her mother knew this, and came across in my client's chart as self-sacrificial, something of a helpless figure, but also as extremely seductive and not above getting her own way by being alluring and mysterious. Though there was no open break between the real parents and they stayed together until the father's death, my client constantly found these archetypes at war in her psyche, often feeling unloved and undervalued, unable to express the love which lay beneath a dominating exterior.

She realized that she saw other men as she did her father and needed to know how she could mend her own relationship and heal the parental split within herself. Mercury conjunct Mars and trine the Moon helped her to see how she might do so. She began to examine how she absented herself from her relationship with her partner and how often she remained unassertive about her emotional needs. Her realization and subsequent change caused some storms and rocky patches in the partnership. Both needed to reach into the underworld of their psyches to understand how their negative traits might transform. This process felt similar to the one Hermes undertook when he mated with Persephone and Hecate, both mystic goddesses associated with the underworld. Emerging from the underworld and her own long and painful search, my client saw that her partner was essentially a loving man who stayed with her through these difficult times. The resulting relationship was more dynamic and rewarding; it felt like something of a new birth for both of them because it showed that previously they had related on the basis of submission and dominance. What underpinned those patterns of behaviour was a fear of breaking away from parental norms and fears of an uncertain future which had to be negotiated carefully.

CHILD OF AN ABSENT GOD

Such a product can be glimpsed in the result of Hermes' liaison with Aphrodite – the birth of Hermaphroditos, the half-male, half-female godling who was later to appear in the history of alchemical Hermes. He was the symbol of the equal intermingling of male and female qualities and can represent the stage of their full integration in both psychotherapy and alchemy. The alchemists saw that he represented the process in which the greatest spiritualizing and physical changes took place. Psychotherapists saw that he stood for both the union of opposites within the psyche and for the realization that one person could find both complementarity and fulfilment by combining with another, while still retaining his or her individuality and respecting individual differences. It was the mating of Hermes and Aphrodite, love and thoughtful wisdom, that the alchemists recognized when they saw Hermaphroditos in the retort. It was only through this process, once he had recognized the way in which he could consciously incorporate his own inner female and male images into a more loving and understanding world view, that Hermes could start to heal the splits within himself, just as my client did.

But Hermaphroditos has a negative image, too. The myths do not state that Hermes took any part in his child's subsequent upbringing and so, as with his other children, he seems to have been something of an absent father himself, replicating his own father's behaviour. Still concerned more with his own survival as masculine intellect divorced from female love, his relations with his children were not governed by much interaction and feeling. Similarly, mercurial people often soak up the feeling of being unwanted by either or both parents at an early stage of their childhood. So human children and Hermes' children were all likely to perpetuate the patriarchal family pattern of unrelatedness. Hermaphroditos, in addition, combined in bodily form his parents' positive attributes, but was sterile and remained self-regarding emotionally, having no need of either male or female, though he could mate with either if he chose. In human terms, a person identifying with this state is likely to become stuck in the image of perfection he or she has achieved. There is no further impulse for development.

This was the case for a woman with Venus and Mercury in the fourth house. Though there was no aspect between them, Venus sextiled Mars in the first house and Mercury sextiled Uranus likewise, while Mars/Uranus were widely conjunct. The woman initially presented her current and long-standing homosexual relationship as well balanced and perfect, with constant surprise and excitement being its binding principle. Some way into the consultation, it became clearer that this was a one-sided image. She did not live with her partner, but with her mother, keeping her partner some distance from the small town in which she lived because it would cause too much personal and social upset to bring the relationship out into the open. It then became clear that her partner was an alcoholic, periodically threatening their relationship, which went through a stuck cycle of drunkenness and drying out. She maintained that the partnership was a spiritually fated one and that her attitude of continuing with it was the right thing to do. Her image of spirituality and perfection had little to do with the awfulness of the reality and she could not bring herself to look at her own lack of commitment or the issues of power and control which were clearly involved.

In this way, the hermaphroditic state of united bliss can become a static instead of a dynamic state, something the alchemists never intended when they used it as a symbol for the product of the sacred marriage, the *hieros gamos*. The hermaphroditic process is only one of many which must be undergone during the alchemical procedure. Even achieving the philosopher's stone is not an end in itself; it is used to transmute base metals into precious ones. Psychotherapists use alchemical symbolism in a similar way, viewing psychological change as an ongoing process. So both the hermetic and the hermaphroditic states can be subject to stuckness when there is no pressurizing motive to change.

UNDEVELOPED MASCULINITY

A further difficulty for Hermes was that his early lack of volition to change repeated itself in the way in which he held on to his youthful image and refused to develop a mature masculinity. Suppression of his own masculine principle, together with fears of his father's obvious powerful maleness, may be related to the type of physical and sexual ambiguity that is often seen in a prepubescent boy. Not yet fully male, but fearful of remaining tied to his mother's relative weakness, the adolescent boy who is to develop maturely has to try to resolve the conflict between the male and female images within himself, and which threatens to overwhelm him. Hermes, at this stage in his development, did not resolve that psychological tension, preferring to remain the youth under his father's jurisdiction rather than developing into the adult man. This is represented symbolically by the retention of his youthful appearance and slight physical form into adulthood. Astrologers are often aware of the youthful appearance and manner of Geminean or Virgoan clients, and though we need to be careful not to equate physical appearance with unresolved and unconscious tensions, sometimes they have a way of manifesting themselves in forms we like least.

This can be seen in the way Hermes' hidden, primitive masculinity revealed itself in the result of one other encounter with Aphrodite. Priapos, the phallic god, was the outcome of this mating. The child was so misshapen with his lolling tongue, distended belly and huge phallus, that Aphrodite abandoned him and Hermes rejected him as too crude and misformed. He became an object of general Olympian laughter. Neither Hermes nor Aphrodite acknowledged their own primitive sexuality, and they both did what they could to avoid facing its consequences; neither protected the child from the gods' laughter.

Priapos was fostered with a herdsman who soon realized that he had an affinity with the land and encouraged him to do what he could to add to the fertility of nature. Though his child eventually benefited from his abandonment, Hermes did himself no service when he subjected Priapos to the gods' derision. However much he denied it and thrust it away from him, the crude power and unformed nature of Hermes' sexuality came to be recognized in the world through the medium of his son. Only in his alchemical form was he able to accept and transmute his own nascent power and ambiguity, but first he had to recognize within himself elements which were wild and untamable. At this time, like some undeveloped mercurial people, he was incapable of doing so, avoidance of the unpleasant and crude being a powerful mercurial characteristic on occasions.

In rejecting his instinctual side, Hermes was also repressing his own history as the Arcadian agricultural and fertility deity which existed prior to patriarchy and the advent of the Olympian gods. As with the human world, so with the mythological realm: Hermes was not above projecting more of his unlived nature on to his children. We most often see him as a rational and civilized god, working cleverly in the male world of the Greeks, able to hide his feelings and instinctive nature, though not without harm to his own growth. Astrologers and therapists often recognize when this archetype is at work in their clients and wonder when another of his sons, Pan, who was the antithesis of Hermes, will come to the surface in reality or in the alembic of the consulting-room.

The son of a wood-nymph, Dryope, and a woodpecker, or, as some mythologers state, of Penelope, Odysseus' wife, Pan never lost his Arcadian origins, or his priapic nature. Archaic Hermes had similar roots, but seemed to disown his primitive origins once he was accepted into the Olympian pantheon and subjected to its civilizing and victorious influence. Pan, in contrast, always retained his association with fertility and was never accepted into the Olympian cult. One god from Arcadia on Olympus was enough to signal that attributes similar to Pan's were accepted and contained by the conquering immortals, and by the culture which worshipped them. But the instinctive god of the woods, whose phallic powers and seduction of pastoral nymphs were legendary, was unmanageable and emotionally free.

Pan had no difficulties in expressing his feelings and no fears of inducing a frenzy in those who did. Such uncontrolled behaviour was alien to classical Hermes, as it is now to some tense and overcontrolled mercurial people; and what Hermes didn't like, as with Priapos, was projected on to his son. But Pan was in the world and could not be ignored. Fathering him ensured that Hermes did not fully escape from his pastoral or instinctual origins, or from the primitive fears which induce panic when they cannot be resolved any other way. Uncovering these basic instincts often takes place painfully over a long period of time in therapy sessions. Even in the much shorter astrological consultations, astrologers are often aware of a reluctance in some mercurial clients to see that these issues need to be accepted as a fundamental part of their own make-up.

Mercurial people who have a history of avoiding the implications of difficult areas of their relational lives often see in their children what they are unable to face in themselves. One child, with Mercury conjunct the Ascendant in Cancer square a Moon/Pluto conjunction in Scorpio, is currently driving his parents to distraction with his constant chattering and need to question, so it seems, every experience, particularly and naturally about sex. The pattern started at the time his younger brother was born and, though a natural way for him to learn about his world, it was also a bid for more attention.

Both his parents are teachers and both are great talkers and intellectually inquisitive themselves, but both had the experience as children that they were best seen and not heard – and sex was not something that was discussed in either family. Though they are reasonably comfortable with their own sexuality, they found it difficult to accept their son's continuing and persistent interest, which seemed excessive to them at times, until they realized that they had internalized their own parents' standards and were projecting these on to their son. They are beginning to acknowledge that, rather than repress their son, they need to allocate special time to him and, in that time, to let him direct their conversations and activities. Initially they found he repeatedly asked for explanations of the meaning of sex, which they learned to deal with without becoming judgemental or irritated. Latterly he seems happier just being in their company while he occupies himself with his toys or other interests. Knowing that this is his time with them, which he doesn't have to share with his siblings, seems to be his most important consideration. His questions about sexuality were honestly answered and his inquisitive and insecure phase seems to be passing. Hermes didn't have such parents and his sexuality was allowed to run rampant, unmeaningful and unchecked.

A PROLIFERATION OF CHILDREN AND GODS

Hermes' numerous other short-lived affairs brought him other children, among them Autolycus, the thief, and Echion, the herald. As with Priapos and Pan, his children echoed his attributes, sometimes in a positive way, more often negatively. He seems to have fathered only one daughter and we know nothing about her: not surprising for a god who had internalized the patriarchal ideology of classical Greece. But, in giving life to his sons, Hermes was able to see, projected and reflected, those instinctive and elemental characteristics which he was to integrate into his own life only in his alchemical future. It took him a long time to recognize that he would keep meeting up with many of his own, denied patterns in the external world until he did something to change them. Producing children was one way of beginning the process, though it was by no means certain that he would carry it through to a conclusion which would free him from his unknown and unnamed fears and longings.

We begin to see something of the change in Hermes when we meet his analogues in other cultures. These hermetic-type gods married. Egyptian Thoth was known to have two wives: Seshat, who was active in the libraries, and Nehmauit, who understood the roots of evil. Both goddesses had attributes to which Thoth gained access through marriage and both goddesses had their roots in pantheons which were older than the one in which Thoth was mythologically active. It seems the Egyptians were aware of the connection between intellect and the need to understand the darker side of the psyche, though the implication is that the goddesses had power over certain aspects of man's behaviour before ever the gods did. Thoth was no more exceptional than Hermes in the way he gained ascendency over the feminine, but there was a realization in Egyptian culture that he had to be associated with it permanently before he could acquire deep knowledge of its skills and wisdom.

The myths of Thoth's marriages may also be a reflection of that part of Egyptian culture which consciously retained its links with the primacy of matriarchal descent until well into Roman times. This same link with the feminine in Egypt was incorporated in some of the gnostic texts deriving from Alexandria, even through the early Christian centuries of conquest and suppression; it went underground, to be revived in Christian cultures in Europe during the twelfth, fourteenth and twentieth centuries. There is still scholarly argument about the dating of the few alchemical texts purporting to come from Alexandria at this time, though less about the gnostic texts of the same period. We are left with having to make a leap of faith that Hermes, in order to recover the meaning of his union with the feminine, travelled the route of the heretical and deviant alchemists, who call on their patron/god, Hermes Trismegistos, to direct their work. As a result, perhaps the work of psychological astrologers and therapists has to be just as subtle, if they are to help divided mercurial clients to integrate love and thoughtful wisdom for their own good, before they then begin to relate in a meaningful way to collective needs.

Resolving the mercurial dilemma may be less easy for those Virgoan and Geminean people who have others of Hermes' cultural counterparts as archetypal images, even where these are married. Celtic mythology represents part of our underculture in Europe and relatively little use is made of its associations with astrology, or, for that matter, with the psychotherapies using collective mythological archetypes. This is because the material is less accessible and less easy to interpret. Apart from the Arthurian legends, which have a long and complicated history of their own, the Celtic myths were written in the Celtic languages and were, for many centuries, overlooked in favour of the classical myths, particularly in education systems which tended to support the ideologies of conquering Latinate cultures.

THE RESULTS OF TREACHERY

It is, perhaps, time to apply some of this collective inheritance, where it is meaningful, to our work. Dominant cultures and their gods do not hold the key to all truths and deny most what they fear will subvert their rule. Though we know more about classical culture, we know something of the mythology of another of Hermes' Celtic analogues, the Welsh Llew Llaw Gyffes, who married the treacherous flower goddess, Blodeuwedd. She eventually betrayed to her lover the secret means by which to kill Llew, for which crime she was turned into an owl. Here, it seems, it was Blodeuwedd who displayed openly the mercurial trait of treacherous duality, both in setting the scene for the fatal encounter between Llew and his rival, and because she represents something of the power still held by Celtic women and fertility goddesses up to the time of the Roman conquest of Britain.

Quite often astrologers and therapists see signs of duality in their more distressed mercurial clients. This can take the form of a constant and draining indecisiveness, or an inability to choose between two relationships, or, a common problem under capitalism and patriarchy, feeling that a choice has to be made between work and personal relationship. Sometimes the choice does not have to be made, because options can be combined in a new and fruitful way; sometimes a choice is imperative if a new direction has to be found. The myth of Llew and Blodeuwedd indicates why. Blodeuwedd's part in it has associations with the matriarchal and sacred sacrifice of the year-king which is necessary for the maintenance of the seasonal fertility of the land and its people. It is also symbolic of the control and destruction of the masculine principle. People with Mercury strong in their charts often have difficulty in sacrificing some of their most cherished if seemingly diverse aims. They may feel that they are betraying themselves and prefer to keep their options open, even when this causes great personal pressure and unhappiness. They often cannot bring their intellects to bear on their difficulties in a clear way, and enter into the kind of mind-spin which continually circles around the same problems, seeing no way out. Blodeu-wedd's story of necessary sacrifice may help them here.

The myth seems to come from a time in Celtic culture when patriarchal power was gaining ascendancy, though this may reflect the fact that the myths were collected and written down well into the Christian era. Llew is revived from his first death, spends some time refinding himself in the Celtic wilderness, and returns with a magician to confront and punish Blodeuwedd and her lover. Patriarchy, it seems, wins out, destroying and usurping female control of the cycle of fertility. We are not told what Llew instituted in its place, other than kingship. Intellectual regeneration and cunning seem to have helped him achieve his aims, though this involves the vengeful sacrifice of Blodeuwedd and her new consort. The safe, known masculine intellect reasserts itself and the myth does not move forward from this point. So, as with classical mythology, the masculine principle does not permanently unite with the feminine, but constantly feels betrayed by it and therefore must destroy its power. Llew's analogies with Hermes and some mercurial people seem apt.

However, neither masculine nor feminine control of the opposing principle is the permanent way out of personal dilemmas. Sometimes it is necessary to strengthen the weakest principle, and during that period it can seem as though the stronger principle has been sacrificed. This is what the myth of Llew and Blodeuwedd represents psychologically: that, at times, both principles need to be confronted, particularly their crueller elements. Quite often those people who are actively Virgoan or Geminean are likely to deny their own cruelty and retreat from facing it. To make the point that this is an aspect of all cultures and individuals at all times, though it comes in different forms, we need to examine other mythologies.

Another, relatively unused part of our collective inheritance may in this case be relevant to astrology and psychotherapy. Closer to us in time than the Celtic cultures, the Norse world left us more easily available evidence of their mythologies. There is, though, still some dispute about whether these collections, put together at a time when northern European culture was being radically changed by the often forced introduction of Christianity, are complete, or even represent the major part of northern mythologies. So while we know rather more about Hermes' Norse counterpart, Odin, than about his Celtic analogues, our knowledge may be fragmented. It is, however, part of our cultural and collective heritage, though gained, in Britain, through conquest and assimilation after the fall of the Roman Empire. The Norse myths may resonate with astrologers and psychotherapists who wish to use them in their work, particularly where they round out the knowledge gained from classical mythology.

This is the case with Odin's relationships and marriage. His wife, Frigg, also known as Frija in the German-speaking lands, was an aspect of the mother goddess. Odin was known for his shamanic and trickster attributes, as famous as Zeus and Hermes for his sexual wanderlust, but he was also a wisdom god and remained married to Frigg, who had affinities with the Norse Fates, the Norns. She was occasionally unfaithful to her husband. Odin's and Frigg's infidelities were publicly known and were both publicly accepted and condemned as the occasion demanded. Psychologically, it seems, both Odin and Frigg found each other lacking in some respects and, unfulfilled and unable or unwilling to confront their own needs or each other's, looked outside their marriage for completion, just as some mercurial people might. What is needed here is a confrontation, both with whatever elements seem to be lacking in the marriage and in themselves, and with the subtle need for, and acceptance of, the punishment and revenge implied in the myth. So Odin and Frigg help us to see that when the tension between opposites is not resolved within the alchemical retort of the marriage, it is projected on to people and events in external reality. What the Norse myths do not help with is the need for people with Mercury active in their charts to integrate and transcend the opposing principles; it is here that mercurial attributes in their hermetic form are much more useful.

THE REBINDING PRINCIPLE

We need an archetypal image which is capable of reintegrating the opposing male and female principles if mercurial clients are to have some hope that they may move beyond the splits in relatedness. The figure of Hermes Trismegistos can be useful here. What we know of him is only in relation to alchemy and hermetic knowledge, but he serves a dual purpose within the tradition. As patron of alchemy, sometimes its god, he is the guardian of the work, able to take the overview necessary to draw it to a successful conclusion. As Mercury, he works within the alchemical process as the unifying principle itself, always volatile, becoming fixed when necessary if the correct procedures are used, but ready to transform to another state again if the work demands it. He seems to have embodied the spiritual and physical attributes of the transmutational process, capable, in this form, of bringing about the internal union of male and female. But Mercury needs his classical mythology to show us how he arrives at the position of transformer.

It is the maturer, wiser Hermes Trismegistos, Mercury in his *senex* form, who can contain and transcend the tension of opposites. Alchemical literature does not always give us personifications of his marriages and matings because it is assumed that he has already reached transcendent status. Unlike Hermaphroditos and mercurial clients stuck with an image of perfection, he contains within himself the knowledge that the great work must continue in other ways, perhaps, initially, beyond the sphere of mating and marriage. Occasionally Sophia, the gnostic goddess of divine wisdom, is spoken of as his wife. The meaning of this marriage is obvious: transcending conflicts can only happen with wisdom's help.

*

The myths of Hermes and his counterparts which tell us of his relationships with women and children are useful because they show how the patriarchal order, whether of gods or men, perpetuates patterns of cruelty towards other people and damages the perpetrators themselves. We see Hermes, whose own inner child was wounded early, unable to break the bonds of his own emotional conditioning either by flight or by intellect. A similar dilemma also confronts those people whose charts show an active but vulnerable Mercury. But we also see in these myths what Hermes and mercurial people need to do to transform their negative complexes.

Sometimes internal or external pressures become apparent as despair at repeated destructive patterns of relationship or partnership failures. These painful situations in outer reality contain the conditions which may impel those mercurial people who need it to look closely at the way they relate at an emotional level to both the inner feminine image of love and destruction and the inner masculine image of conquest and overpowering intellect. Sometimes, and tragically, this inner work can be evaded for a whole lifetime. Fortunately, Hermes himself does not escape the transformation process, but there are other facets of the mercurial character which he must also face before he makes the great change, before he can unite with the goddess of wisdom.

4

The Trickster and the Shaman

HISTORICAL SLIPPERINESS

Hermes is a tricky god to grasp, both in terms of his cultural development and in the way he can help or hinder the work of making psychological connections. In his archaic Greek form, he was an Arcadian pastoral divinity, a 'Master of the Animals', perhaps associated with the Great Goddess of Crete and Asia Minor and fertility cults. He was worshipped in rural areas in the form of a cairn of stones as late as the sixth century BC. The cairns were often found in fields, not far from the roadside. Underlying the layers of myth thrown over him by later, more patriarchal mythographers, we find, not the Hermes of classical Greece with winged helmet and sandals, but a far older, lustier deity concerned with natural propagation, procreation and animal husbandry. This aspect of Hermes is not used in traditional astrology, but it is important because it indicates an affinity with the Virgoan feminine principle which is missing from the classical model we normally use. Though we are aware of the androgyny, some would say bisexuality, of his nature, we tend to concentrate more on Hermes' intellectual attributes. Yet we need to understand the underground sensuous nature of Hermes so that we can see how mercurial people might use this attribute to reach an integration of feeling values and thought processes.

No full myths remain of this older Hermes, though there are traces of his early origins in later myths; but his association with the fertility of his herds was carried over into urban Greece in a conspicuous way. The *Herm* was an oblong pillar with his mask at the top and, some way down, a phallus. By the late sixth century BC it appeared at boundaries and at the entrances to houses and public buildings, a sign of good luck and an emblem of the wish for fertility and increase within and to mark the transition between the outer, busy, sometimes chaotic external world and the world of enclosed order, the home or the meeting place. Later still, once urban life and politics had become an established part of Greek culture as we know it, we begin to see Hermes in his rational aspect, with winged helmet and sandals, carrying the Caduceus, the pleasant-tongued messenger. It is from this time on that we discover more of his patriarchal nature and this knowledge of him is based on the development of the written word and recorded mythology and history.

To increase the mystery surrounding Hermes' evolution still further, we know that he was, by the time of the Roman Empire, openly associated with the Egyptian gods – Thoth, the god of the Moon and wisdom, and Anubis, the divinity associated with death and the underworld. Which god appeared first on the archaic Mediterranean scene is difficult to determine, though it seems likely that Egyptian Thoth and Anubis were the prototypes of Hermes; but by Roman times their cults were known to overlap and they shared many attributes and characteristics. At the same time, each god kept some of his separate cultural determinants. Though all three were known as wonder-workers, mysterious, perhaps shamanistic and having connections with the divinities of the dead, only Greek Hermes seems to be known for his dishonesty and trickery.

By taking into account the historical but unexplained development of Greek Hermes from a phallocentric god connected to the feminine principle and fertility into a rational one whose youthful attributes are more intellectual than sexual, we begin to get some grasp of his slipperiness and shape-shifting abilities. It is also necessary to note his affinity with the death-process when he becomes the guide of souls into the realms of Hades. At core, he has the ability to move between these different states of being, but the problem for mercurial people, as well as the god, is that fear often prevents them from making connections between what seem to be disparate processes. But Hermes is always on the move, always needs to cross thresholds, even though it is sometimes difficult to see when and why he has made the transition from one state to another. So his trickiness has both a positive and a negative value. We can see this at work in

Hermes' cultural history as much as in some of our mercurial clients.

No mythographer explains the cultural development of the cult of Hermes, either in terms of the evolution of the individual and collective psyche in the ancient world, or in terms, even, of the development of written language. We do not know how Hermes came to be the divine carrier of the developing Greek consciousness and intellect; the history of the evolution of the psyche and human consciousness is still a topic of debate and dissent. These attributions may have developed naturally as society evolved, or they may have been assimilated into his cult from other Mediterranean cultures. So any interpretation of what may or may not have been the most important cultural historical trends, events and processes in the cult of Hermes is difficult to sustain from written evidence alone. Greek, Roman and Egyptian historians left only incomplete, sometimes conflicting, accounts of the origins of their gods, and these are the subject of much dispute – and mercurial slipperiness – in the contemporary academic world. As astrologers, then, we are left to fill in the gaps and interpret for ourselves what trickiness and shape-shifting may mean for our clients and why it seems inherent in the collective and archetypal image of Hermes.

THE DENIAL OF PAIN

To do so we need to ask ourselves what function for the psyche such cunning serves; to remember that, for Hermes and mercurial clients, it can have a preserving as well as a damaging aspect. Then we can see how this reveals itself in the birthchart. Astrologers may assess a client's level of openness and awareness of this issue, bearing in mind that it can cause mercurial people personal pain to be honest about themselves and admit to some identification with this trait. The myths of Hermes give strong indications of how such subtlety operates; he was not a god to submit easily to vulnerability, as his childhood lying shows. He was more apt to use denial and, occasionally, when that didn't work, brute force to avoid facing his own pain and woundedness. We see this most clearly in the myth of Argos, which details how Hermes both hurts and saves himself.

After Zeus experienced Hera's rage at his infidelity with Io, he turned Io into a heifer to protect her from his jealous wife. Hera claimed her as her own, captured her and set hundred-eyed Argos to guard her. Zeus, defying Hera, sent Hermes to free her. Hermes knew he could never evade all of Argos' eyes, so he played his pipes until Argos fell asleep, crushed him with a rock and beheaded him. Craft and ingenuity ensured that Hermes achieved his aim, saving himself from harm, but only brute force could be used to cut off Argos' head. Though he used his trickery to lull Argos to sleep, he could not use his trickery to outwit him when awake.

In such a case, even a slippery god will turn killer, and Hermes' normally flexible mind was limited to this solution. But he could only do so by denying the pain death causes, and cutting off from his own feeling response to it. Where he was most wounded, and where his unexamined preconceptions lay behind this act, was in his identification with his father. At no point does Hermes question Zeus' infidelity or Hera's subsequent rage, and in this myth he acts the role of the unquestioning servant. Hermes was unable to connect with any feeling values about Argos' death, so, splitting off from these, logically he carried out Zeus' orders, thus denying any real responsibility for his own part in the killing. This is the mad rationality of the servile warrior who kills not because he has thought through issues for himself in a mature way, or because he has felt the pain of conflicts between his father's orders and his own wishes in the matter, but because he is told to.

Astrologers and counsellors sometimes intuit similar kinds of denial and irresponsibility behind the seemingly rational statements of their clients. One woman, with Mercury conjunct Saturn in Capricorn, both trine Neptune in Virgo, was successful in her career as a teacher and writer and had the ability to communicate well, for the most part, her philosophical ideals and ideas through her work. Where she was less successful was in the sphere of personal relationships, particularly where men could not carry her ideal image of them, or disagreed with some of her more conservative theories and values. Then she would admit disappointment with them, very rationally, and travel on to the next liaison, killing any meaning in her marriages in the process.

Mercury was just out of exact trine with Neptune in Virgo, at the apex of a T-square with Venus and Jupiter, so exacerbating the difficulty; her tendency was to overreact to all imperfect situations, as she viewed them. Acceptance of human imperfection was not the way she chose to work, and she did not allow her consciousness to expand enough to contain her own desire for immediate gratification. During times of stress in relationships, her work suffered and her men were blamed. She denied any responsibility in this process and, instead, felt compelled to finish each relationship when it either challenged her boundaries or seemed not to reach her ideal image. Yet her difficult T-square aspecting Mercury might have meant the development of much sensitivity and loving expression communicated through relationships, had she been willing to work with its negative expression openly and consciously.

THE GOD IN THE MARKET-PLACE

There is a transactional, mercantile character about such negative behaviour – 'If you don't give me what I want, I'll get it by trading myself elsewhere, and I'm not concerned with your feelings about it' – which is represented by Hermes, and, later, by Roman Mercury as the god of merchants and business affairs, legal and illegal alike. His development, split off as it was from the feeling function, was not always helped by his growing knowledge of the use of weights and measures. A functional, practical and a very Virgoan activity when applied to the world of commerce, a necessary adjunct for a god who needed to balance the weight of his words and learning, it also shows where Hermes was tempted to be crooked and undignified. A busy market-place with Hermes as one of the stall-holders would be a place to be aware of the manner in which any business was conducted. He needed a strong moral and feeling component to help him overcome the drive to obtain something for nothing as well as to control the need to use his fluent tongue while engaging in some almost magical sleights-of-hand with the balances.

The acts of weighing and measuring, balancing, bargaining and compromising might be some of the functions mercurial people need to consider in their explorations of the tricky side of the psyche. This involves a capacity for reflection. A hyperactive market-place, both inner and outer, may not be the best place for cultivating it. It is there, though, at the end of the reflective process, that new ways of behaving will be put to use. Hermes does eventually learn to anchor himself enough to do so for the necessary period of time. At this stage, though, he is still potentially volatile in his dealings, his dishonest shadow often planning to get what it could while it could. He did not find breaking away from his old patterns of behaviour very easy.

Sometimes this driven quality of mercurial trickiness is very obvious. Hermes does not always contain his impulse to obtain something of value by stealth rather than work. He often gets what he wants by sowing dissent to hide the essence of the dishonest transaction taking place; then the borders become unclear between what is his and what belongs to other people. He is unable at this stage to empathize with other people's needs enough to prevent himself from acting immorally, or from discovering what is truly his own.

WIT AND SPITE

When he does not act honestly, he displays an unconscious envy of other people's possessions. So the witty god can slip into maliciously enjoying other people's distress. We saw this in the episode where he stole Apollo's cattle. In the myth of Pandora we see no wit, but much repressed spite. Created by the gods, she was a gift from them to Epimetheus, Prometheus' brother. The gods hated Prometheus because he had given their divine fire, that is, consciousness, to mankind. Hermes was given the task of leading the beautiful but inquisitive Pandora to her husband. In her curiosity, she opened the jar in which the gods had enclosed all the world's evils, releasing them to plague mankind. Hermes was well aware that Pandora had been created imperfect, so that, through her, the gods might take revenge on mankind, but he still, unfeelingly, followed Zeus' command to conduct her to Epimetheus, along with the jar the gods had given her. Here Hermes is the carrier of the god's spite, cut off from his own, but willing to let Pandora bear the burden for releasing evil and dissent among men.

He performs the role of the agent and mediator between divine and mortal hatred: where his sense of empathy doesn't operate, the result is inevitably discord and distress for those who are less powerful than the gods. The mercurial qualities apparent in this myth are shadow ones – disconnection and revenge, spite instead of wit, and leaving women to bear the burden for introducing evil into the human world. Perhaps, though, it was necessary for the development of the human psyche that this should happen. People only widen consciousness by becoming aware of the conflict between good and evil, however they define it, and by struggling with the darker sides of their natures. Hermes served as a catalyst in this process, but he was not mature or compassionate enough to mitigate its worst effects. It was Prometheus who put Hope into the jar so that man would not be entirely overwhelmed by misery. Again we see the tricky duality of Hermes; at the same time that he aids the appearance of discord into the world, he also opens the way for a fuller development of consciousness.

Astrologers and counsellors may become aware of a similar duality in some of their clients. Mercurial people of a puckish and immature nature may use this as a way of hiding spite and a need for revenge. A client with the Moon in Gemini at the apex of a T-square to Mercury in Virgo and Saturn in Pisces was known to be a practical joker. His wife, friends and close colleagues were all butts of his sometimes anxiety-provoking jokes. As the years went by, this amusing but mendacious Moon/Mercury characteristic wore very thin with those closest to him and, when finally challenged about his behaviour, he found it difficult to stop. His glib excuse that it was only a joke became less acceptable as people got angrier with him and told him to grow up.

He did have some realization that his watery Saturn, his *senex*, needed to be given conscious life and not used in such an underground way to teach people lessons. He had always found it difficult to be angry, to confront his own anger and to stand firm for his own needs in relationships; he got his revenge at the childish level of practical-joking. It needed quite some work for him to see the cruelty behind his actions; many times in the process he reverted to his Peter Pan mode by being late for sessions or not turning up at all. But facing the pain of openly using his problematic Saturnine strength was the only way he could go in order to start valuing his relationships. Though he hoped for success, he found the work too painful to maintain because other relationship difficulties began to open up. Eventually he chose not to continue with counselling, falling back into using his Moon/Mercury square; and I suspect that afterwards he continued to use his old *puer* traits to survive in what, unconsciously, he felt to be hostile environments.

THE CAPACITY FOR SURVIVAL

This man could not make the transition into maturity because that would have meant the painful death of old habits, and surviving is something Hermes/Mercury knows how to do well. He used it to survive his development from an Arcadian god into one acceptable to the patriarchal Olympian pantheon under Zeus. He used it to survive Apollo's displeasure when he stole his cattle. We occasionally see clients who use the techniques of trickiness and disguise even in relatively friendly environments where there is no real need to keep up defences. Puerile behaviour is one aspect of the mercurial shadow; suspicion is another.

Ovid's Roman tale of Baucis and Philemon shows both Mercury and Jupiter needing to hide and yet test their disbelief in human values. An old couple, Baucis and Philemon, were known to be devout and altruistic although they lived in poverty. Jupiter and Mercury decided to find out how deep their kindness really went, so, disguising themselves, they appeared to the old couple as two travellers in need of food and rest. Baucis and Philemon gladly shared what food they had with them and offered a bed for the night. As a reward for passing the gods' test, when they died they were turned into two trees which stood at the entrance to the shrine they had served throughout their lives. Luckily, here, the true survival was of the old couple's values; the gods' suspicion could not last in the face of such obvious altruism.

The tale tells us perhaps more about Mercury and Jupiter than it does about the old couple. It was the gods who distrusted that two human beings could sustain this degree of altruism with anyone, least of all with strangers, though they were proved wrong in this case. Where there is distrust, people and situations are likely to be put to the test unknowingly and with suspicion, as Philemon and Baucis were. By this action, the gods themselves show their own shadow sides, the quick fall into undifferentiating unconsciousness which displays the more primitive, self-preserving, perhaps arrogant elements of the psyche. Very often uncaring himself, Mercury cannot believe that human beings are capable of sustaining the quality of caring for others. In this he follows his father's lead yet again, appearing unconscious and unrelated. The female quality of continually nurturing feeling values is not displayed by the two gods. Only on proof of their altruism were Baucis and Philemon rewarded, and neither god shows any regard for how they might have acquired it or what they had to do to sustain it.

The ability to sustain relationships, activities or principles is a learned art and one which comes easiest if learned early. Where it is not, trickiness can be used as a quick way out of working steadily on relationship difficulties over the long haul. Such work can often be seen by mercurial people as both boring and constraining. While most astrologers would attribute this characteristic to some people born under Gemini, Virgoans, too, for all the attention they may pay to detail and crafting a piece of work, can fall into this shadow side of Mercury. While they are less likely than Gemineans to admit to boredom, rather than face the routine of painstaking work they will sometimes develop mysterious illnesses or, if it is more appropriate, procrastinate for as long as possible. Virgoans, if unconscious, are unaware that unrelatedness can reveal itself in actions or physical symptoms. Often known as the healers of the Zodiac, they sometimes hide their own woundedness by controlling and ordering their relationships, refusing the chaos of difficult emotions. It is through accepting chaos and lack of control as valuable parts of life's experience, allowing themselves to feel and sustain their vulnerability consciously in this mode, and not evade the meaning of bodily symptoms, that Virgoans are likely to learn most.

ISSUES OF CONTROL

Control was an attribute which classical Hermes delighted in, because, in true patriarchal fashion, with control went power. As his childhood shows, Hermes was not a god to use naked force initially, or the berserker rage of Ares, the martial god, where other means gained him the same ends, though the will to power of both of them was essentially the same. As we have seen, activities which demonstrated the versatile use of physical or mental skills were the ways in which Hermes preferred to gain control. His quickness, dexterity and litheness led to an easy association with boxing and gymnastics, activities associated with men in classical times, as they mostly are now. Evidently Hermes had developed the Virgoan flexibility to roll with the punches or take a fall lightly, just as earlier, in difficult circumstances, he had developed a flexible, Geminean tongue. Both control and suppleness are useful for survival; both traits are double-edged – particularly where they are used involuntarily – and are also interrelated.

It may take mercurial clients some time to become aware of this duality in their bodies, as well as in their personalities and their psyches. Hermes himself begins to do it where the myths show some indications of a shamanistic trait rather than that of the tricky magician. One example of this is when he, the youthful messenger, was given the staff or Caduceus as an emblem of his right to guide souls down into the underworld and to heal. Within the youth are the seeds of the man – or god – who can use his flexibility and control to guide himself and others. This can only happen when he and people with Mercury strong in their charts become sensitive and open to deep and previously unexplored needs, and can devise strategies to protect themselves without harming others or becoming too rigid and frightened of change.

The boundary between remaining open to experience without overdefending against being hurt is a difficult one to maintain. So many balance-points need consciously to be sought for and found between flexibility and control, self and others, pain and harmony, need and satisfaction, that only slowly may the realization dawn on mercurial people that a lifetime's work of conscious maintenance is needed. There is no easy route to gain: some, but not all, are willing to take up that burden or challenge. Yet Hermes' ability to move across thresholds, as he does between life and death, indicates that they are in a good position to benefit from doing so.

One way astrologers may help clients towards achieving that skill is to take note of Hermes' capacity to make connections between consciousness and the unconscious, which is often unknown and feared. He has the dexterity and skill to collect relevant information; he is able to hone his body and his mind and, eventually, his spirit to the level of awareness needed to win honourably, while honouring both joy and pain as essential parts of the learning experience. He has a need to be competitive, but learns to control his drive to be unfairly superior. He learns to respect rather than disdain the skill of his opponents. But he can only complete this work by coming into contact with the healer archetype within his own nature, and that is only reached by plunging into the dark realms of the unconscious. Understanding and learning to contain the crueller, more hate-filled side of the human psyche are also part of the mercurial journey. The myths connecting him with Apollo and Hades indicate that he eventually realizes how important it is for him to do so. As with the gods, so with men and women – or those, at least, who are willing to work in this way.

BROADENING ABILITIES

But the shamanistic traits of classical Hermes have hidden qualities about them which are not fully realized until the development of alchemy, and even then they are not always clear, as we shall see later. There is, however, an indication in earlier Greek mythology that Hermes needs knowledge of more than just a quick mind to make the transition from tricky magician to shaman. He has to learn to bypass the intellect and broaden his range of communication and competitive skills, non-verbal as well as verbal. Yet he also has to learn to use all his skills consciously, including his intellectual ones, to deepen growing feelings of connectedness. He has to learn to face the fears of the unknown and be flexible enough to negotiate difficult situations. This is why his affinity with boxing and gymnastics is as important to his own healing process as his involvement with divination, music, astronomy and the development of the alphabet.

The mixture of rational and irrational characteristics is significant because it tells us how Hermes and mercurial clients might learn to cross boundaries safely and stay conscious of conflicting needs. The difficulty comes for mercurial people when they get stuck with a particular pattern of response or are pulled between seemingly contradictory processes, unable, consciously, to cross the boundaries between thought and feeling. This can be revealed in many forms – overrationalizing, obsessive thinking, indecision, anxiety, and a tendency for them to catapult themselves out of difficulties, destroying relational ties, without really knowing why this process is happening to them.

Such clients need to learn the art of containing their inner contradictions between creativity and destruction rather than projecting their lack of connectedness and integration on to external events and other people. One woman in therapy, of whom I knew nothing astrologically other than that she had a Gemini Sun, had been in a relationship with a man for some years and was aware of her need, but also of her dislike of him.

She was not conscious of her complete identification with her feelings, nor of her tendency to idealize men, and had developed no skills which left her in charge of her feelings. She was driven by them. The only relationship she could maintain with her partner was an on–off one, which left her confused, depressed and almost unable to function in her everyday life.

Initially, she attempted to solve her dilemma in therapy by constantly explaining how she was caught up in the same repetitive thoughts and images day after day. There seemed no escape from them and she had little ego-strength to act consistently by giving up her relationship, by accepting the man as he was or by trying to change the relationship between them. She had no real understanding of her own learned but unexamined values. Any plan of action was compounded by fears of the future, and she did not want the responsibility of accepting the painful consequences of loss involved in making any decision – a very mercurial trait.

She stayed stuck for long months until she became bored and frustrated with the lack of movement and angry that other people were not to blame for the way in which she saw them. Slowly she began to see that only she was holding herself to the pattern of negative thinking, which wouldn't change, by thinking about it even more; that her own fixed patterns of thought were tricking her into thinking there was no way out of her difficulties. She began, very tentatively, to try out new ideas and ways of being, but only after much practice in confronting her own feelings, her fears of the future and her obsessive thought patterns. The quick, mercurial mind which is so overvalued in contemporary society was of little use to this woman. She needed to learn other, less tricky ways of communicating her needs and feelings and to contain and accept the pain of her own slow, suffering steps towards transforming her life – which she cautiously began to do.

This is a similar task to the one which constantly faces Gemineans and Virgoans and certainly faced mythological Hermes. The message is a simple one – as you once learned to walk, so you can learn to know yourself to the best of your ability, contain the suffering and live fully. The route to self-actualization is neither simple nor easy. People undergoing such a life-change need much support and empathy along the way, and those with a strong mercurial streak may need to be held and helped through the period when old pain arises. Mercurial people often need to subject their behaviour and new, fearful feelings to conscious criticism, but in such a way that it supports, rather than undermines, their confidence.

CRAFT AND SKILL

At this point, an astrological counsellor may help a client to realize that ultimately he tricks and deceives only himself into a false sense of security; necessary pain about the wrong use of criticism may have to be faced before transformation truly occurs. Deception and denial may have been survival strategies adopted at a time when a child had neither the knowledge nor the power to challenge stronger adults, but they are inappropriate in a maturing adult who needs to acknowledge his own power and, perhaps, his misuse of it. Astrological Mercury represents a force which can be used to understand and discard old, outworn psychological transactions, as well as assisting the introduction of the new and useful emotional skills. This is a way of gently civilizing the trickster from within its own framework until it becomes acceptably sensible of a range of emotions.

The connection between the cruel trickster and sensible assistant needs much positively used subtlety to be maintained and needs to be informed constantly by a strong feeling component. Once this has occurred then the psyche's trickster element has undergone a profound, perhaps shamanic, perhaps alchemical change. At that point, maturing, mercurial people may become aware that they have added the skills of vigilance and awareness to their repertoire. These are needed because the task ahead of them stays difficult; no once-for-all solution is on offer. Once the philosopher's stone has formed, it then has to be put to use in an imperfect human world – and that process brings with it unknown consequences which also have to be recognized.

We see the shamanic, cultural and useful development of the

Mercury archetype in other areas which come under his patron-
age. In one set of myths, Hermes was said to have helped the
three Fates to invent the alphabet. It was a natural enough
activity for a clever and loquacious god. His part in the process
may have marked the point at which the society in which he
operated shifted from purely oral transmission to recorded statement of facts, history and other cultural and social developments,
lessening the uncertainty of relying on the spoken word. But we
still need to bear in mind the trickster element. Facts can be
subjectively biased or selected for particular propaganda purposes, both consciously and unconsciously, spoken or written. If
the mercurial boundaries are not made clear, much slipperiness
can take place here, as much in the collective as in the personal
psyche. Yet the boundary problem is double-edged. If boundaries
are not passable, then Hermes would find it difficult to move
between the realms of the known and the unknown. But he, and
mercurial people, need to return safely to the known world with
new knowledge and interpretation. Goal-setting might be a
positive asset here. It helps people with a strong Mercury to
know something about what might be achieved as honestly and
feelingly as possible, even if the way and the threshold are not
always clear at the beginning.

There are indications in some of Hermes' other attributes that
cultural developments paralleled the development of consciousness in ancient Greece. In his associations with astronomy, mental
proficiency, his stellar origins and the ability to scribe served him
well. All three were brought together in the field of Greek
astronomy. So, too, were his musical skills. As well as building
the lyre from tortoiseshell as a gift to Apollo, he is credited with
inventing the musical scales. The ancient theory of 'the music of
the spheres', those vibrations that the Greeks thought were
produced by the planets and which influenced the development
of astrology, indicates how Hermes and mercurial people have
the positive ability to combine different areas of knowledge,
perhaps in a way that would once have been labelled shamanic
or magical. Always a versatile and innovative god, Hermes'
ability to bring together separate components to form a new
substance later guaranteed that medieval alchemists regarded him

as a magician of prime importance when any work concerned with great change was undertaken. In the realm of magic, alchemy and science, the ability to synthesize is as important as understanding the changeable nature of the components – as it is with any form of knowledge.

A similar situation exists with divination. Like Apollo, Hermes was originally a prophesying god. Some of the myths relate that he was taught the art of reading the future by the Triae, the nymphs who represent the intuitional female principle. The movement of pebbles in water was their speciality, and perhaps archaic Hermes' affinity with stone cairns helped him with the use of pebbles for prophecy. Other myths tell us that he also made use of knucklebones in divination. Pebbles, water and bones indicate that Hermes, like mercurial people, has to demonstrate his skills concretely and feelingly, that built into his nature is an affinity with form and values; he cannot rely on his airy intellect alone, and diminishes his abilities if he does so. He does need, though, to recognize consciously the depths of meaning in his own symbology.

Yet much ambivalence can occur here, too. We cannot always be sure with Hermes that he is not seeking his own advantage in the easiest way by clouding the issue. Oracles have a way of speaking in riddles and much is left open to later interpretation. Unless prediction is understood and acted upon directly in a way that is acceptable to the gods and the Fates – and the Triae are one form of the Fates – the consequences can range from the confusing to the dire. Men are left with free will to decide whether or not to accept the destiny inherent in their characters which is revealed by a proper interpretation of the oracle. Again the issue is one of boundaries – what needs to be done, who has to be appeased, what new areas of experience and learning have to be brought into operation and what choices have to be made – and much pain may be confronted or avoided.

This was clear from the chart of one woman who came for an astrological consultation. She had Gemini rising sextile Mercury in Leo and also a Sun/Pluto conjunction which was conjunct her Leo IC; the conjunction opposed her Moon. She studied occult practices; was convinced that she had a gift and that her predictions were rarely wrong. She had a partner, the latest of many, whom she could only control by periodically threatening to leave. The myth guiding her life was that what she could not control, she left – and blamed her partners for being unpredictable. Her unshakeable belief in her powers of divination was similar to the way in which she conducted her relationships and she resisted any attempts to raise the issue of letting go of controls. Predictably, what she wanted from me was a one-off reading which looked at future trends. I was also to be controlled. She saw no relationship between the ways she wished to control both the future and her partner. She was not at the stage where her Sun/Pluto conjunction could allow her to take charge of her own development in a very conscious way through the Asc./Mercury sextile, though the potential was there. Though she was not happy with the way she related to people, she was unwilling to take responsibility for her part in the process. Sadly, she went away, I feel, not much wiser than when she came and with her control mechanisms intact.

The quality of intactness is very much a Virgoan one. Though a Mercury-ruled mutable sign, it is still in the element of earth, but earth gives form as well as being resistant to change. The positive, form-giving side of Virgo is indicated by the purity with which Virgoans can express their dexterity and craftiness. They are often clever with their hands and are able to craft their environments with considerable skill. What Gemineans can do with their minds and speech, Virgos are able to put, sensibly, to practical use. The meaning underlying both, however, is similar; the emphasis is on using learned skills in an ingenious way to find an individual path through the world, but one which connects them with an understanding of other people's needs as well as their own. Unconsciously, the trickster element may still arise; Virgo has the capacity to cut corners impatiently and shape-shift as much as Gemini has, though their fields of operation may differ. It is here that positive craftiness of intent can easily slip over into its opposite form of a dishonest craftiness of action, which may then turn destructive.

CUNNING AND DESTRUCTION

This much can be seen in one of the myths which is attached to Loki in Norse mythology. He appears to have, in some respects, similar characteristics to the Amerindian Trickster, of whom Paul Radin has made a study. Loki is foster-brother to Odin and the son of two giants. In the earlier myths we see his trickster aspect most clearly. He is involved in the loss of the goddess Idun's golden apples, but helps find them again; he cuts the goddess Sif's long, golden hair, but makes reparation; he helps to build the wall around the gods' homestead, Asgard, by trickery – all easily, quickly and magically. But in the later myths Loki seems to become the enemy of the gods, setting up impossible situations which eventually lead them to their own downfall, to Ragnarok. There is an essential cruelty in the way he arranges that mistletoe should kill blind Balder, and aids his daughter, Hel, in preventing Balder from returning to life. For his part in the process, Loki was bound in chains by the gods, much as Prometheus was by the Olympians, and placed where a snake could drip venom on him until the end of the world came. Before he was caught and chained, however, he attempted to elude his captors by shape-shifting, turning himself into a salmon. Not that it helped him much; the gods were used to his wiles by that time.

The myth of Loki indicates what happens when the trickster turns life-threateningly bitter and cruel, something that does not openly happen to classical Hermes in recorded mythology, even in his darkest aspect. Hermes learns, eventually, to use and transmute his inner darkness and chaos; Loki is taken over by, and acts out, the more destructive aspects of the unconscious, wreaking full-scale vengeance on the gods and the world. Poisoned himself, Loki ultimately ensures that the whole of creation is doomed, and, at Ragnarok, all the gods and most of the world are destroyed by his monstrous children, Hel, the goddess of the underworld, Fenrir, the wolf and Jormungard, the Midgard serpent.

Loki and his children, too, do not survive. Here we see how the trickster god, and some mercurial people, sometimes remain prisoners of their own self-regarding slyness and find no deeper creative meaning in their relations with any quality, divine or human; they then lose control of the inhuman monsters they have raised from the depths of the psyche to help them in their work of destruction. Mercurial people who have dropped into a nihilistic world-view can then find no reason why a creation which they do not value, whatever form it takes, should continue. They may not realize that by destroying all of creation they are ultimately destroying themselves.

None of Odin's shamanic qualities seem to help at Ragnarok; he perishes along with the other gods. Odin himself wasn't a creator god, though he descended from those who were, and he is unable to bring order out of ultimate chaos and survive the process. Tricksterish though it is, it may be that Ragnarok is a necessary destruction, akin to the biblical Armageddon in its effects. The Eddas tell us that after the world is destroyed a new world arises, and a new life, with younger gods, some resurrected gods and a continuation of the human race. Loki himself was not resurrected. Though this myth may reflect the succession of Norse culture by Christianity, or may be a development of early Near Eastern destruction myths, it also has implications for psychological development.

Loki's fall into the unconscious and destructive side of the trickster eventually resolves into a new form of consciousness, and this is something that may happen to mercurial people whether or not they choose to face their pain. Events may conspire to bring about the end of old patterns of behaviour, but there needs to be some glimmer of understanding from the person involved in the process for it to result in new life and new hope. This was where Loki failed; he could not separate from the chaos and was consumed by it. Unlike Loki, alchemical Hermes eventually chose a less cataclysmic and more time-consuming way of reaching new consciousness, though even that process had its risks.

No myths of Loki show us that he ever attempted to struggle with the shadow side of his nature, and none show us that Thoth or classical Hermes did either. We are only given descriptions of the underground aspects of the latter two, and we know that Hermes connects the upper and lower worlds in his role of soul-guide. We do not know how he came to recognize the trickiness of his own nature and to use that quality positively to light the way between consciousness and unconsciousness. This leaves psychological astrology with a delicate task, which is as slippery as is Hermes himself.

We are left to assume that, because Hermes is associated with travelling and the underworld, he has successfully made the transition. It is godlike not to fear the boundaries or the travelling, but people are not gods; they have to struggle to recognize and cross the boundaries between thought and feeling, lower and upper, consciousness and unconsciousness – and they need to learn how they might return safely. Some mercurial people might fear the going, others fear the return and the responsibility that it brings with it. So we have a responsibility to ensure, as best we can, that mercurial clients who fear change or depth are not pushed beyond their capabilities at the time of consultations. What we may do is gently open the way for them so they may see more of how to use and extend their abilities, but to leave the choice to them about whether they wish to make the journey. This way we guard ourselves from falling into Hermes' trap of separating our knowledge from our clients' feelings.

It also means that we have become aware of some of the difficulties which cultures, as well as individuals, have had to undergo in the past because too much accent has been placed on the more masculine development of the intellect, while underplaying the necessity of balancing it with more feminine and supportive feeling values. We need to restore to the archetypal image of Hermes not only the values of feeling but also those of intuition and sensation, all of which are inherent in Hermes' myths – particularly those related to his travelling, healing and alchemical attributes. It is this part of his journey we shall trace in the following chapters.

5

The Traveller and Soul-guide

COMPANIONSHIP AND COURAGE

Not only is classical Hermes the traveller and transactor above ground in the world of commerce and merchants, but he carries the same attributes underground in his role of Infernal Hermes, one of the death gods, carrying out the commands of both Zeus and Hades. We know that at some point in the history of his cult he was made psychopomp to Hades, guiding the souls of the dead to the dark regions. In the myths concerning the death process we see similarities between the Greek myths and those from Egypt about Thoth and Anubis, both Lords of the Underworld. The assumption is often made that the cults of Hermes and Anubis merged only in Alexandrian and Ptolemaic Egypt, after which the joint cult was brought to Rome around the time of the Roman conquest of Egypt. As we have seen, there is still some scholarly dispute concerning whether or not the Egyptian, and perhaps Phoenician, cults of the dead penetrated Greek culture in the second millennium BC. If it is eventually accepted that such cross-cultural influences did occur so early, then Hermes' connection with many Mediterranean dying and reborn gods, and so, psychologically, with the death of old consciousness and the rebirth of the new, is much older than we have thought.

This has implications for psychological astrology today, because it seems that the struggle between discarding the inappropriate and introducing new, more helpful elements into the developing psyche is common, in some form, to all past and present cultures. While the Greeks may not have been fully aware of these psychic struggles within themselves at the individual level, we cannot make the assumption that they were never so. All we can say now is that they had made an appearance in the collective culture by classical times – hence the plays of Aeschylus and

Sophocles and the Homeric poems and odes, as well as the need for religious cults and rituals; they may or may not have reflected individual struggles.

It is not proven that men developed self-orientated reflective and inward-looking characteristics at this particular point in historical time; nor is it proven that human consciousness at this stage of its evolution was mostly directed towards the needs of the collective. We can be fairly sure, though, that as consciousness and conceptual and symbolic language developed, so men would have had more tools at their service to help them deepen their psychological understanding. Psychological astrologers nowadays may take this a step further and can consciously draw analogies between psychological growth and Hermes' development through time.

We can watch the way in which he processes useful attributes from his time as a phallic god and expands his range of responses to life. Tracing the passage of his development into Hermes Trismegistos, and into the figure who is now used both in psychology and astrology, is one of the methods we can use to explore unconscious depths. He seems to pass through the stages of displaying primitive instincts, to youthful error-ridden explorations of his environment when he tests out the gods' reactions to the theft of his brother's cattle, through to containment of his functions as psychopomp to Hades, and then on to a recognition and management of all his attributes as the alchemical Hermes Trismegistos. For him to be most useful in psychological astrology we need to know that he can help mercurial clients to reach previously unexplored material which resides in the lower regions of the psyche and to put it to good use in the upper world.

One of the tasks often faced in therapy is for the therapist to be with a client as a friend along the way while he or she becomes aware of less developed inner resources and struggles to integrate these into consciousness. Often in mercurial clients the struggle is to balance the overvalued intellect with developing feeling values. There is a need, too, for such a person to search for connections they might make between their bodies, psyches and spirits. This can only be done by consciously descending into the unknown realms of the unconscious, willingly submitting to the powers of the dark gods for a time, as Hermes did to both Hades and Zeus. They may take with them, not only the myths of Hermes for guidance and protection, but also the powers of an inquiring intellect in a purposefully deep search for as much wholeness as they can encompass. This journey involves a risk which not everybody is willing to take. To go underground in the psychological sense is to face, perhaps, death or madness, very much as the Celtic bards and poets did when they spent their nights of initiation in the open, on the top of a death-barrow. Great gifts could be brought back from the realms of the dead, but at the risk of being destroyed in the process.

In the Greek myths, we see Hermes accepting this underworld role when he is given Hades' helmet of invisibility, which helps make his activities less accessible to men. It ensures that he can pass unharmed between the lands of the living and the dead. The helmet also indicated that Hermes appeared to have a quicker-than-thought, intuitive reflex. His thinking processes were not at all obvious and this was a useful trait when quick responses and actions were called for. Zeus had also given him a staff when he made him messenger to the gods, and by doing so positively used his restless and mutable qualities. His flighty mercurial nature was now contained within the meaning of the appropriate symbols. Initially, there is a need for mercurial clients to separate the functions symbolized by the helmet and staff, fully recogniz-ing them, and how they operate, before reintegrating them in a more useful and expanded way. New thinking and new ways of being are then firmly founded on the co-ordination of the four Jungian functions, thinking, feeling, sensation and intuition. At the level of integration the aim is to realize that the mind is a good servant but a bad master: not all functions are to be reduced to the level of mind alone.

So Hermes does acquire from Zeus and Hades the attributes he needs to connect and travel between the god of the mountain-tops and the god of the depths. Acquisitiveness is a useful mercurial quality for psychological astrologers to bear in mind when they and their clients are deep in the consultation process. Hermes needs his tools and he knows how to get them; mercurial clients need them also. Perhaps his means of acquiring them are slippery initially, but, at the point where Hermes connects with the death principle through his association with Hades, there is something inexorable and honest about him. Death cannot be avoided or outwitted, and it is easier for mercurial clients to plumb the depths of the psyche if they befriend Hermes and take their intellects with them on the inward journey. If they do not, there is a danger of perpetuating the obvious, defensive dodging and weaving of the intellectual process which shows that an outdated mode of behaviour is still operating.

What happens when the old defensive cycle still continues we can see from the myth of Sisyphus. He tried to outwit death itself. Condemned to Tartaros by Zeus for revealing the god's abduction of Aegina, he, before dying, told his wife, Merope, to leave his body unburied. On reaching Tartaros he went to Persephone and said that he had no right to be there because his body remained unburied. He begged to go back, promising to return in three days. Persephone agreed. Sisyphus returned to the upper world and then refused to return. Hermes had to drag him back by force. That god will listen to no argument, respond to no trickery when men fail to submit to death's call — and people with Mercury prominent in their charts often are pushed to answer Hermes' call when they will not go willingly.

A man with Mercury in Capricorn square to Neptune in Libra and quincunx to a Pluto/North Node conjunction in Leo was called to respond in this way. His Mercury was also sesqui-quadrate Jupiter in Leo. He had made a successful career in business and decided to risk expanding his operations quite significantly. This happened after he had settled a series of difficult staff disputes, acting as sole judge on all staff issues. Initially, he seemed quite successful, but had a time-limit within which to make a profit. When this didn't occur, he chose to make cutbacks. The process still did not result in the required profit and he eventually had to resign, returning to his original career. He was called upon to respond to the logic of the market-place and face the death process involving his own risky expansion. His previous mercurial success failed him in the new business and Hermes exacted his price when he refused to behave in a realistic manner, preferring to speculate and take his chance with success.

This man had chosen to live out his life at the collective level, unaware that the experiences he underwent could be drawn back into himself and used to examine his own life purposes and processes. For him, the external world was the real, the concrete, and he had no awareness that events in his everyday life might have mirrored his inner world. The descent into unconscious life may have been too risky to make because, by doing so, he would then have had to contend with coming to terms with some of his shadow characteristics concerning the abuse of power, arrogance and unwise speculation. This time of facing dark fears echoes the alchemical stage of the *nigredo* which, in psychological terms, can bring with it much pain and depression. A man who values his outward life very much would defend himself against making the descent, fearing that it would prevent him from acting effectively in the outside world, much as Hermes feared the same process before he became Hades' psychopomp.

Yet Hermes can also be a companion on the road to facing death in a conscious way. He has the ability to go beyond ordinary boundaries and to bring himself and his companions safely back to the upper world and consciousness. When Herakles was set the task of descending into Tartaros to capture Cerberos, the three-headed dog which guards the way to Hades' kingdom, Hermes went with him. Herakles, the hero who continually challenged the gods by his labours, courageous though he was, needed a god to guide him. He had set out to capture an attribute of death, not to conquer death itself, and by choosing his target carefully he did not commit the sin of hubris, which was unpardonable insolence towards the gods, thus honouring and propitiating Hades. Hades himself then set the conditions for Herakles' task. Cerberos was only his if he could master him without using either club or arrows. Herakles agreed, did so, and, with Hermes' help, brought Cerberos back to the upper ground.

Here we see how the intellectual function may be used to lead the way to facing the monsters which may lurk in the depths of the psyche. Hopefully, the expanded psyche may eventually learn how to manage them. Gemineans and Virgoans often find this task a difficult one; Gemineans particularly are adept at making the quick intellectual connection and then taking off in pursuit of another train of thought. This is often to avoid deepening the process of finding meanings for their actions, and to evade acting in an individually moral way. They may find it difficult to move away from this particular way of behaving. By not doing so, they often, quite unwittingly, subvert their own mercurial suppleness of thought: their behaviour then becomes fixed, predictable and inappropriate. It may be necessary for them, at some point, to face the death of inappropriate ways of being, as Herakles does. This may free them enough to bring to consciousness some of the raging energy for change which may then be tamed and used to expand their own range of conscious behaviour.

The process takes much courage. Even with Hermes as a companion, it is not easy for mercurial people to pit only their own capacities against unconscious forces and use no unfair or artificial weapons. Like Herakles, mercurial clients who decide to face this task need to strengthen and increase their resources to withstand any onslaught a monster like Cerberos can make. As well as understanding their emotional lives more fully, Gemineans and Virgoans may need to become more consciously aware of their bodies and material surroundings, studying their connection with their physical environments in an effort to ground their more air-inspired ideas, but guarding against becoming too rooted through fear of change. Gemineans, particularly, may benefit from this process, while Virgoans sometimes may have difficulties trusting their more intuitive faculties. Their search in the underworld of the psyche may include finding and developing these sometimes elusive faculties.

Some ego-distance is needed to judge appropriate responses and make conscious choices of action, as much in the underworld as in the daylight of consciousness. Hermes' function of separation and detachment and the Virgoan one of discrimination are useful here; they are not split off from Hades' realms of unconscious feeling when applied in this way. For some mercurial clients, this may be the first time that they meet up with raw feeling values. The work is then about how they consciously manage the fluctuations of feeling in external life. Seeing where detachment can be used both negatively and positively may give them an insight about the best possible choice to make according to the circumstances. The process entails examining old thoughts and reactions by mining the unconscious and rooting out the obsolete and distorted.

A JOURNEY PARTLY COMPLETED

Though Hermes can help with this process and can lead heroes safely back to the upper world, as he did Herakles, there are some instances where he definitely partitions life from death. Here mercurial people are left with no choice but to dissociate and compartmentalize, mourning, sometimes very consciously, sometimes not, their loss of relatedness and completion, experiencing where the upper and lower worlds cannot meet because some vow has been violated, some promise broken. This happens most often when defensive boundaries in some areas of the personality become fixed rather than permeable; sometimes they are open enough for people to realize where they can make no further progress.

We see this most clearly in Hermes' role in the myth of Orpheus. When Orpheus, one of Apollo's sons, descended into the underworld to reclaim his dead wife, Eurydice, Hermes was with him as psychopomp. Persephone was moved by his pleas and his music, persuading Hades to make an exception and let Eurydice return to life. Hades gave his consent, but only on condition that Orpheus did not look back to see if Eurydice was following him out of the land of the dead. Orpheus broke that command, breaking faith with Hades; Eurydice faded back into Tartaros and was lost to the living Orpheus for ever. As he continued to mourn her loss in the upper world, his power to create music faded and he was finally killed and dismembered by his own followers. Only on his proper and complete death was he reunited with Eurydice, and then only in the underworld.

Hermes had not returned to light his way to the underworld for a second time during his life, and, for Orpheus, the boundaries between trust and distrust, the upper and lower worlds, consciousness and unconsciousness became rigid and impassable for the rest of the time he spent on earth.

It seems that Orpheus had taken on more than he could cope with, not having the strength of a Herakles to complete his task. He did, though, have enough of Hermes' awareness to know that he had failed to complete his own inner journey. Hermes does not guide him on his return from Tartaros; he chooses to rely on his own resources to lead Eurydice towards the light and they are not strong enough to sustain him in his task. He appears presumptuous in taking over Hermes' role. He cannot trust that Eurydice is behind him, doubts the faith implied in Hades' command and so loses her. He cannot trust, by implication, that his intellectual function will stay firm of purpose in the underworld of the unconscious.

In extremity, if there is no faith and trust, then mercurial people may find it difficult to connect responsibly with much-needed feeling values embedded in the unconscious. They find it difficult to take the long view. Like Orpheus, having partly made the journey into the dark realms of the psyche, they may unconsciously sabotage their efforts. Once they have attempted the journey inwards, however, they may return partially conscious of what they have lost, of how they have dissociated. Having to hold that pain, as Orpheus did for the rest of his life, means that full healing cannot take place. A deep woundedness and loneliness always remain because they have chosen to compartmentalize their lives and live a restricted existence.

This was shown in the chart of one client whose Mercury was in Aquarius and conjunct Venus. Mercury, while opposing Uranus in Leo, also squared Mars in Taurus and Neptune in Scorpio. He came for counselling because he could not choose between returning to his former wife or deepening his commitment to his present partner. A very articulate person, he said he wanted to resolve this problem and came into therapy to do so. As the sessions progressed, it became clear that there was a life-history of lack of trust, always to do with relationships and ultimately connected with disowning responsibility for his own decisions. Yet he was in agonies because he had a strong need for relatedness, as his Mercury trine Jupiter/Moon conjunction indicated. He had chosen to live alone at that time because he wanted less pressure from both women. He expected that therapy would provide him with magical answers and he resisted any attempts to look at the deeper implications of his behaviour. Eventually he realized that the responsibility for working with this issue was his, but didn't trust that therapy could help with this process. He discontinued, and his ego-defences remained unaltered. Sadly, some time later, he developed cancer. Though this was operated on successfully, he did not resolve his difficulties, choosing to continue to live alone although he was desperately unhappy and depressed.

Defensive boundaries such as this man erected can only be breached with Infernal Hermes' aid. We see this in *The Oresteia* of Aeschylus when Orestes needs to contact the ghost of his dead father, after swearing before Zeus to avenge Agamemnon's murder by Clytemnestra and her lover. He invokes Hermes:

> Hermes, he-god, who can go in and out of the ground,
> he-god still wary to keep power with the fathers,
> now I have need of you, back home from long exile.
> This is the gravemound of Agamemnon, my father.
> Help my cries through the ground to his ghost.[1]

Hermes does help and Orestes contacts his father. It is obvious from Aeschylus' drama that Hermes still acts from the masculine principle, even in his underground aspect. *The Oresteia* is about the establishment of patriarchal power in Greek culture and a question of mercurial slipperiness arises at this point. How far was classical Hermes prepared to go in helping to plumb the depths of the plutonian world of unconscious feelings when this conflicted with preserving the egoic and jupiterian power of the fathers?

An understanding of mythology helps here. We are told that Hermes performs both roles. In his mythology there seems no conflict between the two, but Hermes had Zeus' permission to travel between Olympus and Tartaros. My client mentioned above did not. His ego would not let him penetrate his own defence system, even under the most severe pressure. Acting on the commands from the unconscious is often too fearful a process for strongly mercurial clients to undertake; they certainly need all the help they can get before they even attempt the descent.

RETRIBUTION AND JUSTICE

Sometimes a violation of principles in the conscious realm can lead to it commanding the death process. Retribution can be equally as cruel and remorseless at this level – and Hermes is sometimes involved. After he had attended a banquet on Olympus, Ixion, the son of a Lapith king, planned to seduce Hera. Zeus suspected what was about to happen and fashioned a cloud in Hera's form which Ixion then attempted to seduce while the gods watched. On revealing himself to the surprised Ixion, Zeus ordered Hermes to thrash him, then tie him to a fiery wheel that was thrown into the night sky, where it turned ceaselessly. Hermes obeyed Zeus. The light, prancing, loquacious god disappeared and was replaced by the god who did not question his master's motives.

Ixion had committed hubris through lack of common sense and restraint, so Hermes acted as his outraged intellectual function, pinning him to the flaming wheel of his own fiery consciousness for eternity. The form of retribution handed out in this myth has a very Virgoan quality. Ixion is not allowed to die and be led by Hermes into the death process, but must remain conscious and eternally alive to his misdeeds without the hope of ever correcting them, without ever coming off the wheel. Quite often we see Virgoan clients who are pinned to their own ever-circulating, anxiety-producing patterns of thought, caught in a mind-web. It is a defence mechanism against plunging into the lower levels of their sometimes turbulent and feared psychic depths and indicates that they are unable to take Infernal Hermes with them. They are unable, without help, to use their intellectual functions to discover the hidden emotional meaning behind the troubled workings of their minds.

We see these principles of retribution and justice most clearly in the myths attached to Hermes' Egyptian counterparts, Thoth and Anubis. Both gods of the underworld, embedded in the rituals surrounding death and judgement in the afterlife, they represent the capacity of souls, or of people, to reassess the meaning of their lives, to survive judgement. It needs a clear mind, well-contained observation skills and considerable insight to reveal and judge the weight of a life. Neither Thoth nor Anubis can improvise here; quicksilver solutions and mercurial skating over the surface when choosing between possibilities are not appropriate. The process needs profundity and depth. The profundity also needs to be accompanied by a capacity for judgement without harsh criticism or self-condemnation; enough of that happens as the consequence of unconscious choices in a life anyway, as the harsher myths of the Egyptian gods show. Mercy as well as judgement is necessary, though punishment may not be avoided if the laws of life and death have been violated.

The capacity for judgement is apparent in the functions of Egyptian Anubis, the jackal-headed god, the ruler of tombs and embalming, who, after weighing the hearts of the dead in the underworld, guided souls to Osiris' throne for judgement. Anubis tests the beam of the balance to ensure that the weight is true before placing the heart in the scale-pan. In one pan rests the heart of the dead man; in the other is the feather of Ma'at, the goddess of harmony and justice. Only if the heart outweighs Ma'at's feather will the dead soul be given refuge by Osiris. Like Hermes, Anubis is a psychopomp and acquainted with commerce, always finding the point of balance. He extends Hermes' previously more tricky use of commerce into the hall of judgement, where all has to be seen to be fair. He also sees to the preservation of the body, because only proper preservation could ensure eternal life. Like Hermes, he was associated with the dogs of death who act as guardians in the underworld, constraining souls to act according to the laws of the dead. Like Hermes, too, he does not seem to judge directly, but sets up the conditions for judgement.

It is not surprising, then, that in Ptolemaic times his cult became fused with that of Hermes and they were worshipped as Hermanubis in many places, including Rome, where, we are told, he always appeared with a dog's head, holding in his hands a palm frond and the healing Caduceus. This development shows how closely, despite his apparently more elusive nature in Greek mythology, Hermes became linked to transformative potentials within the body symbolized by the process of mummification, and so with healing processes of resurrection as well as death. Though more likely to be associated with earthy Virgo, Gemini, too, has the capacity to link his or her mind to body functions and awareness. Psychological astrologers may find that one of their tasks with mercurial clients is to help open up issues to do with the separation and reintegration of the four Jungian functions, taking bodily health into account. All these are part of a life's development which is examined in the realm of Anubis and Thoth.

In Anubis' functions we see that mercurial slipperiness has been transformed. It has become the means by which not only a life's worth is weighed, but also how it is lived after judgement in the Halls of the Dead. For strongly mercurial people, not all dies in the realms of the dead, the unknown unconscious. What is preserved, though it may be unrealized, is the potential to make use of the separated intellect to perform fair judgements and to discriminate between good and harmful intentions and actions – a very Virgoan quality when performed well and with feeling. The aim is to make the process conscious, to invoke the mercurial function, so that it can be chosen for use at an appropriate time in the upper world.

Before this can happen, mercurial people need to be able to use their intellects to develop a talent for recording those traits which need to be readjusted. Thoth, the ibis-headed, sometimes the baboon-headed, is the god most associated with Hermes in this area of operation. Originally a Moon god, his cult at Hermapolis was a cosmological one. Worshipped where the Sun god, Ra, was thought to have arisen for the first time, he is the author of the *Book of the Dead*. He holds both the tablet and the reed of the scribe, and he records the deeds of the dead souls before they are brought to Osiris. He was, as Hermes was, too, the inventor of the alphabet and there are myths which state that Hermes took the alphabet to Egypt, or acquired it there. These indicate that there may have been some interaction between Egypt and Greece at a time around the invention of written language. It is yet another hint that the connection between Hermes/Anubis/Thoth might have been established earlier than the Ptolemaic period. If so, the very compressed Greek myths concerning Hermes' involvement with death rites may have once been more elaborate than we now know.

Unlike Hermes, Thoth is capable of acting on his own initiative, particularly when acting out his shadow, perhaps dissociated side. The early pyramid texts indicate that he had no time for liars and was quite capable of cutting off their heads and ripping out their hearts. Yet this may be a necessary function for a god of truth who is compelled to act forcefully in the face of constant denial. In psychological language, it may be an indication of the strength the mercurial intellect needs to get to the heart of matters under question. Thoth ensures that, in the period of judgement, the buried shadow is transmuted into awareness, however painfully and radically: he records everything; he forgets nothing. Getting at the truth of oneself is part of the process of self-awareness and self-development during life, and, some would say, after death.

It is a characteristic that maturing Virgoans and Gemineans can develop, but it may be a painful one. Consciously holding the shadow side, with its overemphasis on details, a disregard for the truth and a tendency to punish harshly and critically, means constant hard work. Often the mercurial journey into the unconscious is the only way to realize that the shadow is the flip-side of the other, more acceptable qualities. The aim is to learn how to accept and integrate both, so that constructive choices can be made – an alchemical product that brings with it an understanding of the need for constant awareness, refinement and practice.

Happily, Thoth also had gentler qualities. The god of scribes and knowledge, lord of hieroglyphs and writing, having first invented the alphabet, he then set about acquiring scientific and literary talents, as well as magic, astronomy, music and arithmetic. Although we are not told how he acquired these attributes, it is easy to see the similarities between him and Hermes. This Egyptian god of intelligence was also the keeper of sacred books, in both the underworld and temple libraries. The herald of the gods, like Hermes, he was known as the true record-keeper in his underworld aspect. His overground activities included the recording of divine and kingly archives, keeping careful records of royal births and pharaonic successions. His Gemini-like versatility and his Virgo-like hard-working nature are impressive. As a result, he was often referred to as 'mightiest of the gods'.

All these achievements would seem quite a weight for mortal Virgoans and Gemineans to carry, but the functions attributed to Thoth show that he travels very consciously, and as well as Hermes, in connecting his underworld activities with those that take place on earth. Where we translate godlike functions to the human plane, we can see that one of the benefits of a mercurial plunge into the realms of the unconscious may be to release the wealth of talents and gifts buried there. Not for nothing, at least in Greek mythology, was Pluto known as the god of buried wealth – and an active and positive mercurial function can help clients to access their own hidden treasures and resources which may help them to understand the nature of their own development.

THE UNDERGROUND FEMININE

Another growth-point of Hermes is often hidden behind the myths which show him in his death-role. This is the part of him which is connected with the unconscious and underworld feminine principle. On Zeus' orders he once again travelled to the realms of the dead to escort Persephone, Demeter's daughter, back to earth after she had been abducted by Hades. We know that he was affiliated to Hecate, also an underworld goddess, and that she was often shown in triune form accompanied by a three-headed dog. Originally, she was a Great Goddess in triple form, and she is likely to have been the crone form of the Persephone/Demeter/Hecate triad. By the time the Greek myths came to be written, only her underworld aspect was mentioned.

Like Hermes, her representation was often placed at crossroads or by the wayside. Significantly, it was Hecate who saw Persephone's abduction by Hades and who later ensured that Hades kept his vow to return Persephone to the upper world for the spring and summer months of the year.

Hermes' connection with the underground goddesses is not clear from the myths that remain. That they are fragmentary may indicate their antiquity, predating the development of the written word. They may also represent a submergence of the early Greek, more feminine-honouring deities beneath the weight of the classical and patriarchal Olympian pantheon. Mythographers, too, are representative of their culture and are likely to select, consciously or not, myths which show something of their own cultural bias. The Greek mythographers, in the main, were writing at a time when male dominance was reaching supremacy in Greek culture. We have noted previously the importance of Hermes' connection with nymphs and goddesses in the upper world; there is, then, every reason to study his relationship with the underground goddesses, the hidden feminine, particularly as he travels so easily between the realms of the living and the dead.

We can be fairly sure, given the mythological evidence, that Infernal Hermes worked harmoniously with the death goddesses. He is known to Hecate, and nobody could approach that goddess if they feared rather than honoured her power. Both she and he guard the traveller's way and the turning-point on the road. We know this to be an important mercurial function which is useful on the journey to discovering the unconscious realms; we now find that Hermes has an accompanying female principle to balance out the results of the search and to help him become used to the death process – something mercurial clients must do if they are to explore the underworld of their own psyches. We also see that he guides underworld Persephone into her springtime, overworld self, a sign that they, too, are both embedded fairly deeply in death/rebirth rituals and processes – as client, astrologer and therapist also are when exploring the meaning of a life.

We find the theme of the underworld feminine, too, in

British-Celtic mythology and lore. Here, the link is clearer than in the Greek myths. Annwyn, the god of the dead, sometimes seen in various guises above ground hunting with a pack of hounds, is thought to be intimately connected with Morgaine, known as Morgan le Fay in Arthurian legend; some say she was his daughter. She seems to have been a psychopomp, just as Hermes was, and her role is obvious when she and three dark queens take the dying Arthur to the Isle of Avalon in their black-draped barge. The queens openly mourn for, and comfort, the dying king, honouring that process. None the less, they take Arthur with them to the land of the dead. Nowhere do we find Hermes grieving in his underworld role, but in this myth we see the women grieve, displaying a value for the long process of necessary mourning, much as Demeter did when Persephone was abducted into Tartaros.

Like the Greeks, the Celts believed in an afterlife. Arthur was to be healed in Avalon to await the time when he is recalled to Britain to help her in her darkest hour. We see more clearly in the Celtic myth how compassionately the feminine principle leads souls into the underworld and so, by analogy, into the unconscious. This myth might be used to round out the definite knowledge lacking of Hermes' connection with the death process itself and with the death goddesses of the Greek world. If this is carried through, we may find that Hermes, and mercurial clients, are more intimately connected with finding both male and female feeling values deep in the recesses of the psyche than appears on the surface of the myths. They may find that they have the capacity to incorporate both the intellectual and the medial in their search for the meaning of life and death.

CONTAINMENT OF THE DARK FEMININE

In contrast, the later myth of Perseus and the Gorgon seems to show us Hermes at his most patriarchal. He was instrumental, indirectly, in the death of Medusa, one of the three Gorgons, whose looks could turn men to stone. Medusa had violated Athene's temple by coupling with Poseidon there, and, though he had forced the Gorgon, the goddess of wisdom vowed vengeance on her. Athene presented Perseus with a polished shield to ward off Medusa's stony stare, while Hermes gave him a sickle with which to cut off her head. Hermes' direct role in the myth ended there, but he was associated with the other attributes Perseus had to acquire before he could slay Medusa. He needed Hades' helmet of invisibility, a pair of winged sandals and a wallet in which to put Medusa's head.

We have seen Hermes' connection with the helmet and winged sandals prior to this, but the wallet is a new addition, typifying the patriarchal need to contain the destroying glance of the dark mother. In this myth Hermes seems in danger of losing his connection with the underground aspect of female power; more so, perhaps, because he shows no awareness that he is doing anything other than handing over the instruments of death. Hermes, it seems, has 'gone unconscious'. Perseus was then free to force the Graeae, the sisters of the Gorgons, to help him in his search for helmet and sandals, after which he set about destroying Medusa.

Perseus' approach to the underground female principle, the terrible feminine, is to force it, kill it, cut it off, not come to terms with it, nor honour its rage and destructive qualities. On the surface, there is nothing in the myth to connect Perseus with an understanding of female outrage and power which can petrify; rather, he seems intent on destroying it. Yet destructive rage, male or female, does eventually need to be contained, even when it arises as part of the therapeutic process. The symbol of the depotentiated Gorgon's head, contained within the wallet, has a positive value, too, provided its power is honoured and appeased.

We know that, ever afterwards, Athene carried the Gorgon's image on her breast, symbolizing, perhaps, that the raging power of the feminine had been contained and could be used constructively, though we are not told how. Conversely, this part of the myth could mean that female power has been conquered and is not available to the woman who develops under patriarchy – and we know that Athene was a patriarchal goddess, born from Zeus' head. So Hermes' involvement with the myth again shows us the double-sided nature both of the development of the human psyche and of the interpretation of mythology. Shamanic and tricksterish qualities are important to Hermes when he operates underground or behind the scenes. We shall see more of this later when the alchemical implications of this myth are examined more closely.

Perseus' return from his adventure, like that of many heroes from the more patriarchal myths, has nothing of a long, reflective process about it. All we are told is that he gave the Gorgon's head to Athene. The hero's task in this myth, it seems, is to have difficulties at the beginning of the adventure, not at the end. In real life, it takes some time for mercurial clients to make the return from pyschological depths and the changes they have been exploring. As the way into the unconscious is sometimes long and difficult, so, for Virgoans and Gemineans, the way back might be hard to accomplish. The way back may require a long transitional period so that they can assimilate the new knowledge and understanding. Their new ego-boundaries need to expand safely. This is a more feminine, medial process than most heroes bent on action are willing to undertake. To rush this phase of the work is to risk cracking the *alembic*, the alchemical container, letting go of the old ego too soon, and losing the valuable, perfected contents of their experiences. With care, taking the long way back, mercurial people may avoid Orpheus' fate. Then there is hope that they can retain the best of the old in transmuted form, and introduce the new elements necessary for psychological growth.

We can see something of this process in the chart of one client whose first house Mercury was conjunct his Gemini Ascendant. Mercury was at the apex of a T-square to Saturn and Neptune and trined his Aquarian Moon. In early middle age he decided that he wanted to set up an art business. He received, initially, little support from his wife, because she found his reasons for wanting to do so beyond her comprehension. Relations between them worsened.

He came for counselling because he felt that his marriage would be under more strain if he carried out his wishes, yet he wanted more richness of meaning in his life than he had at that time. He felt he needed to resolve the dilemma. It took him some time to work through the issue and, during the period of counselling, he had a cancer scare and underwent a number of tests. He was in touch enough with his body to be aware that the cancer scare was a symbol of something deeper, though he wasn't quite sure what it meant. It was the change in his wife's attitude and her concern about him at this time which made him look at his marriage in a new light. After a period of reassessment, he decided to stay with his wife and eventually persuaded her that he should set up in business. Staying with the painful dilemma for quite some time led him to the position where he could renew his commitment to his marriage and remain strong about wanting a new career. His way back from the underworld was a long, difficult process, but he achieved considerable insight about his own needs and motives on the way.

THE GO-BETWEEN

Hermes was, in his death aspect, acquainted with this more human side of pain and grief. It is most clearly visible in his intervention in the Trojan War on Priam's behalf after his son, Hector, had been killed by Achilles in revenge for the death of his close companion, Patroclus. Hermes led the grief-filled old king, Priam, into the Greek camp after dark and persuaded the raging Achilles to accept a ransom for Hector's body. Hermes used his eloquence and negotiating skills to induce the half-mad Achilles to part with the body, calling forth Achilles' own grief at the death of his loved friend. He compared it with Priam's sorrow for his own unburied and defiled son.

This story from Homer's *Iliad* shows how Hermes combined his underworld role and versatile tongue to serve the interests of both men. Occasionally, as here, he is called on to act as a catalyst between mortals stuck at an impasse because they are overwhelmed by emotion and incapable of acting wisely. There are dangers in using such mercurial detachment because there is a risk of once more separating intellect from feeling. But the detached mercurial intellect, if wisely used, can stand back and play the observer, seeing what has to be done to remedy the situation, and in this myth Hermes acts maturely. He is able to empathize with the emotional conditions of both men, is in touch with his own and their feeling natures, and so is able to act beneficially for all concerned.

Mercurial people are often able to act as go-betweens and negotiators when their empathic functions are working well, but these are characteristics which usually have to be acquired quite consciously. One man with Mercury in Libra sextile his eighth house Pluto and sextile his Ascendant in Sagittarius, had a sister who died when Pluto transmitted his natal Pluto. He came from a large family and his mother went to pieces at the time of her daughter's death, which is reflected in the man's natal Mercury/ Moon/Uranus T-square. While empathizing with his mother's desperate grief, which he was himself feeling, he found himself in the role of chief go-between to family members on funeral arrangements and the money they had inherited in such a sad way. At the time, he was carrying a full workload and felt he could not take time off because this might have affected his promotion prospects. Though it was difficult, and a time of great strain, he fulfilled both roles satisfactorily. Later he realized that it was possible to function effectively in the world while carrying a painful emotional load – something he had never been able to do before. He could do this only because he fully acknowledged his own grief, as well as his mother's, and neither buried nor repressed it. He said long after the funeral that it had profoundly deepened his relatedness to people in grief and bereavement. Before that time it had never occurred to him how he might react to death and he had, indeed, been scared of it.

Sometimes psychological astrologers meet mature Gemineans and Virgoans who have undergone and understood this process. They act as friends along the way with people who are grieving, until the bereavement period has passed and a new life is under way. The process of mercurial travelling and conscious self-discovery often has something of the homoeopathic principle about it – it may have to get worse before it gets better. Empathy is a necessary condition in this process and it can bring with it much healing capacity. We have seen, buried in the legend of Arthur's death, how healing might take place in the dead lands and, by analogy, in the unconscious. We might also consider why, at some historical time in the development of his mythology, Hermes' staff, an emblem of the messenger, changed into the snake-entwined Caduceus, a symbol of healing associated both with Apollo and his healer son, Asklepios.

It is also useful to encourage clients, slowly and carefully, to put their new-found knowledge to use in the upper world once they have made the long transition back from the depths of the unconscious. Often, the plunge into the depths is a lonely and frightening one, but it may also reveal rich treasures. Once back in the upper world, there may be an impulse to act without realizing the effect new discoveries may have on other people and pre-existing situations. Here, the Virgoan quality of discrimination is of use in helping to judge and negotiate sometimes difficult changes in everyday life.

The process is not always a painless one and may bring up other issues to be explored and brought into consciousness, but nobody comes back from the dark realms unchanged. Of necessity, external circumstances and other people are always affected in some way, sometimes painfully so. The going is hard and the return contains a further duality – the possibility of success and failure. This time, though, the duality is likely to be conscious; the hope is that the profound understanding of both pain and pleasure gained in the underworld may be consciously held.

6
The Healer Gods

CONNECTION AND CURE

Currently, astrologers mainly allocate healing capacities to Virgo and the sixth house. We do not often directly associate Mercury with healing capacities and tend to concentrate more on that planet's Geminean connective and intellectual functions during the process. Hidden within the myths of Hermes are the signs that he once had many more connections with healing attributes than now. It is these that give us a greater understanding of Mercury's rulership of Virgo and the sixth house.

It is interesting that Hermes' association with the healer gods, Apollo and his son, Asklepios, does not seem to have begun until the classical period in Greece. Certainly the myths and dramas of this period underline how father-right and patriarchy had superseded mother-right and how this process retained its power in the collective psyche. We know that Apollo was a late addition to the Olympian pantheon. His cult overcame and absorbed that of the oracular and intercessionary Pythia, the serpent priestess of the mother goddess, at Delphi. He was a god of pestilence, but it seems he acquired his healing attributes by adopting the wisdom of the serpent cult. Snakes were always associated with transformative potential and wisdom in the ancient world and Apollo was keen to seize both. To be accepted by the inhabitants of mainland Greece and the Aegean islands and their gods, the cult of Apollo needed a formal liaison with these cultures. The myths are a form of propaganda which show this. Over time, these conflated myths affected the perceptions of later cultures. Generally, assumptions are made that Apollo was the only Greek god of healing.

According to Michael Astour, Asklepios was an ancient healing god, possibly of Akkadian origins, who was associated with the

Aegean island of Kos. The characteristics of his cult had some affinities with the healing bird gods and goddesses of the Near East, particularly with the short-eared owl, known to be an emblem of wisdom. Athene later took over the cult of the owl, much as she took over Hermes' function as a wisdom god. The Aegean islands, like the inland Arcadia of Hermes, were eventually conquered by the patriarchal Achaeans, who would have needed to assimilate, influence and be influenced by indigenous cultures. In this way, over time, both Hermes and Asklepios were subsumed into the healing cult of Apollo. In the late classical period, Asklepios became the most important healer god of the trio, but by then his cult was well assimilated into Greek culture – and he was still subservient to Apollo.

Apollo and Asklepios appear, from the viewpoint of the twentieth century, to be the archetypal carriers of the traditional view of curing by taking medicines and remedies. This view does not encompass the more shamanic and psychic range of their healing skills, or Apollo's acquired prophetic powers. Even so, they do seem to perform a very different function from Hermes in classical mythology and seem more concerned with the cure of bodily and material ills. Hermes, in this context, is associated more with the development of a consciousness which recognizes the pattern of disease. He also seems to play a part in connecting the disease with a particular cure, and the interface between them may not easily be understood by the layman. In healing, Hermes is the connecting principle and he exercises it by adopting both a shamanic and alchemical role. This is how the Geminean skill for linking seemingly disparate pieces of knowledge becomes allied to the Virgoan affinity with healing.

Essentially, it is what mercurial healing is all about. Hermes' skills are less easy to decipher and ascertain than those of Apollo and Asklepios because he so often operates in the realms of the invisible. We begin to move towards an understanding of his capabilities only after we track his connection between the living and the dead on his journeys to and from Pluto's kingdom. He and we are brought to accept that a living realization and experience of both pain and joy are necessary preconditions of healing at all levels, from body through to spirit, individually

and collectively. This is the turning-point in Hermes' development; at a later historical point it is reflected in the alchemical
process. It seems, on the surface, appropriate that, in the myths
that remain to us, Apollo should have guided Hermes' early
education in this field, much as he later guided his own son, the
lame god Asklepios. But when we look closely at the myths,
though Hermes' part in the medical arts is now mostly obscured,
the beginnings of the connection between him and curative
powers are just about visible and stem from his prepatriarchal,
Arcadian days.

Hermes had learned augury; his art of divination for a medical
diagnosis is a useful one in shamanic cultures, and just as useful
as Apollo's was in the later, pan-Hellenic cultures. Divination is
the intuitive tapping of unconscious knowledge which may
reveal something about the course of a disease. It is not so very
distant from the intuition some medical practitioners use to
enhance their usual diagnostic techniques. Virgoans who are
associated with the healing professions, especially where Mercury
is strong in the chart, are often very aware of this quality.
Through this, what we also discover about Hermes, as we know
more certainly with Apollo, is that those who learn to diagnose
disease are also associated with its cure – an indication that
within the afflicted body itself is the potential for healing. It is
this potential that medical practicioners, therapists and psychological astrologers alike attempt to help their clients reach. The
hope is that they can then heal themselves.

One woman therapist who has learned to tap this potential has
what is, at core, an unintegrated Mercury in her chart. In
Sagittarius and the third house, it is sesquiquadrate the Moon,
semi-sextile Venus, bi-quintile her strong Saturn and quincunx
the MC. Originally trained as a nurse, she has had her own
health issues to deal with: cancer of the thyroid at the age of
twenty-three and, in latter years, a necessary hysterectomy. The
Moon square her Saturn/Pluto conjunction on the MC is one
indicator in her chart of the wounded who can also heal in the
collective, and she has used her Mercury to become conscious of
the underlying difficulties in relation to her inner feminine.
While doing so, she left nursing, took an Open University

degree, trained in psychosynthesis, worked and still works with women on health and therapeutic issues and currently teaches health studies and counselling at university level.

She is able to use her Sagittarian Mercury in the third house to reach into her own unconscious processes and then to relate her own learning to her students' and clients' needs. She has managed to combine a love for work with a psychological necessity to carry it out, and she has only achieved this position after struggling with feeling that she had been left behind at an early stage of her own education, emotionally unsupported by her father and mother. She learned to stay with the pain and the joys of this process and, because she has integrated this with her training and experience, now feels that she has a useful understanding of the psychological process, the results of which she can offer to her clients. Diagnosis of her own issues were part of her cure, which she also recognizes as ongoing.

We see this process reflected most clearly in the myth of Odysseus when Hermes handed him the drug *moly*, perhaps wild garlic, so that the wanderer could safeguard himself against Circe's black arts. Circe was herself a death goddess and seems to have had some of the powers that Hades also had. However, historically, female power over the realms of the dead was to be curtailed and trickery was an essential part of achieving this. It is here that Hermes' essential ambivalence becomes obvious. The myth indicates that the god had gathered a thorough knowledge of herbs and their medical functions and shows how he began to use his medical skills in men's favour. We note, though, that he did so by deception, thus depriving Circe of her right to grant life or death. Hermes would not have done that to Hades – even the gods, and so their archetypes, are influenced by the culture within which they are embedded.

BOUNDARIES AND ETHICS

In order to cure one ill, and stretch the boundaries of human and divine power, Hermes was prepared to fence in and cut short the power of another deity. There is a certain amorality about this position; no boundary that comes under Hermes' jurisdiction remains fixed for long, particularly when the boundaries are shifting under the influence of patriarchy and the weight of collective culture.

Boundaries also shift at the psychological and physical levels when Hermes combines the healing and magical arts. Odysseus ate the drug to ward off the sleep-inducing concoction Circe had mixed with his meal, but it had, in addition, the magical property of protecting people against the effects of evil. No doubt to people of the ancient world any medical cure or protection was seen as a magical act because the effects of a medicine are internal and invisible. The process of physical healing is an unseen, alchemical act requiring the careful control of volatile forces and chemical reactions if a cure is to take place – and some medical procedures, especially in the preparation of drugs, are the same ones used in the alchemical workshops of the past. Hermes' behaviour towards Odysseus shows an awareness of this process at the medical level. It reveals, too, that, like Gemini and Virgo, his knowledge could extend beyond the bodily and into the metaphysical field.

His action saved the lives of Odysseus and his men; otherwise they would have been turned permanently into pigs, the totem animals of the archaic death goddess, Circe. His behaviour was a benign act towards men, but, as ever with Hermes, the duplicitous god, it served a double purpose. Death was cheated of some of its victims for a time and, indirectly, Hermes aided the process. Even for a god, outwitting death is a tricky task to perform and Hermes saved Odysseus and his men from the deadly Circe, only to have them submit at the end of the tale to the underworld and Hades. Something very patriarchal seems to be happening here. By his action, Hermes helps to disempower the Circean death cult; stripping women of their power was a favourite Hermetic pastime, as we have seen. His intervention on Odysseus' behalf has all the makings of a well-thought-out plan, structured to ensure that more than one desirable goal is reached. Or perhaps this was the goal of the mythographers, unconsciously supporting, as they seemed to, the role of the patriarchs embedded in the collective unconscious of literate

Greece – always supposing that the myth was not conscious propaganda in the first place. One can never be too sure of the motives behind the actions when Hermes is around.

What we do see in the myth is that Hermes has some knowledge of the relationship between healing and death. This seems at odds with the usual picture of him as the light-hearted Olympian messenger whose serpent-entwined staff of office, the Caduceus, was given to him by Apollo – a set of characteristics more usually ascribed to the *puer*-type Geminean. This is why his connection with Apollo becomes doubly important. Mythology reflects cultural and social processes and we have seen that the incidents which took place between the two gods indicate how the later healing cult of Apollo superseded the older Arcadian cult of Hermes. If so, Hermes was out to show, in his usual bivalent fashion, that the Hellenic gods needed to reach an accommodation with him, as much as a conquest of him, and that he was not as shallow as he is sometimes depicted.

Cunning and persuasive, Hermes needed these healing attributes because they meant survival, even if his form and role changed under the Olympians. Brute force and open displays of power would have been of little use against omnipotent invaders and their gods. Stealth, guile and trickery were still necessary to obtain recognition for himself, much as they would have been for those Arcadians who preceded and were assimilated into pan-Hellenic rule. Here, however, he used them to retain some of his old healing capacities and to fuse them with the new knowledge acquired through his association with the Apollonian and Asklepian healing cults. We often see this process at work in Gemini and Virgo. The ability to retain what is useful of the old, after discarding what is no longer appropriate, and synthesize it effectively with new knowledge is one we recognize when Gemini and Virgo are working well.

THE ATTRIBUTES OF HEALING

So the snake-entwined Caduceus becomes an important symbol in establishing the healing link between Hermes, Apollo and Asklepios. The latter god, too, was given a healing Caduceus by

Apollo, while Hermes' turned all to profit – or death when he used it to conduct souls into the underworld. We will never know which of the three gods first had the Caduceus historically, but we do know that the symbol of snakes and staff is an ancient one in the religions and mythologies of the Near East. They appear as emblems of Ninazu, the Lord Physician, in Sumerian mythology, and of Moses and Aaron in the Old Testament, and were used for curative as well as magical purposes. A statue of Asklepios at Epidauros shows him with a staff in one hand, the other resting on a serpent, while Moses and Aaron use the staff and the serpent against Pharaoh's magicians prior to the Exodus.

The snake is often an emblem of healing in archaic cultures because it contains transformative potential. It sheds its skin and survives the process, vulnerable at the time, but afterwards a larger, more adult version of itself. We know that if the serpent's fangs are milked, its venom can be used for healing under the homoeopathic principle that ' like cures like'. We also know that the venom of some snakes may induce a hallucinatory state reminiscent of the trance-like states mediums may encourage by other means.

So poisonous totems in the ancient world, whether they are scorpions or snakes, had power over human beings. They needed propitiation, special rites and a priesthood within which their powers were recognized, honoured, regulated and made available to humans. In early cultures, priestly and medical functions were often synonymous because the powers residing in natural forces and totem animals alike were dangerously transformative; they were both life-giving and death-dealing. It is not always clear to the uninitiated which was which; mercurial consciousness is necessary to distinguish between the two and to indicate where one property turns into another. Much the same process is undergone at the material level in the administration of medicines and herbs.

The staff, as a symbol, is equated with the exercise of power and the act of will that begins the process of change. We see it in the magician's rod used by Aaron and Pharaoh's wizards. It forms the basis of our collective image of the medieval mage – cloak, pointed hat, alchemical apparatus and all. Zeus' thunderbolts and the sceptre in the British coronation regalia contain a similar meaning. Whoever wields power has the capacity to generate change at whatever level is required, political, social, psychological, religious and physical. Neither the snake nor the staff is an easy attribute for Gemini or Virgo to carry; with great power and transformative potential comes the burden and recognition of mature responsibility, or the avoidance of it. Moses discovered what happens when its power is misused. In doubting anger, he struck a rock in the desert because the Israelites craved water. The punishment visited on him was that he would see the promised land, but not cross into it. The skills he had taken years to perfect were rendered personally useless because he let anger direct his actions.

THE INITIATION OF THE HEALER

This is why the initiation or training of healers is necessary; it ensures consciousness of both healing properties and their correct usage. The healer's decisions then need to be imbued with a moral choice – the standpoint the *puer*-type Hermes finds difficult to adopt consciously, but which is embedded in the Hippocratic Oath with, even today, its calls to Asklepios as healer. The moral choice, too, was part of the alchemist's world-view. By looking behind the myths and symbols, once again we see the close connection between the healing gods.

We have written evidence of it in the *Corpus Hermeticum*. There the three gods, Hermes, Thoth and Asklepios, are to be found conversing about the nature and metaphysics of healing and Hermes takes the role of teacher and connector of the body with the mind and spirit, very much reflecting the neo-platonism adopted in Alexandria. So we see that though, in later classical times, the cult and healing temples of Asklepios on the island of Kos predominated, and Asklepian principles are now reflected in orthodox medical developments, Thoth and Hermes never entirely lost their connection with the healing arts. Hermes, especially, became associated with more esoteric forms of healing and learning and moved beyond the cure of only physical ills, able to act as tutor to us as well as to Asklepios.

Neither god, though, suffered the fate of Asklepios, who was killed by Zeus because he unlawfully brought a man back to life. Asklepios had inflated, made the wrong moral choice, and stepped beyond the bounds of his designated function. Hermes never did so in relation to the laws of life and death, except under orders, though there were many other instances in which he blurred the boundaries and slipped across them during the healing process. In healing he has the ability to contain his slipperiness within the process itself, if it is carefully managed and fully understood, as doctors, therapists and alchemists know. If he doesn't, or the healer's eye has been taken off the process, he can be volatile and ultimately destroy the work. Hermes as healer and the one to be healed has to obey the laws of containment, otherwise the disease, collective and individual, mental and emotional, physical and spiritual, rages out of control. The folktale of 'The Sorcerer's Apprentice' indicates what can happen when the forces are not contained or are used for the wrong purpose. The apprentice wishes to emulate his master and sets spells in action to clean the house; because he has no way of stopping them, they eventually destroy all his master's work. However, unlike Asklepios, he was not killed, only castigated and made to clear up the mess – a further learning process in itself.

Sometimes Gemineans and Virgoans can show fear of responsibility at this level and refuse to enter the process of change, or lose, through panic and anxiety, overall management of what they have undertaken. They may, then, either fragment and allow Mercury to become volatile and destructive, or refuse to learn from the results of their actions. The mercurial mind, to function well, has to ensure a management of the overall process. It has to have an understanding of the mechanics of each part of the work, and to become flexible enough to respond to the different stages of change. This is why Mercury in astrology is associated with intelligence. It also allows us to understand why some mercurial clients balk fearfully at change; the responsibility and awareness needed are enormous. Essentially, the client is responsible for his own cure, however much help he receives along the way.

THE PARADOX OF HEALING

The classical myths show that Hermes was capable of maintaining the links between body, mind and spirit. His affinity with death, magic and healing at all levels is very obvious in the myth of Tantalos and Pelops. Tantalos, a mighty king who wished to teach the gods a lesson, invited the Olympians to a banquet. The main dish was his son, Pelops, whom he killed and served up in a stew. Tantalos' actions were discovered and it was Hermes, on Zeus' orders, who brought the boy back to life, replacing a shoulder eaten by Demeter with one of gold. This is Hermes in an unfamiliar role − that of a god of resurrection as well as healer, connecting the physical and the spiritual. In this, Hermes acts out his underworld role, unseen, connecting the parts which are unreachable by other means. He could only do so, however, after one of the Fates had said that it was not yet time for the boy to die. No god or man could defy what the Fates decreed, because they were a far older, far deeper psychological force than any god. Even Hades himself could not escape their rule; nor could Hermes.

Here we see Hermes restoring to life a boy whose future was scarred, changed and deepened by a life-shattering experience suffered at the hands of a destructive and overambitious father. The repercussions of that act resounded down the generations of the house of Atreus until after the fall of Troy. When we read the tales of human tragedy, destruction, suppression of the feminine and madness contained within that saga, we may well ask about the purpose of Hermes' healing of Pelops. Human healing and transformation, it seems, have a temporary quality about them; no one ultimately escapes his or her fate. Hermes was around throughout the duration of the saga to ensure that, down the generations, the Fates had their way and were eventually propitiated by regular blood sacrifices and the correct rites of passage. Simultaneously, he heals, and we are left to resolve and encompass the paradox, or, at least, get a glimpse of how one part of the process fits with another. This is a realization we would often like to see our more fearful mercurial clients reach.

The process, though, not only works at the level of the individual; sometimes we see Hermes just as deeply at work in the collective. At the level of a developing collective consciousness, the myth seems to have begun its emergence at a time when the cult of Zeus was superseding those of cannibalism and human sacrifice, according to Robert Graves. The Greek culture reflected in mythology was becoming relatively more civilized and the religious cults show us the shift towards a greater respect for human life in some areas. There were still many anomalies, including the suppression of women and the aggressive destruction of enemies. Hermes, moreover, was acting on his father's orders. Intelligently, he carried out his task with some dexterity, indicating a considerable knowledge of human anatomy and the need for connectedness in all things. Putting pieces together was one of Hermes' skills, as it can be for Gemini and Virgo, and, perhaps unconsciously, he was laying the foundations of future alchemical work in his successful attempts at the recombination of parts of Pelops' human body, soul and spirit.

The dual nature and essential ambiguity of the god becomes more apparent when this myth is placed beside those in which Hermes acts as psychopomp to Hades. In this role he allows no man to escape the necessity of death and no man is allowed to bargain for a longer stay on earth. At the moment of death, though, no one can be quite sure whether Hermes will appear as psychopomp, healer or deliverer. Through his ambivalence, he ensures his place as one of the gods who control both life and death, though in a less direct way than warlike Ares or justice-dispensing Zeus. A hermetic death is likely to be not what it seems because it contains the potential for both on-going transformation and oblivion. The dead go below ground, where seeds die or germinate; they need to experience the turn of the winter season's deathlike grip on their own roots before they can spring up to life and light, if at all, for Hermes promises nothing and fixes nothing permanently. It is a recipe for both hope and dread and such an end is likely to freeze an immature man's emotions with fear when he senses but does not understand its contrariness.

Essentially, the cycle of life-to-death-to-life-again is beyond patriarchal control and is not a process which is governed by the intellect. The intellect can only aid an understanding and deep acceptance of its inexorability. So Hermes has to put the power of his fluid intellect on hold and accept the dictates of the process itself, and of gods stronger than he – Zeus, Hades and, beyond even their jurisdiction, the Fates and Necessity. By becoming familiar with the human life and death process and associating with the strong psychological powers these gods represented, Hermes was acquiring knowledge of the ways in which he himself would be changed by his interaction with others. Not even a god can escape transformation and death, as he was to come to know through alchemical magic, and as we can see from his history.

Something of this process is apparent in the chart of a woman whose Mercury in Capricorn and in the sixth forms a Grand Trine with Neptune and Uranus. It also is in bi-quintile to Saturn and square the MC. She took a degree in psychology and worked for some time in mental hospitals, at the same time suffering from emotional disturbances herself and unaware, at the time, that she suffered from emotional unrelatedness, which is shown by the Moon in square to a Mars/Uranus conjunction, and her need to project this on to her husband, which is shown by her Aquarian Sun in the seventh house. In early adulthood, neither her sixth house Capricornian Mercury, nor her eleventh house Saturn could help her to structure her own inner nurturing environment and she was hospitalized on one occasion with a catatonic panic reaction to the stress induced by exams.

Unable to help herself, emotionally or rationally, she put herself in a position where she was unable to help others. Only after two broken marriages and many years' inner work was she able to accept her lack of emotional relatedness. She recognized that she was projecting her own need to be emotionally healed not only on to her husbands, but also on to the patients with whom she worked. This made her very unhappy for a while, but she realized that she could not continue to work with people in the unconscious way she had previously, though she knew that it was important for her to continue working with them. At that point she changed her job, while continuing to work as a part-time counsellor; she is now happier with the way in which she relates to people.

It takes much maturity to face the end of all intellectualized knowledge and submit to the life-and-death cycle itself. For Hermes, as for Gemini and Virgo, this acceptance of ambiguity, paradox and unconsciousness is the self-healing factor which, simultaneously, helps him face his own fears. Like Ariel in *The Tempest*, he needs to be able to put a girdle around the world, encompassing the whole, in order to do so.

But not before he had acted ambiguously throughout the Trojan saga. It was he who delivered the apple to Paris. The mythological consequences of that act, after Paris gave the apple to Aphrodite and enraged both Hera and Athene, resulted in the Trojan War. The Olympian pantheon was split between those gods who supported the Trojans and those who supported the Greeks. Good though he was at capitalizing from such splitting, Hermes remained Zeus' messenger and, on occasions, acted as the go-between at various points of the war, particularly where death rites were being violated. It was he who soothed the half-mad Achilles and persuaded him to surrender Hector's body to his father, Priam.

In his own raging grief for his dead companion whom Hector had killed, Achilles had savagely mutilated the corpse and denied Hector burial. Initially, Hermes had wanted to steal the body, but Zeus had ordered that its return be negotiated. So, in this myth, Hermes wants to act as the splitter and is ordered to be the one who attempts to heal the rifts. Achilles, though, cannot overcome his initial rage without Hermes' intervention. But in this myth Hermes, even if he is constrained by Zeus and not by his own conscience, moves beyond the capacity of some mercurial clients who are unaware of the distress caused by their actions. The childish, 'It wasn't my fault, he made me do it,' which we see in Achilles' behaviour is often how we know immature Hermes is at work: the child has not grown up.

It seems as though Hermes is compelled to act with double purpose in whatever he does, but consciousness of this trait brings with it the pain of both decision and indecision. Whichever choice is made, even the choice of indecision, something is always left behind, dies and has to be buried. There is heartache in consciously seeing potential wither, and grief in letting go of possibilities. Many Virgoans and Gemineans would recognize the truth of that, but in the healing process even disease, as well as dis-ease, has to die. No doubt microbes and viruses find their own deaths painful, but it is necessary if a member of another species is to survive. A conscious awareness of, and responsibility towards, the imperfections and unfairness of life, even if the process involves pain, is something we often hope our more mercurial clients may be able to acquire.

A WILLINGNESS TO CHANGE

To make the aware mercurial choice means to embrace death and embrace it willingly, even while mourning, even while not seeing the new potential which might arise. Risk-taking of this nature is not an attribute a god of connections and transitions acquires easily. Fear of the risks and lost potential is behind much of Gemini's indecision and Virgo's procrastination. Yet to remain in these psychological states when they are not appropriate is also painful. Being caught on the hook of pain, consciously, not knowing which way to turn, may show maturity, but does nothing to diminish the pain. We often see clients who have made the unconscious decision to stay out of that troublesome state by cutting off from it, refusing to recognize repeating patterns in their lives and unaware of how they are stifling their own development. But the choice to move forward into pain and awareness is theirs and cannot be forced, however we as astrologers and therapists might feel about it. Compassion is of more use here, at the point of alchemical agony and transformation, than criticism.

That painful mercurial course continues to operate in cultures as well as in individual psyches. We see a similar duality of purpose, physical, mental and spiritual, reflected in the Judaic and Christian mythology which underpins many current religious beliefs in the West. As with the Trojan War, it starts with an apple. The pain of consciousness came when Adam and Eve ate of the tree of the knowledge of good and evil and were expelled from the garden of Eden, the uroboric paradise of the unified psyche. Christ entered the world to redeem that split by showing how to work towards complete union with the divine. His agony in the garden of Gethsemane is concerned with his recognition that he has to suffer a death to heal the split between good and evil, accepting the will of the divine quite consciously. The watchers who sleep, like hundred-eyed Argos when Hermes killed him, have little knowledge of what is really taking place. What began with a snake in a garden, the place of growth, ended in a garden; both suffering and transformation are a result of the conflict between human feeling and divine knowledge. Christ, in essence, clearly parallels the development of the mature and aware Hermes, becomes one who moves beyond patriarchy and collective values. He faces the pain inherent in his own choice in his agony in the garden, and so redeems Adam.

There is further evidence of Hermes' connection with pain and healing in Judaic mythology. In cabbalistic astrology, Mercury is equated with the angel Raphael, the healing presence of God. One of the seven watchers of the heavens who stand near to God's throne, he has the ability to cure by correct understanding and the communication of knowledge. He only ever appears to men in response to the divine command and, like Hermes, is limited to a particular function. He is not allowed, by divine law, to act beyond his designated powers. What he brings to men is an awareness of how the divine operates in all matters. Like Hermes, he can represent the conscious part of the transcendent function which comprehends and moves beyond all pain and all healing, yet he can also acquaint himself with human pain and distress.

In the Apocrypha, it is he who appears in the *Book of Tobit* to cure Tobit of his blindness and his wife's, Anna's, distress by finding a wife for their son, Tobias. It seems that Raphael is able to operate very precisely in the areas of greatest human need and distress. Precision is a characteristic we regularly ascribe to Virgo and, to some extent, Gemini. Raphael also has the capacity to use that trait, ensuring, as he does so, the continuation and growth of Tobit's family. Throughout the book Raphael accompanies and aids Tobias in his healing of Sara, his wife. Eventually, he reveals himself to father and son, praising their obedience to God through their acts of humanity. In a very real sense, though he appears in this myth as a vision, Raphael is the principle which connects the human with the divine, and pain with healing.

NURTURANCE AS WELL AS PAIN

As well as his connections with death, pain, the subversion of the feminine and the collective, Hermes is, in at least two instances, also involved with fostering growth. Ambiguity is present here, too. A late myth about Dionysos informs us that, after Zeus had consumed by fire his mother, the pregnant moon goddess, Semele, Hermes rescued the unborn child and sewed him into Zeus' thigh. As he did Athene, Zeus bore Dionysos three months later, Hermes helping in the birth process itself. To save the child from Hera's jealousy, Zeus ordered Hermes to take the child into safety. Hermes temporarily turned him into a ram and gave him over to the Nysian nymphs, the nymphs who traditionally attended birth. They brought him up near Heliconian Mount Nysa, far from Olympus and Hera's anger.

Here we see elements of the patriarchal and older, matriarchal myths. Zeus does nothing to prevent Semele's ultimate destruction, even brings it about, but enlists Hermes' aid to save his son. Interestingly, Hermes turns to his own archaic roots as ram-bearer, very much like Christ the Good Shepherd, to save the child. Though a clever solution, it indicates that recorded myth cannot quite shake off its preliterate origins, though it can disguise them somewhat. It may indicate a commonality at the root of all myths in the Mediterranean region, if not beyond, which suggests an overlapping of cultural, collective and human experience.

It also shows Hermes' affinity with the nurturing, healing and salvation principles, even when he carries out Zeus' patriarchal orders. This paradox is the result of the process where Hermes has been at his most alchemical. Held, but usually unseen within it, are the strands which make up our mercurial complexity – history, myth and the development of consciousness, both individual and collective. The resolution, the cure, comes somewhere in the process of consciously weaving all these strands together. At what point, we cannot always tell, but we do sense that Hermes has been active again. All we can hope is that our mercurial clients recognize some of the parallels in their own lives and know that they can set their own healing processes in action and stay aware of the paradoxes involved.

Healing, nurturing and salvation are also very apparent in the chart of a man who has Mercury strongly aspected. In Aries in the fourth house, conjunct the Sun, opposite Saturn, Neptune and the MC, it is in a T-square formation to Uranus. It is also in a Grand Trine with Pluto and the Ascendant. His wife died very suddenly, leaving him solely responsible for their children. He and his wife worked in the same business, so he was able to incorporate his wife's work into his own. He then decided to work from home so that he could be more closely involved with his children. Though he had fears that he might not be able to withstand so many changes in so short a time, he set up his support systems and found, after some years, that he had changed and was much closer to the children than he had been while his wife was alive. He found that the talents he had previously exercised only at work – a good sense of structure and sound financial sense – were very much needed as he reorganized his life, continuing his wife's work in the process and ensuring that their children received the support and nurturance they needed.

It was a responsibility that would have flattened many people, but he later said that he throve on it, eventually rediscovering a spirit of idealism and adventure in his work that he had projected on to his wife when she was alive. Simultaneously, he discovered that he had given away a large part of his power and had unconsciously fallen in with patriarchal attitudes. For a time he was very angry, with both his wife and himself. Later he realized that he had been harbouring envious feelings, which were both released and accepted as he became more confident about combining his need to work with bringing up the children. He had broken through to feelings that he was, in essence, powerfully nurturing as well as a provider.

In Greek mythology, unhappily, the nurturing female potential is often not allowed to develop fully. We see this in the
myth of Hermes which involves him in Asklepios' birth. Apollo
had fathered him on Coronis. She was an archaic raven goddess
associated with healing cults and she died in similar circumstances
to Semele, who had challenged Zeus' power. She had wanted to
see Apollo in his full glory. He let her reluctantly and the sight
killed her. She was pregnant with Asklepios and Apollo begged
Hermes to save the child. Hermes cut him from his mother's
womb when she was on her funeral pyre. It seems that one of
Hermes' tasks is to rescue the children of goddesses who have
died while challenging male supremacy. In this way, he helps to
preserve a synthesis of two cultures and two psychological
inheritances. It is yet another instance where he serves a dual
function.

Duality, recognizing the flip-side of every coin, is an important
function in these myths. It does not give us a pretty picture of
what Hermes is sometimes about. Male children are saved while
females are sacrificed. Hermes develops a crafty surgeon's skill,
but does nothing to save their mothers. He tacitly supports the
male principle in all its death-dealing actions, yet is aware of the
techniques of Caesarean section, a boon to some child-bearing
women today, though not used often in the ancient world.
When it was, the operation indicated that a choice had been
made in favour of the borne, not the bearer. The meaning of the
myths are that the life-bringer must die so that the life-holder
can live, at least in a patriarchal culture. Zeus then shows some
mercurial ambivalence about the importance of the life-bringer.
As with Athene, he sews the embryonic Dionysos, the twice-
born, into his thigh so that he can emulate the natural birth
process. It indicates some grudging recognition that the female
womb has a rightful place in the procreation cycle and is one
that conquering gods and men perhaps envy. The couvade, in
which men mimic the birth process while their women are
actually in labour, is a rite that has been recognized in many
cultures and is not unknown in the present.

So the act of birth becomes, by assumption under patriarchy
and the classical collective conscious, a male prerogative and the

female role is diminished. This time, we see Hermes constantly and unnaturally having to shape-shift during the birth and healing process. We are not told whether he awarely and alchemically holds the tension between life and death, between fostering growth and cutting it short, and we know nothing of the pain of his decision-making, if, indeed, he felt any. Patriarchy seems peculiarly involved in cutting off from pain and a knowing participation in the life process. Yet Zeus must have suffered at the time of the sewing in and birth of Dionysos. It seems that the pain of staying in control is preferable to the pain of relinquishing it — another psychological state familiar to both Virgo and Gemini and one that is often reinforced by collective behaviour.

THE THRESHOLD OF CONSCIOUSNESS

What we do know is that, awarely or not, Hermes is continually involved in the connections between the apparently different phases of life; he was very much a god of the spaces and places between, where nothing visibly exists, though all things may. He was also a god of the threshold between the known and the unknown, and of the place where the meaning of an event turns into its opposite. Liminality and a sense of continual change are Hermes' domains as much as trickiness is. When we study the myths of Egyptian Thoth, we clearly see why.

He was the deity who took charge of the process of restoring the vegetation god, Osiris, to eternal life. The cult of Osiris could only gain and retain ascendancy if it included the attributes of the earlier gods, or could command their service. Thoth responded in true Virgoan fashion. After Osiris' transmutation, Thoth served him and his family well, it seems, guarding and guiding the child Horus, son of Isis and Osiris. So well did he carry out his duties that once, after Horus had been stung by a scorpion, Thoth got rid of the poison by sucking it out and restoring him to health. Thoth, in his wisdom, guarantees the continuity of the holy family and, in order to do so, needs to be aware of the sometimes dangerous acts that must be undertaken at the threshold of life and death. He must also be able to carry them out.

Thoth's affiliation to healing, medicine and surgery was well known both to Greeks and to Egyptians and it has entered the mainstream of Egyptian mythology known to us. The myths of the Egyptian death guardian, Anubis, are also reasonably well known. This cannot be said about the association between Hermes, Thoth and Asklepios. It remains outside the main body of Greek myth which has travelled down the centuries. This is because the *Corpus Hermeticum*, the syncretic and alchemical writings which contain more certain evidence of their association, stems from the centuries in which Alexandrian Greek power gradually became supplanted by Roman supremacy. They are not part of our dominant collective heritage, but are part of our submerged culture. The progress of Christianity ensured that they remained in that state; gnostic philosophies are too threatening to established orthodoxies.

The composite figure which emerges from this process is the alchemical, platonic and gnostic Hermes Trismegistos, a representation of Hermes in his *senex* form. He attained this form after he had undergone pain and purification by the elements, but he was without power in the cultures in which he is embedded. He never became a deity associated with a particular national culture. He became, instead, the guardian, perhaps god, of a small number of adepts who preserved his identity throughout the conflict of those cultures which eventually became Christian and Islamic. In a sense, he and the other gods went underground in order to survive, became part of the collective unconscious, but still worked away, in secret and unobserved, much like the alchemical process we can sometimes see at work in our mercurial clients.

What is missing from this picture of the development of Hermes are the shamanic powers, the knowledge of the spaces between, by which he develops his own history, changes and heals himself and acts as a model for the evolution of individual and collective consciousness. By the time the classical myths had come to be written, Hermes' shamanism was no longer obvious and seems lost beneath his patriarchal acquisitions. There are, though, hints in his myths that he was once such a deity, as we have seen in a previous chapter. Shape-changing, trickiness and slipperiness are all characteristics of the shaman-as-healer; so is a knowledge of both the human and the spirit world and the ability to go beyond ordinary human knowledge in search of the vision and wisdom which underlie the effectiveness of a cure. Both are characteristics we recognize in relation to the healing qualities of Virgo and connective functions of Gemini.

In the pantheon of a culture closer to our own time, we can see clearly how hermetic shamanism might have operated. Odin, chief of the Aesir, the Norse battle gods, had other attributes than the ability to win battles and decide on the dates of men's deaths. He was a shape-changer, who, like Hermes, ruled by the use of magic and craft. On his shoulders perched two ravens, Huginn and Muninn, Thought and Memory, who brought to him all the news he needed from the world of men. He was the god of law, poetry and wisdom and could be benevolent, knowing how to give wise counsel and cure illness. In this we see again some of the attributes of Hermes. Like most shamanic gods, Odin had acquired his magical attributes and healing powers by undergoing a series of tests and initiations. We do not have direct knowledge of this process for Hermes and can only work by analogy, speculating on some affinity between Hermes and Odin.

To increase his powers, Odin wished to drink from the fountain of knowledge which was near the root of the world-tree, Yggdrasil. He consulted the disembodied head of his uncle, Mimir, and was told that he must forfeit one of his eyes in return. He must be willing to sacrifice himself on the world-tree, hanging upside down for nine nights, pierced by a spear. At the end of that time, Odin found that he could see to the ends of the earth, see what was in men's hearts and had become the repository of all wisdom and magic among the gods. But Odin was also remembered as a tyrannical god, fierce and harsh in judgement. Those who make the conscious sacrifice risk raising the shadow as well as the treasure. This is not unlike Adam's and Eve's condition after eating of the tree of knowledge of good and evil.

Again we see that conscious suffering has to be accepted before wisdom can be acquired, but this time, unlike the Hermes myths, we are told more about the process. Odin loses one eye and gains the ability to see the whole world, externally through his ravens and also because the loss of an eye can denote the further development of the inward eye of wisdom. He has to sacrifice himself on the world-tree. Damaged by experience of the world, he finally understands that that experience is a necessary if painful way of getting to know how men think and feel. Pain and loss are indispensable parts of the curative process.

He hangs upside down on the tree, an indication that this knowledge can only be gained by abnormal and unusual means. Hanging there for nine nights ensures that he knows that gaining wisdom is a lengthy process that has to be endured; it is not an attribute acquired overnight. He is pierced by a spear which ensures that he will not forget that he learned through pain, nor that he came near to death. We are not told that, like Christ, he died on the tree, so we cannot say that he was resurrected in the Christian sense. What we can say is that he would have been irrevocably changed by the experience, which is a kind of resurrection. Again, like Christ, all this requires his voluntary and conscious submission to experience and an acceptance of the will of the unifying principle. Paradoxically, he cures himself of ignorance by sacrificing himself to himself in order to gain wisdom.

What happens in myth can replicate what happens at the bodily, psychological and cultural level, as we have seen in relation to the journey Mercury makes through his own myths and history. The Celtic cultures, too, contained gods and myths which show how the deities of healing and death acquire their attributes and learn through experience. Nudd, the god of healing, often recognized as one of the Celtic avatars of Hermes, was the father of Gwyn ap Nudd, the patron of death and battle. He has sometimes been equated with Annwyn, the underworld deity. As Nuada, the silver-handed, he fought against the early mythological inhabitants of Ireland, the Fir Bolgs, and lost his left hand in the battle. It was replaced by one of silver, much as Pelops' shoulder was replaced by one of gold. The implication of Nuada's myth is that, much as Odin does, in order to heal, he must first suffer the wound and know how pain feels. Further, he must suffer it in battle. Only then, like Hermes and Odin, can he cure. The problem with Hermes is that we never see him undergoing suffering; he is too quick and glib for that. It is only in his alchemical form that we see what he has to undergo in order to transform. We do not see him battling, like Nuada, in order to extract what is right and pure from a life-threatening situation. This is often a mercurial characteristic, the ability to slip away from strife, not facing the consequences, but Nuada's myth indicates that standing firm is sometimes necessary.

We see another aspect of the healing process in a further avatar of Nudd, Nodens, the Romano-Celtic healing god, whose sleep temple at Lydney in Gloucestershire was excavated earlier in the twentieth century by Mortimer Wheeler. Similar sleep temples dedicated to Asklepios have been found on the island of Kos and healing rites were discovered to be part of his cult at Epidauros. Ritual sleep and dreaming, perhaps induced by drugs, and dream interpretation were known in the ancient world to be part of the cure for some illnesses, processes by which healing transformation could take place. The importance given to them shows us something of the way in which unconscious processes were raised to consciousness in the ancient world. Hermes and Odin submit to the pain of delving into, honouring and enduring the realms of the invisible and the inaccessible. While they do not second-guess the outcome, they have some awareness that the process of crossing the boundaries between the known and the unknown worlds is a necessary and an inexorable one, if they are to acquire the wisdom and healing which they need.

The analogies between Hermes, Odin, Nudd, Christ and other Greek, Roman and Egyptian deities are very close and may lead us to conjecture that healing, gaining wisdom and the development of maturity have similar components in all cultures and for all men. The common elements are the pain involved in becoming conscious of the duality of all actions, learning that wisdom is only gained through making sometimes painful choices which involve the death of some possibilities, recognizing the thresholds which lead us into living our lives in a particular way. Only through understanding our own pain and healing ourselves first can we develop the capacity to be of service to others, individually and collectively. This is the maturity towards which Virgo and Gemini strive. The whole process, though, is a volatile one, as Hermes knows, and as the next chapter hopes to show.

7
The Wonder-working Alchemist

THE HISTORY OF A PROCESS

Almost certainly it was the Alexandrian Greeks who continued
the tradition of Thoth, the great author and magician, according
him even greater status as the prime source of all learning and
wisdom. He owed to them the power of the name, three times
great Thoth, afterwards translated as Hermes Trismegistos, indicates G. R. S. Mead. His cult arose during the four centuries
straddling the start of the Christian era when the Mediterranean
world was a ferment of doctrines and sects. At this stage of
historical development, not only do we find worship of the
classical gods, Egyptian, Greek and Roman, but also the growth
of gnosticism, which was to influence Judaism and early Christianity. As we have seen in a previous chapter, gnosticism
informed a number of doctrines and sects, many of which were
later described as heretical by the Roman and Orthodox
churches. It took the Council of Nicaea in the fourth century
AD, held under the auspices of Constantine the Great, to begin to
systematize the body of knowledge that was to coalesce into
Christian theology in the following centuries.

Over the next few centuries many of the early Christian texts
and gospels were expunged from official Christian records.
During the same period, many other influential texts from
Alexandria, Greece, Persia and Palestine were lost to the West
for hundreds of years after the Islamic conquests of the Mediterranean regions and the burning of the library at Alexandria.
Leaders and followers of the sects which adhered to the rejected
doctrines were either anathematized, or, like some of the early
dissenting Christian fathers, were cruelly martyred in order to
establish a body of essentially Roman Christian theology which
would supersede all others. This happened during the time of the

slow dissolution of the political and polytheistic Roman Empire; later other empires were to grow – those of the Roman church in Western Europe and Greek Orthodoxy in Eastern Europe.

The doctrines which made up gnosticism were varied and relied on a direct experience of the divine by the participant, which did away with the need for the intercessionary priesthood growing up around early Christianity. Direct, if visionary, experience of the divine was a threat to any body which was in the process of establishing and institutionalizing itself. It also meant that different gnostic sects tended to form around their own particular texts and doctrines. Mainly, though, these doctrines had their roots in the Hellenic, Alexandrine, Zoroastrian and the Essene tradition, as far as we can tell at present, and so they are both a fusion and an extension of religious thought current at the time. Complex religious philosophies, practices and beliefs were being reflected in an increasing number of books and texts – a very mercurial process which tracked the diversity and depth of intellectual development in the Mediterranean region around the beginning of the Christian era. Paradoxically, it was from this same seed-bed that Christianity arose.

A basic tenet of Christian gnosticism, though there were many variants, was that the world was essentially evil and was created, not by God, but by the 'demiurge' created by him, usually equated with Satan or Lucifer. God and his son, Christ, retained their purity by dissociating themselves from the material world. This dualistic view of the forces of good and evil ensured that man was trapped in the world of matter and the world of the spirit was veiled from him. There are hints here of some similarities with the cabbalistic, Buddhist and Hindu cosmologies, in which man had to learn how to penetrate the veil of illusion, or *maya*, before he could become one with the spirit. He could only achieve this through gnosis – knowing himself – a doctrine which, in European culture, is most directly attributable to the apollonian cult and to later pythagorean and platonic philosophy which influenced certain Alexandrian philosophers, among them, Plotinus and Iamblichus. There is some conjecture that Alexandrians had some contact with the philosophies of the Indian subcontinent. Certainly Alexander himself did on his attempted conquest of India, so it is hardly surprising to see some affinity between these and gnostic doctrines.

Mercury's need to gather and disseminate knowledge from apparently disconnected sources is paramount in the development of this tradition, but the received history of Hermes Trismegistos and alchemy seems a long way from it until we start to examine the *Corpus Hermeticum* and the Smaragdine Tablet. These works almost certainly derive from the first two or three centuries of the Christian era, most probably from Alexandria itself in the time of Valentinus the Gnostic, who aspired, St Jerome tells us, to be bishop of Rome; there is still some academic dispute about their dates. The *Corpus Hermeticum*, often taking the form of a dialogue between Hermes Trismegistos, Thoth and Asklepios, among others, states that to know God is to experience him inwardly and directly, growing beyond the corporeal, realizing his immeasurable greatness:

> 'Now fix your thought upon the Light,' he said, 'and learn to know it.' And when he had thus spoken, he gazed long upon me, eye to eye, so that I trembled at his aspect. And when I raised my head again, I saw in my mind that the Light consisted of innumerable Powers, and had come to be an ordered world, but a world without bounds. [Libellus 1][1]

This is what is meant by the direct knowledge of God and it accords with the dictum above the doorway of Apollo's temple at Delphi, 'Know thyself', because no man knows God until he first knows his own mind. The acts of cognition in this passage are reflective, receptive, imaginal and active; paradoxes which all find a home in the human mind. It is here that we begin to see the classical and the gnostic, if spiritualized, Hermes at work in the form of his later counterpart, Hermes Trismegistos.

The earliest mention of the Smaragdine Tablet is in the work of Jabir ibn Hayyan, an eighth-century alchemist who lived and worked in Baghdad. The Latin original of the tablet tells us not only more about the nature of gnosticism, but also about the early roots of alchemy, traditionally thought to have been founded in Alexandria and practised there as a form of spiritual and material chemistry by Maria Prophetissa at the end of the first century AD. From it we see how Hermes Trismegistos came to be known for his ability to combine gnostic experience, mysticism and magic. The tablet indicates that the material world is a reflection of the spiritual world and is the workshop in which we can strive to attain unity with the perfect essence of creation. The creating power can separate the gross from the subtle and translate itself from the divine to the mundane, so uniting them. All this was performed in the name of Hermes Trismegistos and is written as a very brief alchemical formula:

The Emerald Tablet

It is true, without lying, sure and very true.
What is below is as it is above, and what is above is as it is
    below, to perform the wonders of the one thing.
And as all things were from the one by reflection on the one,
    so all things were born by adaptation from the one thing.
The father of it is the Sun; its mother is the Moon.
The wind has borne it in its belly; the earth is its nurse.
It is the progenitor of all marvellous works throughout the
    whole world.
Its power is entire if it is turned on to the earth.
Separate the earth from the fire, the subtle from the gross,
    sweetly, with much ingenuity.
It rises from earth to heaven, and descends again to earth, and
    it receives power from above and below. So you will have
    the glory of all the world. The idea of darkness will fly
    from you.
This is the complete firmness of courageous strength; for it
    masters all subtle things and penetrates all that is solid.
So there will be miraculous changes and this is the manner of
    it.
Therefore I am called Hermes Trismegistos because I have
    three parts of the wisdom of the whole world.
What I have said about the work of the Sun is complete.
                                        [Author's translation][2]

Hermes is very obviously acting as the translator and traveller between corporeal and spiritual existence, extending his classical past as psychopomp into the neo-platonic Alexandrian present as spirit.

We see from the tablet that alchemy is closely associated with this movement towards the attainment of wholeness and unity, a point not lost on Jung when, centuries later, he adapted alchemical principles for psychological work, psychic wholeness being the first stage on the journey towards spiritual wholeness. We know that by medieval times Hermes Trismegistos had been adopted as patron by the alchemists and that Mercury was to be used, transformed into his spiritual essence and fixed by the Great Work. What we see in the writings of the alchemists is a fusion of gnostic, neo-platonic and Judaeo-Christian beliefs, underpinned by the symbology of chemical processes. But the body of beliefs had passed, in mercurial fashion, through many centuries and different cultures before it reached Christianized Europe.

After its early beginnings in Alexandria, alchemy's esoteric and spiritualized knowledge was developed by Islamic scholars who protected the platonic philosophies. It re-entered Europe first by way of the Moors' conquest of Africa and Spain and later by way of the flood of gnostic and neo-platonic literature bought up by the Medici princes and others after the conquest of Byzantium by the Sultan Mehmet II. It is also thought that the Crusaders and Knights Templar may have had some contact with the esoteric doctrines of the Near East.

So Hermes travelled many of history's highways and byways before we see him emerge as the two interrelated forms of Hermes Trismegistos in the writings of medieval alchemists. He was the god of all the arts of alchemy, the keeper of all changes which took place inside the hermetically sealed retort and the protector of alchemists themselves. He was also Mercury, still the god, and, in addition, the spirit which corresponded to the alchemical quicksilver. That itself was a spiritualized form of the liquid metal which changed its own substance within the retort. In this way, Hermes Trismegistos, the wisdom god, descendant of the now paganized Greek Hermes, Roman Mercury and Egyptian Thoth and Anubis, became associated with heresy, magic and alchemy. His respectable philosophical antecedents were suppressed and forgotten. Hermes became demonized and went underground, always surfacing again when the time and conditions ripened.

The history of alchemy does not reveal clearly how classical Hermes changed into gnostic Hermes Trismegistos, or how they both came to be associated with alchemy. We are left, also, to deduce how this process happens at the individual level. Any attempts to bring about a rational and spiritual interaction between life and death would result in a change within the personality of the god, or chemist, or psychological man performing the work, as we have seen in previous chapters. Eventually, the transformation and the means of transformation would become conscious to an intrigued and reflective personality, and we know that Hermes was always a god curious to learn new skills. A Virgoan precision, attention to detail and purification of the results were the process by which he was to illuminate himself, casting light on his own shadow and integrating this new knowledge with what he knew before. An understanding of alchemical transmutation was to be his own best healer, but this could only happen after he had acquired the wisdom of Thoth in Alexandria.

THE GREAT WORK

What happens at the cultural level is often reflected in individual attainments. We quite often see this process at work in mercurial clients who begin to come to terms with the complexity and depth of their own life development. Both Virgoans and Gemineans have the capacity to become intrigued by what happens to them once they are even slightly aware of their life paths; Virgoans, particularly, may find the process healing. It is no coincidence that Hermes is associated with Thothian and Asklepian healing in the *Corpus Hermeticum*, in terms of both his own deepened understanding and application of knowledge, and the ability, then, to offer it as a teaching and a therapy to people in need. The translation of skills to others is a mercurial process, and some strongly mercurial people do develop their skills to a high level of operation.

One woman with a Virgo MC, has a kite formation with Pluto in the ninth house conjunct the MC and opposing a Sun/

Mercury conjunction in the third house. The Moon and Saturn are both in Grand Trine to Pluto, and are in the fifth and second houses respectively. Mercury is also trine a twelfth house Jupiter/Neptune conjunction. Not unexpectedly, this woman has moved into healing work as her main career. She started, conventionally, as a graduate in the sciences and began research work for her doctorate, then realized that she enjoyed teaching and wanted to explore the possibilities of healing work, hoping to combine both. She also suffered from a long-term skin complaint which, she said, made her more sympathetic towards people who were ill and in need. It and her search for more creativity led her away from the institutional medical field and research. She was aware of her need for security through her work when she left university, trained in acupuncture and set up her own practice, so decided to retain some conventional teaching. She is still studying alternative forms of treatment and while she does not yet formally teach them, she has been approached to give the occasional lecture. She is able to combine an understanding of her own needs with those of other people in the field she has chosen to work in and she continues to deepen and extend her own knowledge concerning her work.

She recognizes and values the emotional component of her work and, unsurprisingly for someone who has the Moon in the fifth house, it pervades her leisure activities. She has taken up painting after a lapse of some years and a constant theme is the sea or water. Quite how she might combine this with her work she does not yet know, though she is aware of the emotional undertow in her paintings. At present she uses it more as a relaxation from work, and it is a prominent part of her leisure life. Here we can see the alchemical process at work. Some of her activities – those concerning her work – are part of an integral process in her life; at the same time, she is unsure how her painting reflects the rest of her life, or her inner and spiritual development, though she is open to exploring that. Her sense of observation is keen and she may, in time, become more conscious of the meaning of her need to paint.

In a sense, these few details of her life reflect the unevenness of the alchemical stages mercurial people may go through in the journey from unconsciousness to consciousness, and to move from a mundane to a more spiritually centred existence. Virgoans may find the implied chaos very threatening, while Gemineans could find themselves having to struggle with those parts of their lives which are split off from consciousness. The alchemical process is not always a comfortable, orderly one.

Similarly, unevenness of development is reflected in and among those alchemical texts which survive. Authors of the texts differ in the number and sequence of the stages of the work they lay out for our inspection and it is sometimes confusing to attempt a comparison of the explanations. As we know, Hermes can confuse the very process he is involved in, if the result is to protect himself. In alchemy's terms, it is more to protect the meaning of the work that confusion and secrecy prevail. The stages explored below do, in the main, appear in most medieval and Renaissance texts, though the names sometimes differ. The differences occur because each alchemist, particularly if chemical compounds were being used, performed the work alone and relied on his own powers of observation to track the changes. Most alchemists, as well, took pains to make deliberately incomplete records of the stages and the materials involved in the process. This helped to ensure that alchemy remained an individual activity rather than a collective one. Followers are given some guidelines, but ultimately have to find their own way through to the completion of the work. Again, Hermes ensures that we each follow our own path, that we individuate, to use the Jungian term, that we become masters, if we can, and do not remain stuck in the phase of the eternal apprentice whose powers of understanding are limited and repetitive.

For this process to operate, alchemy, as well as depth psychology, needs a base substance, a *prima materia*, in a state ready to be acted upon. While it is the raw material of the process of change, it cannot be changed until the time and conditions are right. One of those conditions is the recognition that change needs to be contained, cannot be allowed to become volatile to the extent that the work is destroyed. So, to heal himself and to bring about his own transformation, Hermes would need to become the *vas Hermeticum* itself, sealing himself into that round glass bottle in which all alchemical change, re-creation and dynamic life took place.

To the uninitiated, and to those watching the process from the outside, that seemed to be magic and trickery. The alchemists who supposedly embodied these characteristics were both denounced and encouraged by the uninitiated and greedy in medieval and Renaissance times. Similarly, anyone undergoing the work in a therapeutic environment is vulnerable to the same support or lack of encouragement from people around them, with the result that the process might be destabilized. This was a further reason why the alchemists of old kept their work as secret as possible. So mercurial awareness has to operate from the point at which the work begins, if there is to be any success. Again, we see that what happens at the cultural level is reflected in the individual process.

CALCINATIO

As well as being the container, Hermes was also the captured mercurial spirit which was put over a carefully watched and regulated fire and subjected to sometimes slow, sometimes fierce heat, which brought about a death of the old substance and the emergence of a new one, something in the manner of the phoenix arising from its own ashes. The low fire prevented the alembic from cracking, and Hermes, in the form of the spirit of Mercury, from escaping. It was of little use to speed up the cooking process; burning slowly to the point of perfection, changing from within the substance, amalgamating all that was within the retort, were his tasks and his destiny. Burning in a fierce fire indicated an intense and painfully quick transmutation which was sometimes necessary at certain stages, but ran the risk of becoming uncontrolled and volatile, destroying the base substance on which so much time and care had been lavished. This process, quick or slow, was known as the *calcinatio*, one of the many procedures by which the base substance was purified.

It is a process which is difficult to withstand. Cherished ideas, beliefs and behaviours are reduced to an essence which is devoid of emotional content and old feeling values – all water is evaporated in the *calcinatio*. Thought processes may be seen to be stale, redundant and uninvigorated by emotional expression. Mercury-ruled Gemini and Virgo would find this part of the procedure uncomfortable, fearing the heat when confronted by the fire, stifled by the hot air which is produced, unable to escape without ruining the chance of the work succeeding. Hermes imprisoned and cooked is not a happy god and may not be until he realizes consciously the pain of a spirit trapped in imperfect matter and willingly undergoes his trial by fire. It may seem to mercurial people that at this stage they feel spiritless and lifeless.

This is a necessary stage because the spirit of Mercury can only be freed from the base material, though still contained within the alembic, by undergoing the *calcinatio*. Even in his alchemical aspect Hermes was a tricky god to handle. In the form of ordinary Mercury he was variously described by different alchemists as metal, fire and water, but his essence, his ethereal being, was contained within a special kind of quicksilver known for its fleeting, volatile, airy quality. It became, contained within the alembic, the *servus fugitivus*, the fugitive slave, which would transform eventually into the Philosophical Mercury. At this point, Mercury was both spirit and soul, a life-giving power able to hold the concrete world and the spiritual world together. Hermes' famous duality, his ability to recognize both sides of the same coin, was to be put to constructive use at last, as an act of transcendent unification. In some ways, Zeus and Hades had been good masters, but now Hermes had to learn how to operate under his own mastery, humbly and industriously. He came to embrace the polarities of love and hate, good and evil, life and death, rise above them in volatile form and bring back his purified understanding of the totality of his experience to enact change both in himself and in his relationships with others.

In so doing, the opposing forces within him became one; Hermes was both unifier and unified. He was able to work with, and on, and from within the *prima materia*, the source, in order to bring about the *ultima materia*, the perfected stone. In some alchemical traditions he is seen to be synonymous with the philosopher's stone itself. More than that, he was also the process of metamorphosis himself, the beginning, middle and end of the work. Any work of alchemical change is both Hermes and the means by which he achieves transformation. In psychological terms, those means are love of self and others, and attention and courage in the face of life and death; the meanings of which, at the individual level, are gained in experience of the world and its realities.

Staying with the process meant that he had to trust it, whatever the outcome. Fear that the outcome might be failure is likely to make mercurial people fear the start of the work. Though the work can fail at any stage, it is usually the first fear that seems the most difficult to face, but this is where dualistic Hermes is able to help others and himself. He may fare better when he learns to recognize consciously those previously unreachable qualities which reside deep within the psyche. Knowing that the goal is attainable may be both comforting and daunting to mercurial clients.

SOLUTIO, CONIUNCTIO AND SEPARATIO

Though alchemical Hermes is often associated with gnostic Sophia, the wise feminine principle, a deeper re-examination of some of the classical myths we have already looked at indicates that, in Hermes' earlier experiences, lay the seeds of later alchemical understanding. Though he was never able to marry her, Aphrodite was the goddess who effected the initial change in Hermes' attitude to women. In her he was unable to escape the embodiment of love freely given, even if she herself was unobtainable because she was still married to Hephaistos. His union with Aphrodite, brief as it was, indicates a marriage of feeling values and intellect.

Those feelings which Hermes had resisted for so long were revealed to him in Aphrodite's bed, even if, at that time, he was not consciously aware of them. Love needs to embrace all human and divine attributes, including the intellect, if it is to encompass both earthly and spiritual understanding. It needs to recognize and reflect that knowledge. Hermes was faced with the possibility of the first great change in himself when he sought wholeness through skilful service in the craft of love itself. He had used his known need for connection and communication to good effect when he loved Aphrodite. His experience indicated that he could both dissolve into the love act itself and separate properly from Aphrodite afterwards. Here we have the next three alchemical stages – *solutio*, the stage of dissolution in the act of love, *coniunctio*, the act of lovemaking itself, and *separatio*, the ability to draw away from the lover. The *coniunctio* is also referred to as the *heiros gamos*, the sacred marriage, without which the stage of wholeness or unification cannot be reached. In psychological work these three stages indicate that our mercurial clients need to recognize that both merging and separation are part of the process of relatedness.

The result showed in the fruit of their union, Hermaphroditos, the godling and symbol of the alchemical *coniunctio*, in which two bodies were made one. Alchemical symbolism often depicts this in drawings of the hermaphrodite, shown as half-woman, half-man. Alchemists themselves recognized the necessity of the equal union of male and female energies within the work and in the world. There is evidence that some alchemists took female partners, sometimes their wives, as equal partners in alchemical work. Nicolas Flamel, working in France in the fourteenth century, acknowledged his wife's interest and support. If the alchemical process is to succeed, what happens at the internal, individual level will also be reflected in the relationship to the world – one of the lessons Hermes has to understand in his transformation to Hermes Trismegistos. However, we cannot say that recognition of this process results in sweeping changes in collective attitudes towards women; it clearly does not. But alchemy helped to develop and keep alive a belief that has received some cultural recognition, if not full implementation, in the twentieth century.

In both alchemy and Jungian psychology physical union represents the psychic union of opposites, within which Hermes had allowed himself to submit to, and dissolve into, the feminine. To recognize, understand and transcend the wounded feminine bequeathed him by his mother was one stage of his transformation; the unification of body, mind and spirit was the desired outcome. The conscious Hermes could no more escape the meaning of the birth of Hermaphroditos than he could escape the more primitive meaning of the birth of Priapos. He needed to come to terms with his own, raw masculinity before he could attempt a mature relationship with the feminine, loving and sometimes destructive qualities embodied in Aphrodite and the purified essence of Sophia.

PUTREFACTIO AND NIGREDO

But Aphrodite was an earth goddess of life and light, though born from the sea. If Hermes were to achieve his magical and alchemical aim of uniting the worlds of earth and spirit, he needed knowledge of the death process, the psychological depressive stage, to help him do so. This corresponds to the alchemical stages of *putrefactio* or *nigredo*, which we examined in a previous chapter. We can clearly see this process at work in the chart of Roberto Assagioli, the Italian psychiatrist, psychotherapist and founder of psychosynthesis, who was born in Venice in 1888 (see p. 143). His work was known to Jung and Freud from as early as 1909 and he trained at Burgholzli, where Bleuler, one of Jung's teachers, was then director.

On returning to Italy he published a series of articles, worked further on his own understanding of psychotherapy, married and, in 1926, opened the Istituto di Cultura e Terapia Psichica, concentrating on both individual therapy and therapy in relation to education, investing it with the results of his studies in many fields of spirituality and creativity. By 1936, the *istituto* was under surveillance from the Fascist government, not least because Assagioli was Jewish. By 1938, he was under pressure to close down the organization and was also imprisoned for a few months. He survived the war by hiding on occasions in the rural depths of Italy, and, at its close, founded the Istituto Psicosintesi, branches of which have subsequently spread across the world. His work is alive with influences drawn from Christian, Jewish, neo-platonic and Buddhist cultures and spiritual traditions. A writer of two books and numerous articles on his methods, Assagioli died in Italy in 1974.

We see in the chart a number of disparate themes, the most influential being the Grand Cross in Mutable signs which pulls in the mercurial influence, not only through the MC/IC Axis, but also through the wide conjunction of Mercury to the Sun. The Grand Cross indicates a personality which is able to raise unconsciously powerful issues up to the conscious light, in so doing imbuing them with an understanding of their feeling components before disseminating their meaning. Assagioli was both teacher and writer as well as a psychiatrist. The Ascendant and MC in Water signs would indicate a caring persona, but perhaps somebody who is not comfortable with the shadow side of human nature. Pluto in Gemini in the twelfth house would tend to exacerbate that trait. It is significant that in his work he tended to emphasize the transforming and life-enhancing nature of his view of psychotherapy, though he did acknowledge the power of unconscious complexes. His Sun/Mercury conjunction in Pisces would sensitize him to the chaos of life and he would need, in his work, to emphasize an underlying unity of all life in order to contain the fear of disintegration – hence his work on synthesis and the transcendent.

The minor aspects Mercury makes in the chart are also of some importance. The planet makes a semi-square to Venus in Aquarius and a quincunx to an unaspected Uranus in Libra. Venus and Saturn oppose each other in the eighth and second houses respectively. Mercury also rules the Moon and the IC in Virgo. Here we can see that any disordering of the intellectual processes might cause a feeling of psychic insecurity and there could be a tendency to dissociate from the emotions, and to experience other people as cold. Certainly, there would be fears of emotional closeness, and the Moon in the fourth house would tend to heighten that feeling. How far Assagioli was aware of this process in himself we do not yet know. We know little of his interactions with significant people in his life or of his continuing work on himself. What we can say is that, in true mercurial fashion, he was able to translate his perceptions,

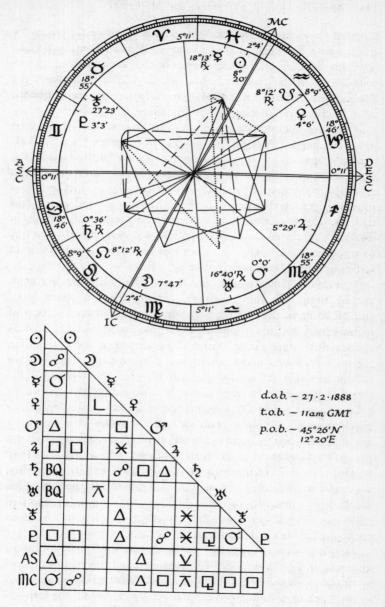

Birthchart for Roberto Assagioli.[3]

whether they came from his observations of himself or from his studies, into his work in the collective. We can also say that, at some level, Assagioli had experience of the death process; no one with Pluto in the twelfth house, Venus in the eighth and the Moon in the fourth can escape that. Whether he was conscious of it, or chose to live it out in the collective, is arguable.

It is here that we see Mercury at his trickiest. The chart indicates that for Assagioli to be able to propound a transcendental psychotherapy, he must have had a sense of the *nigredo*, but the facts inherent in his work do not necessarily bear this out. In actuality, he warned against too much delving into unconscious processes, stating that defences were there for a good reason and that to release unconscious contents too soon could result in explosive emotions and drives. While not denying the potency of unconscious contents, he does not seem too comfortable in working directly and consciously with them.

This raises a delicate issue concerning Assagioli's imprisonment and his flight into the countryside during the war years. Pluto and Neptune in the twelfth house might indicate a condition of reclusiveness, spiritual transformation, and could, further, be associated with incarceration. Pursued by an unjust and totalitarian regime which was noted for its barbarity towards the Jews, we cannot say that he complied with his fate and lived out the *nigredo* unconsciously as a result of misreading the nature of collective pressures; there is no interpretation, astrological or psychological, that can explain away the atrocities committed by any political regime, or that can tell us much about the stage of a person's awareness at a particular moment in time. All that may be said is that his imprisonment was a *nigredo* experience. What is certain is that, after the war, he continued and deepened his work in psychosynthesis, offering it as a healing to a wounded collective. Whatever form his *nigredo* took, he was able to complete his life's work with some success.

In some ways, Assagioli's work is not dissimilar to Jung's either in aim or in method. Both encouraged the creative use of symbols to establish a meaningful link with unconscious processes; both were concerned to establish, *contra* Freud, the importance of an integrating and inner Self or Higher Self which had a transpersonal and spiritual connotation; both approached their patients as doctors trained in diagnosing and curing abnormalities. Their big difference was over Jung's emphasis on the importance of the collective unconscious. Assagioli asserted that a sense of spirituality came from a personal centre within man and not from a common cultural pool, though he did acknowledge a collective influence on people's development. How far he is right is debatable, but it did lead to his need to help people to a realization of their unconsciously competing subpersonalities. He put the accent on the conscious transcendence of multiplicities rather than on the Jungian transcendence of opposites. This bears out the influence of his Grand Cross in Mutable signs.

He emphasized the development of the right use of will as part of this process, aligning it with a higher purpose once the natural progress towards synthesis is revealed, rather than using it as a driving, sometimes punishing force. This indicates some resolution of the conflict residing in his Pluto/Jupiter opposition. The aim was to live much more from the viewpoint of the Higher Self, thereby avoiding the projection of unconscious material on to the environment and other people. For Assagioli, a transpersonal sense of unity was the purpose of life and this aligns him quite strongly with the Buddhist tradition, with which he was familiar. Unity could only be achieved by a conscious synthesis of formerly unconscious processes which undergo a deep, inner transformation. So psychosynthesis can be seen as a very mercurial and spiritualized therapy.

In alchemy, the *nigredo* cannot be neglected; mythology tells us why. We are informed that Hermes became the lover of both Persephone and Hecate in Hades' kingdom. Where Aphrodite was extrovert, a direct and lusty goddess, Persephone and Hecate represented the inner, feminine realm of the spirit, both being, in essence, death goddesses. Since they were elusive and difficult to understand because of their more introspective natures, Hermes needed experience of their interior world, their feminine knowledge of the death process; they had been there before him and so had powers he also wished to hold. Both goddesses had some of the characteristics of his mother, elusive and ultimately mysterious, but by binding himself to Hades' service as psychopomp, he was repeatedly drawn back to seek his soulmates, both old and young, in the dead lands. The lively and and airy Hermes was to fix himself, putrefy, then incubate beneath the earth as he engaged in resolving within himself the tension and conflict between life and death.

CONGELATIO

Hermes, through his knowledge of Persephone, was forced to recognize the strength of the great earth mother, Demeter. Her grief over her lost daughter roused Zeus to bargain with his brother, Hades, for her return to earth for at least part of the year. Hermes was sent, under Zeus' orders, to conduct Persephone back through the realms of the dead to the upper world, so ensuring that life and death were united in an eternal, seasonal cycle. This part of the myth indicates that, though he could interact with the feminine attributes of his nature while still in the underworld, he still needed Zeus' external mastery to help him unite this-world and other-worldly feminine values. So Hermes does learn to mediate between corporeality and the spirit because, for the first time, he was witness to the depth of feeling of a mother who was attached to and grieved for her child. This was a bond he had not known with his own star-directed and emotionally elusive mother. Demeter mirrored back his own deprivation and need for attachment.

We can see this process at work in mercurial clients who start to become aware of their own pain. Finding a nurturing part of the psyche which can grieve with, and support, the wounded feminine within is part of the journey and the task. What can help to give hope to mercurial development is that, in some myths, Persephone gives birth in the underworld to Hermes' child, a process which reflects Hermaphroditos' birth in the world above. Repetition of the same process in a different realm helps fix the universality of the experience and corresponds to the alchemical stage of *congelatio*. Hermes needed more than one experience before he could see a repeating theme which helps to make real and solidify experience. Only then is healing a possibility. Gemineans and Virgoans would recognize this pattern; both are used to collecting and gathering, though perhaps Virgoans find it rather easier to bring the disparate parts together and make sense of them.

The *congelatio* contains within it the recognition that all experience needs to be included if the work is to be completed successfully. Mercurial people are often aware of many aspects of their life experiences, but they may not be aware that one small part reflects, in microcosm, all the others. So there are aspects of his own myth that Hermes needed to accommodate before his final transmutation into the wisdom god, Hermes Trismegistos. Though he learned to accommodate the hetaira Aphrodite, medial Persephone and Hecate and maternal Demeter, he had greater difficulty doing so directly with the amazonian and intellectual attributes of Athene and with the queenly, ruling qualities of Hera. He showed recognition of these feminine archetypes through male intermediaries, Perseus and Herakles, whose myths we have partly examined in previous chapters.

Poseidon had raped Medusa at Athene's shrine, so violating it. For some reason unable to act against her brother god, but needing to protect her emotionally controlled virginal image, Athene sought to obtain the magical amulet of Medusa's head, whose glance could turn men to stone. Hermes could not face or understand Athene's steely vengeance directly, having misused too many women himself to put himself under the goddess's power without protection, but another son of Zeus' could. Perseus, the 'destroyer', could allow himself more immediately than Hermes to befriend the goddess who chose to live in her aloneness, cut off from her femininity by the terrible power of Zeus. She, however, still remained an embodiment of female wisdom in its most civilizing, if patriarchal, form. To reclaim their primal, split-off identities, all Zeus' children resorted to, or were implicated in, death of some sort, whether by natural means or by murder. Medusa represented that dissociated aspect of civilized Athene's personality, the murderous sense of outrage against men that could freeze their blood. So, in the language of myth, Medusa had to die for Athene to reclaim it.

In this case, by supplying Perseus with the weapons and

attributes he needed to kill Medusa, the raging power of the destructive feminine, Hermes perhaps showed more awareness of his half-sister's need to retain her protective cover than the myth at first glance reveals. In accepting Athene's need for self-protection, Hermes took on himself a brotherly protective role, giving Perseus what was necessary to overcome the destructive power of the Gorgon. At the same time, by using Perseus as a cover, he also protected himself against too much pain when he found himself having to understand Athene's wounded feminine nature. Sometimes such protection is necessary for mercurial people, though we do not know if Hermes was, by this time, aware of his own need. The alchemical process occasionally uses a catalyst to further the process and the myth indicates that Hermes was certainly aware of using Perseus in that way.

The complexity of this myth indicates what subtle mercurial awareness is subsumed in the *congelatio*. Perseus stands behind the reflecting shield to kill Medusa. Behind Perseus stands Hermes with his helpful gifts. Behind Hermes stands Athene, who herself is protecting Zeus' power while liberating some of her own. Mercury-ruled people need a clear and continual alertness to integrate such subtleties into the constancy of the *congelatio*.

Coming to terms with the power of feminine rule was, for Hermes, just as difficult and just as indirect. Herakles, the hero, was the protector of Hera in her matriarchal form of divine ruler, but he needed guidance from the gods on his many labours and, often, protection from Hera's wrath. In his last great labour with death itself, raising Cerberos from Tartaros, Athene and Hermes, the two intellectual immortals, and one a psychopomp, accompanied him in and out of Hades' kingdom, reassuring him and helping the labour to a successful conclusion. Though Hera was protectress of Herakles, his many excesses often displeased her, but she could not afford to have him fail, otherwise Zeus' power over her would have been supreme. Hera, unlike Hermes' mother, constantly fought for her position as Zeus' wife and co-ruler on Olympus, and, through his perception of the conflict, Hermes experienced again how important a balance of power between male and female was. So we see him, not under obvious orders from Zeus this time, accompanying

Herakles to ensure his success, again uniting the worlds of the living and the dead, the free spirit who can also fix himself when necessary.

CIBATIO

In doing so, Hermes became more aware of the need to be his own master. The more experiences he had in different spheres of operation, the more those experiences fed his understanding. There seems to be a clear correlation with this and the alchemical stage of *cibatio*. By acting on his own initiative in the last of Herakles' labours, Hermes breaks away from the power of the father and, accepting the world of the feminine in its entirety, brings it into balance with his emerging, mature nature. The more he does so, the more complex and independent his thinking becomes. Hermes was now to be recognized for the depth of the connections he could make, using, too, a skilful intuition. Study of and service to the father of the gods meant that Hermes developed the capacity to outgrow his father's sovereignty. In order to act alchemically on himself, he became more aware of the limit and extent of his father's influence. Once he had independent and mature control of his own life, he was in a position to assume control over his own death and descent into the underworld.

The life and chart of Elizabeth Kubler-Ross indicates clearly the process of *cibatio*, the constant feeding into and learning from a theme (see p. 151). She is the oldest of triplets, born in Switzerland in 1926. She had a conventionally comfortable middle-class upbringing, but quarrelled with her authoritarian father over her desire to go to medical school. Eventually she supported herself through her medical studies by working as a laboratory assistant. Prior to attending college she worked as a volunteer with refugees to Switzerland from Nazi Germany. When the war was over she took a back-packing trip through Europe, visiting Majdanek, a concentration camp near the Russo-Polish border, an experience which shook her deeply.

Returning to medical school, she completed her studies, met

and married her husband, also a doctor, and set off for America, where, by 1964, she was working and lecturing at the University of Denver. It was here that she first became aware of the need for terminal care of the dying and prepared a lecture for her students on that topic. By 1966 she was working in Chicago and her interest in terminal care struck a chord with people, other than doctors, who were concerned with the dying. Her medical colleagues were not so impressed. Her work was opposed by all except one physician, but she continued in the face of pressure.

By 1969 she had published her first book, *On Death and Dying*, and it received world-wide recognition within months. The publicity triggered stronger opposition from her medical colleagues and she left the university, embarking on a programme of lectures and seminars. Eventually she was involved in founding the organization Shanti Nilaya, which concentrates on the organization of lectures and seminars, teaching the skills needed to help treat the terminally ill. Her interest in the spiritual aspects of dying has increased throughout the years and is somewhat in line with Buddhist precepts. At her workshops, she stresses the need to live life fully, even with the realization of impending death, rather than just pass through it unawarely. She has continued to write on many aspects of death and dying, publishing many books, and her work is now recognized throughout the world.

When we look at her chart we see Mutable axes, with Mercury-ruled Gemini on the IC and Virgo on the Descendant. Mercury is in sixth house Leo and is sextile Venus, trine Mars, square Saturn and quincunx the Ascendant. Her Pisces Ascendant, a Pluto/Sun/North Node conjunction in Cancer and the Moon also in Cancer, allows us to see a person who knows the transformative and compassionate values of the emotions in relation to life and death and can make creative use of them, or one who fears them. Kubler-Ross's life story indicates that she has been willing to stand by her work and beliefs in the face of strong opposition, making creative use of her talents and profound understanding of the transformation process of life and death. Mercury, seemingly, has both helped and hindered her in this process. Again, there is the fear that the god Hermes is not quite what he appears to be. It was her first book that brought

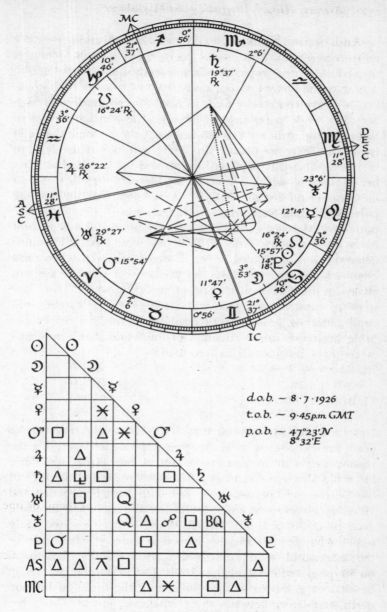

Birthchart for Elizabeth Kubler-Ross.[4]

her both acclaim from the world and disapprobation from her more conventional and critical peers; there are echoes of this theme in Mercury's rulership of the seventh and fourth houses.

Not one to concede defeat easily, we see how her sixth house Leo Mercury continually feeds its need for recognition through her daily work in the field of healing. The Mercury square to Saturn in eighth house Scorpio bears out the Plutonic theme in her chart. There are obstacles to communication if she dares to step beyond socially approved norms and yet her need to share her knowledge, which is indicated by Mercury's sextile to Venus in Gemini and by the MC/IC Axis falling in the teaching polarity, Gemini–Sagittarius, is imperative and is strongly supported by Mercury's trine to a very dynamic and independent Mars in first house Aries. The result would be a continual determination to succeed in her chosen work even when most criticized. She writes, lectures and teaches on a regular basis, not always in the institutional world of medical practice. This is the stage of *cibatio*, where constant feeding of the learning and communicating process about death and dying has helped her bring her work to the attention of the world. She seems well aware that fears about death need to die.

SUBLIMATIO

Hermes knew, in addition, that death had to die; that out of death came regeneration of the spirit. He led men and gods, the representatives of his own psychic forces, into Hades' kingdom. He could also lead them out again, with assent and the help of life-affirming properties, as he did with both Persephone and Herakles. He grew to know the power and usefulness of death, even psychic death, and learned when Hades could be justly opposed by life itself. He also learned to know when the rules of the underworld could not be broken, as he did when he insisted on Sisyphus' return to the dead lands. The alchemical Hermes, in his maturity, was to balance judiciously the forces of life and death, translating between them with ease, just as Thoth and Odin did in their respective cultures. To be fair-minded, show mercy and give proper retribution in the halls of the dead, within the alchemical retort, meant that Hermes had to have a conscious understanding of how his experiences and emotions could integrate positively with his flexible intellect. This, then, is the stage of the alchemical *sublimatio*, where body and spirit are shown to be one in the psychological lands of the living and the dead. Virgoans and Gemineans, through recognizing the correspondence of life experience with their own internal processes, have the capacity to realize this unification.

FERMENTATIO AND EXULTATIO

Once understanding has taken place, that the tension of opposites within is safely held and the opposites themselves are seen to be of the same nature, then Hermes is in a position to recognize those who have as deep an understanding of the same process. This is the stage of *fermentatio*, where gold is added to gold to make it more active. We are shown this in the Egyptian myth of Thoth's two wives, Nehmauit, who understood the roots of good and evil, and Seshat, the record-keeper and guardian of libraries. Hermes in his Egyptian aspect and alchemical form was seen to work with, rather than against, his own nature. Nehmauit represents his mature ability to contain and understand his own actions; Seshat, his capacity to record painful and truthful experiences, storing them carefully so they could act as a guide to those who had access to the sacred libraries. At that point, civilization and self-regulation of an unruly spirit take place, fixed and are constant, yet remain flexible and responsive. Only at that point can Hermes safely proclaim his achievement; its alchemical correlate is the *exultatio*.

MULTIPLICATIO AND PROJECTIO

We see whither this leads in the myth where Thoth accompanies Anubis and Osiris on a mission to civilize the world. Only at the point where he is reconciled with his own shadow, able to act

independently of others, but in a contained fashion, fully accepting, on all occasions, the depth of communication necessary for
any reconciliation between opposing psychic forces, could
Hermes be said to act maturely. So he became both guide and
guided, apprentice turned teacher, showing his capacity for
studious undertakings and wisdom in his later form of Hermes
Trismegistos. In this later role he was able to ingest his skilfully
acquired knowledge and transmute his earlier, irresponsible way
of being into a considered, dependable one, always capable of
assessing, accepting and encompassing in his world the true
worth of human and spiritual values and to continue to pass
these values on to others. These, then, are the last processes in the
alchemical work, the *multiplicatio* and *projectio*. They are the
stages by which the original base matter resolves into the perfected philosopher's stone and by which Hermes also becomes
the Philosophical Mercury and Trismegistos, thrice-greatest.

But the hermetic work does not stop with the fixing of the
stone. In the world, and in the psyche, this is a work which
continues in many forms, life-long and, some would say, beyond
life. This shape-shifting aspect of Hermes/Mercury not only
aligns him more closely with Odin, but shows us, also, how the
hidden god who seemed, initially, to be morally neutral within
the retort, became the impeccable force which could reconcile
the opposites of weak and strong, death and resurrection, old
and young, wise and foolish, collective and individual. Hermes
needed his mercurial fluidity if he were to reveal an embodied
but incorruptible spirituality. To do so, he was forced to explore
and accept his own dark shadow, the shiftiness and superficiality,
the lack of understanding of the feeling side of nature, the
inability to trust and the selfish need to plan events to his own
advantage. He had to learn how to turn his shadow characteristics
to good effect in the alchemical retort, the conscious depths of
his own psyche.

The alchemical Hermes grew into an acceptance of consciously
trusting, rather than unconsciously manipulating the deep need
for change, when this was seen to be a necessary part of his own
transformation and development. The god of thieves and magicians used his own magic and trickery to transform himself into

the alchemical and psychological unifier and unified in the world without and the world within. He becomes, in effect, the true spiritual heart of the process of transformation and change, constant and free simultaneously. At each stage of the process he reflects the historical, cultural and individual development of the human psyche, and the interlocking of its component parts. It is a process for the evolution of consciousness which finds its mirror in the complexities of the birthchart and may also reveal a life-path for all those people in whom Mercury resonates strongly.

PART TWO

ASTROLOGICAL MERCURY

8

Aspects to Mercury

Mercury's aspects to the other planets, the angles and nodal axis are indicative of the way a person's curiosity and intellect function, not only in the external world, but also inwardly. Internal reality is where we make sense of our lives and where we discover our values and sense of meaning. If Mercury's connective function is working well, then he is able to translate between the worlds of inner and outer reality, ideas and environment, self and other, so that the process of growth and change is kept fresh and alive. Aspects between planets show us how the essential planetary functions and energies combine to produce a particular effect in a person's life. How Mercury translates that effect when he is one of the planets in the combination depends on which of his wise, tricky, changeable, adaptable or versatile qualities is uppermost at the time. There are, though, core combinations of effects, and these become more apparent when we look at the interaction of the archetypes – or gods – in mythology.

SUN – MERCURY

The Sun and Mercury can never be more than twenty-eight degrees apart, so the two planets can only ever make a conjunction. Astrologers up to the middle years of the twentieth century used two further cases for Sun/Mercury conjunctions: *combust*, where Mercury was within four degrees of the Sun and which indicated a mind that was weakened or burned up by the Sun's rays; and *casimi*, which occurred when Mercury was within thirty degrees of the Sun and was supposed to indicate a very powerful intellect. Contemporary astrologers, on the whole, disagree with this and put forward a number of ways in which the Sun/Mercury conjunction can work.

In this combination, intellect-orientated Mercury entwines itself with the Sun's vitality and will-power, giving lively and alert minds. People with aspects between these two planets can be self-sufficient thinkers with a need to gather knowledge and to communicate this. The exchanges between Hermes and Apollo in their joint myths indicate as much. The sternness and insistence on the truth that Apollo displayed generated Hermes' glib but lively tongue. We sense that his mind was on full alert as he searched for ways to defend himself and appease Apollo's anger.

Appealing to the softer, musical side of Apollo, Hermes offered him the lyre made from the shell of a tortoise. His ability to survive by his wits was legendary, but he needed the vitality of Apollo, and what the Sun god possessed, to bring him to the point where he began to deepen and regard other people – and gods – less as objects to be manipulated and more as individuals in their own right. This ability to heal the mercurial split between thought and feelings is the real meaning of Hermes' later association with the healing gods, Apollo and Asklepios.

Often accused of gathering facts in a superficial way and for their own sake, mature people with this aspect strong in their charts can combine and make connections between different areas of knowledge in a thorough manner. They may have a powerful need to make the knowledge they have acquired accessible to others, as Hermes, Apollo and Asklepios did when they propagated the healing arts. Curious, and with a keen sense for well-thought-out arguments, they can be rational and logical, enjoying stimulating conversation and discussion in a lively, chatty atmosphere, anxious to make connections between people and ideas. It is with Sun/Mercury aspects that we can see the potential to begin work at a much deeper, healing level of psychological development. The intellectual function of Mercury can be used with the light-shedding power of the Sun to explore the darker realms of the unconscious.

Conversely, people with aspects between the Sun and Mercury may have minds which are too powerful, inclining others to see them as stubborn and opinionated, unable to see anyone else's viewpoint but their own. There is always a tendency to remain flexible in argument on the surface, but it soon becomes apparent that, underneath, they may not have moved from their original positions. Often this is through fear of relinquishing old and redundant patterns of behaviour and development. In the dissent between Hermes and Apollo over the theft of the cattle, it was Zeus who had to intervene to help to resolve the dispute.

Left to themselves, the half-brothers might have argued for ever, neither willing to give up their original positions in case they had to change their attitudes. We can see this more negative side of the aspect at work in people who overemphasize the intellect, forgetting that feelings and values can add greater depth to life's experiences. In fact, they might find it difficult to get in touch with and contain their own feelings. When the boundaries to their egos and independence of thought are threatened, they are likely to see the attacks as a way of devaluing their minds and ideas, just as Apollo and Hermes did. Identifying with their minds so strongly, they may fall back on rationalizing their feelings in an uncontrolled manner.

Houses, signs and aspects to other planets will also affect the way in which the Sun/Mercury aspect behaves. For instance, the dark god of the underworld, Pluto, may represent the hidden, perhaps destructive, portion of the psyche. So Pluto square either of the planets can lead a person to repress or hide the dark nature of his thoughts altogether, or it could indicate someone with a spiteful and wounding tongue – a very different image from the bright and vital characteristics of Apollo and Hermes at their best. The duo's aspects to Pluto can also indicate the type of work a person undertakes, and the methods which might be used, depending on house placements and signs. The combination can show up in the person who has a deeply perceptive mind with a powerful motive to get to the root of matters, which is the meaning of travelling in the mythological underworld; it is a useful characteristic for anyone seriously engaged in research or investigation. Sometimes all three character traits can be observed in the same person at different times, which suggests that planetary aspects are often lived out in a number of ways which may conflict or combine with one another.

MOON – MERCURY

Aspects to Mercury from the Moon indicate that the mind works in association with fluctuating emotions, depending on whether the aspects are hard or soft. We see this in Hermes' mother, Maia. She both berates her child over the theft of Apollo's cattle and defends him from his brother by lying. People whose charts contain this combination are likely to be very conscious of their own emotions and their responses to others; consequently, they often have a good sense of humour, a good practical reasoning ability, as well as showing a witty understanding of other people's ideas. They may develop a tactful form of expression and give emphasis to easing communications between themselves and others. This Maia did, when she said that the baby could not have stolen his half-brother's cattle because he was too young, and anyway was asleep in bed. Though it was a perversion of the tact which operates when the aspect is working well, it does indicate the need to ease emotional communications between people. Close observers of domestic and daily life, people with the aspect, may develop the ability to talk in a calming way with those who need to discuss their own emotional difficulties, and to be sympathetic listeners. At their best, they are quick to perceive the emotional undertow of any situation and are well able to balance feeling with reason. They are able to put their thoughts into practical action, showing much sensitivity to the needs of others.

Where the combination does not work well, or the planets are badly aspected, there is often a compulsion to talk. Certainly Hermes' early childhood days with his mother indicated that he was in the right environment to develop a continual verbal patter, as we may judge from his inventive conversations with Apollo and Zeus. It operated from the moment he decided that he wanted recognition from his father. Constant chatting is sometimes the way in which these people show how nervously emotional they are and how feelings can override their reasoning capacities. They may find it difficult to control their thought processes and can dwell too much on the past and their own emotional history, but without reaching definite conclusions.

Being mentally trapped in the past, and perhaps too rational in assessing their own feelings, can make them boring and irritating to others and frustrating to themselves because old emotional issues never seem to be resolved. Where these characteristics are suppressed, they may find themselves similarly irritated and bored by others who refer to their own past. In these circumstances, it is a way of exercising control over other people's emotional reactions, letting the mind override the emotions much as Hermes did when he attempted to talk his way out of the theft of Apollo's cattle. But we see this operating in a positive, caring way when we see the more mature and contained Hermes interceding with Achilles on Priam's behalf for the return of Hector's body.

Difficulties between the functions of these two planets can also indicate changeable feelings and minds, with a high degree of muddle-headedness and emotional confusion. Passing moods and mutable opinions may cause others to see them as overconcerned with trivialities and too whimsical and, in a sense, quite absent from the realities which face them daily. Often there may be problems in reaching a decision because this, in some situations, is a way of warding off the fear and pain involved in making a commitment. It is here that we get a sense of the emotional absence of Hermes' mother, shown in the myths by her nightly disappearance into the heavens. The tendency to live in their heads, or fly sky high, may be observed in people whose charts contain the Moon/Mercury combination, particularly where no rational solution can be found to ease emotional issues.

Aspects to other planets can also affect Moon/Mercury. Mercury trine the Moon, for example, where the Moon also squares Mars, indicates a person who may be emotionally sensitive, has a strong desire to be independent, but may not be able to communicate this in sensible and non-threatening ways. The Mars principle stirs up and energizes any aspect it contacts, much as the god of war did in mythology. Any integration is likely to occur only where a person has seen the need to work purposefully on previously conflicting characteristics. More probably, people with this combination are likely to split off from the Mars principle, unable to contain their own angry feelings. They may repress them, or find it difficult to work with others, particularly women, in acts of projection which leave them free of the responsibility of own their anger. By itself, Moon square Mars can indicate that problems stem from an angry or selfish mother, perhaps one who repressed these tendencies. This is one interpretation of the myths of Maia. If this is the stronger characteristic, then Moon trine Mercury may not be able to communicate its feelings in domestic situations very easily and perhaps may only be able to operate well, if at all, outside the home or at work where its practical business sense may be put to good use. Hermes was away from his mother's home as soon as he possibly could be, putting his wits to work in the world. As with all aspects, the signs and house placements of this combination would need to be taken into account before giving an interpretation.

MERCURY – VENUS

Mercury and Venus are always found less than seventy-six degrees apart, so the only aspects they can make to each other are the conjunction, sextile, quintile, semi-sextile and the semi-square. Aspects between the two planets are reasonably common in birthcharts, as are aspects which both make to the Sun. The nature of Mercury/Venus is to combine, or not, the world of feelings with that of the intellect. Understanding the nature of the emotions and valuing the insights of a perceptive mind seem to be the tasks set when the two planets are combined.

When it is working well, the combination brings about a diplomatic and communicative nature which helps people to act on ideas in a harmonious way. People with aspects between Mercury and Venus may have literary or artistic talent and may try to work out their ideas in partnership with others. They often need to express the beauty of ideas in a readily observable form. The relationship between the intellect and the emotions is recognized and people with the aspect often appreciate the beauty of ideas, often opening up to talk about values which mean much to them; it is the core meaning of the joint myths of Hermes and Aphrodite. They have the ability to communicate with others in a refined way, easily attracting others by their amusing personalities, and with much charm. Their sometimes overactive minds are steadied in a loving way by rooting themselves in physical experience, while overindulgence of the senses is contained by strong powers of discrimination and insight.

The myths of Hermes and Aphrodite are very active here. No matter what the circumstances surrounding their mating, these two divinities found pleasure in each other's company, for a brief while, and were fruitful because their love was freely given and taken, harmonious and beautifying. This is the positive indication of a Mercury/Venus aspect, where the intellect recognizes the connective power of love. It is often devotion to the principle of love, which Aphrodite represents in her positive form, that can strengthen the mercurial aim to accept other people and themselves more compassionately.

Where there is lack of awareness of the meaning of the Venus/Mercury principle, people may find themselves easily seduced by words and show a degree of mental laziness, or indulgence in the sound of words for their own sake. They can be overly agreeable and unable to see that verbal expression needs to be meaningful before true relatedness can take place. Something of the kind can be seen in the myths of the love-affair between Hermes and Aphrodite. There was no thought of Hephaistos' feelings and no thought of what fate might have in store for Priapos and Hermaphroditos, the results of their mating.

Some stress may be experienced in relating the needs of the body to those of the mind and the combination can exacerbate flightiness and superficiality, often in relationships. As a result, partnerships can be short-lived because mental processes are disconnected from the emotions. This is apparent in many of Hermes' relationships with women and goddesses – his flightiness and escapism most often make him fickle. Sometimes people with this combination feel that there is no depth to their relationships, or they may be wary of being hurt and attempt to keep all relationships at a light-hearted, uncommitted level. Luxury-loving to a degree, they may be in danger of becoming conceited and vain, blinding themselves to other people's need in relationships and losing a balanced sense of values along the way.

Other planets in aspect to Mercury/Venus will colour the nature of the combination considerably. Mercury semi-square Venus, for instance, where Venus opposes Jupiter, indicates a nature which may overindulge in sensuous and sensual gratification, without using much discrimination to discover what is worth while. People who have this configuration in their charts may forever be looking for unrealistic and total fulfilment in romantic attachments, whether to other people or to ideas, and may come across to others as verbally sentimental, gushing or overenthusiastic. The Venus/Jupiter opposition is likely to be the stronger aspect, while Mercury/Venus acts to exacerbate an already difficult situation. For the meaning of this combination of planets to be integrated successfully into the personality, grandiose and inflated ideas of self-worth and emotional expression would need to be put into a realistic and thoughtful perspective, particularly where there is a tendency to project these less easily owned qualities on to other people.

MERCURY – MARS

This combination of planets indicates people who may have a keen awareness of the world around them. Having quick and agile minds and an abundance of mental energy, they may be direct in speech and are able to act on decisions incisively. The task for these people is to co-ordinate the flexible, hermaphroditic quality of Mercury with the masculine dynamism of Mars.

Where the combination works benignly, they may develop a practical turn of mind, even if they are rather competitive about putting ideas into action. Unafraid of being assertive when the occasion demands, they know their own minds and what they want; they are often quite intense in communicating their ideas to others. Used to observing closely the people and conditions which surround them, their quick thinking and verbal dexterity often make them sharp-minded and witty. The discovery of

Ares' and Aphrodite's mating, and their shaming by the Olympians, illustrates this well. It was Hermes who stood at the side of the bed laughing and commenting on the plight of the lovers as they lay tangled in Hephaistos' net. All very clever, but it did not take on board the lovers' shame and Hephaistos' distress. People who have this combination of planets may not themselves appreciate being at the sharp end of the joke. Developing and deepening their thinking and acting skills will often help these people calm their sometimes over-ready tongues and too inquisitive minds.

But the combination also has a negative polarity. Occasionally these people can give vent to aggressive outbursts which are often the result of extreme nervous tension that has found little outlet in practical action. It was Hermes who released Ares from thirteen months' imprisonment in a brass jar by one of the sons of the giant Aloeus. Though Ares was a shadow of his former blustering self when he crawled out of the jar, and his voice was almost gone, he hadn't stopped protesting from the time he was imprisoned. Hermes, as the tale shows, needs to engage Ares' activity constructively, rather than suppressing it or wasting it.

For people with this combination, letting fly verbally means that others may see them as impatient, irritable and sharp-tongued, unable to listen to anybody's opinions but their own. This tendency often damages their relationships because other people can see them as essentially uncooperative, even when this is not really the case. If their ever-active minds are not fruitfully engaged in putting ideas into action, or their plans are thwarted in some way, the resulting boredom, as well as tension, can make them argumentative and aggressively opinionated. On the other hand, they can also act impulsively, not stopping to think about the results of their actions or explain what they are doing – another tendency which can alienate people.

The aspects that Mercury/Mars makes to other planets can considerably affect the way the combination operates. Mercury trine Mars, where Mars conjuncts Uranus, may show up in a person who is extremely highly strung and is affected powerfully, and perhaps debilitatingly, by the quality of communication with other people. But that same quality of communication is needed in order to exchange ideas, even if the intensity isn't so desirable. This is the person who can find it difficult to sleep because his or her mind is a constantly churning and sometimes uncontrollable whirlpool of thoughts and worries. This is reminiscent of the myth of Ares when he lay yelling and screaming on the battlefield at Troy, thrashing around uselessly in rage because Athene had felled him. The myth gives an indication of what happens when the mind is overactive and cannot be switched off – nothing is resolved, and the mental processes continue to circulate uselessly.

Sometimes, with this combination of planets, overimpulsive action and speech are present which is made worse by a uranian tendency to rebel unthinkingly against established and conventional ideas. On other occasions, ideas which are freely expressed and exchanged with others will be put into action in very original ways. People with this combination of planets would need periods of physical activity interspersed with periods of relaxation to offset the intensity of the way in which they think. They would also need to be aware of a tendency to be disruptive or overforceful in speech or action, or, perhaps, of projecting these traits on to other people and significant partners.

MERCURY – JUPITER

People with Mercury and Jupiter in combination can have broad, tolerant minds with the potential to communicate easily in a philosophical cause. They have the ability to express their ideas confidently and fluently and so may be drawn to teaching, or otherwise inspiring people. Tending to be more attracted to ideas than practicalities, they have wide-ranging interests, sometimes travelling great distances in the pursuit of knowledge, as Mercury and Jupiter did on their visit to Baucis and Philemon. The travelling, though, may be embarked on inwardly, to find the connections between morally uplifting and philosophical ways of thinking. These people could have expansive, intuitive minds, with a supporting ability to balance ideas and judgements. Though they are intuitive, they are also careful about the way they pick and choose ideas to give weight to their intellectual arguments. We can see something of this in the tale where Zeus arbitrates between Apollo and Hermes. He is not willing only to condemn his younger son, but is concerned to place Hermes' qualities within a broader perspective which makes better use of his sometimes too-flexible tongue. It's the reason why he made Hermes into his messenger – containment can sometimes lead to better judgement.

When the combination works negatively, it does so in two ways. People may become intellectually arrogant and conceited, fixated on one idea and exaggerating it out of proportion to the idea's actual worth. These are the people who tend to be bombastic in speech and overly talkative in defence of their own thoughts. Other people may see them as overconfident and lacking in judgement and discrimination, unrealistic in the way they tackle the practicalities of everyday life. Hermes on his own is not liable to bombast, but he can inflate the truth – with Jupiter's help.

If they are blown up with ideas of grandiosity, people who use this combination negatively may misconstrue the meaning of their own or other people's ideas. Jupiter's need is always to see the wider perspective, but he may not accept that he has missed some of the smaller details which would make that perspective a truly representative one. On the other hand, some people manifest the combination's negative qualities by being indecisive and woolly-minded. They can be so lost in their own thoughts and ideas that they have difficulty taking in the reality of the world around them. They do not find it easy to choose the most relevant arguments to support their cause and are apt to gather knowledge for the sake of it rather than to communicate it in a meaningful way.

When Mercury quincunxes Jupiter and also sextiles Neptune, for instance, people have a very sensitive ability to pick up on the thoughts and feelings of others and to translate these into a creative form of expression. On occasions, though, they may have a nagging suspicion that they have overdramatized their original impressions, or have, in some way, not made honest sense of them. Their doubts can be communicated in a rather muddled way, which sometimes makes other people impatient with them. In these cases, Jupiter's intuitional abilities and Neptune's emotional sensitivities may be at odds if Mercury cannot translate freely between the two processes. These people do not always realize the full worth of their ability to communicate delicate sensitivities which others either do not see or ignore. At best this is a combination which favours creative work, combining a strong imagination and an inspirational approach to life, particularly because Mercury sextile Neptune is likely to be the strongest aspect in the combination. Where the planetary grouping is not working well, these people may need to ensure that they have not distorted their first perceptions and have organized their work into a coherent form.

MERCURY – SATURN

There are no myths extant of any direct relationship between Hermes and Cronos, the Greek Saturn. To Hermes, Cronos was the grandfather god who, long before his grandson's reception on Olympus, had been shut up in Tartaros by Zeus for eating his children as they were born. Only Zeus escaped this fate, and it was he who led the rescue of his siblings, forcing his father to vomit them up. What Cronos had been trying to do was to preserve his own reign; any interference with the structures he had built up, or the threat of usurpation by his children, would be met by force and containment, if not outright destruction. Many of the gods on Olympus were either children or grandchildren of Cronos and, though Cronos himself had been incarcerated, his characteristics of discipline and fear would have filtered down the generations, even if they had become hidden in the unconscious in the process.

Where these two planets act together in a chart, people are often logical thinkers with sound judgement and disciplined minds. They are able to focus their thinking on the task in hand and have the ability to screen out any intruding thoughts or behaviour when it is necessary to get through the work. The planets in combination can indicate an aptitude for thorough study and learning, and, where it is strong in the birthchart, people may be drawn to teaching, or other practical expression of the intellectual arts. Those people who appreciate highly structured learning with a practical application might find themselves developing abilities in the scientific or mathematical fields.

Whatever form the education process takes, these people want the extent of their learning recognized and are prepared to go to considerable trouble to plan careers which give them the recognition they feel they deserve. Saturn gives structure and form to the intellectual processes, something that is necessary if the mercurial function is to develop the ability to delve into the unconscious. Most often, though, people with aspects between these two planets feel more comfortable when they can see their intellectual life actualized through some contribution to worldly responsibility.

On the other hand, they can be worriers who are dismissive of unconventional ideas which they feel threaten their carefully ordered thought processes. Here, the saturnian principle of destruction, through fear of being usurped, overwhelms Mercury's flexibility. Saturn then becomes another dark god ruling from the underworld. So, as a protection, people whose charts contain Mercury and Saturn in aspect could be highly critical of others. They may overcompensate by becoming domineering, perhaps garrulous, and attempting to control the way in which people around them think. Sometimes they can appear to be closed-minded, much like Saturn shut up in Tartaros, lacking in imagination and placing too much emphasis on tried and tested ways of thought.

When they are in this mood, it is often difficult to get through to them because they have an ability to shut out what they do not want to hear. They may become taciturn and morose as a defence against rethinking any of their ideas. At root, there may be two reasons for this: they may have a fear of learning which stems from having their intellectual capacities cramped when they were young and so have not learned to express themselves spontaneously – the image of Saturn eating his own children springs to mind here; or they may have been so criticized as children that, as adults, they are highly self-critical of their own work, and fear and resent it when they feel other people are adding a second burden of unnecessary fault-finding.

Where, for example, Mercury conjuncts Saturn, which, in turn, squares Pluto, people may find themselves blocked from learning by collective forces which they feel are beyond their control. Two gods of the depths, one fearful and the other at home with the dark powers, may bring to bear a feeling of oppression where the weight of other people's intellects may seem too powerful. They may feel that they cannot express themselves adequately or as powerfully. At an unconscious level, they may fear being overwhelmed and destroyed by people who attempt to control the way they think. Perhaps, when young, they had difficulty settling into any intellectual work, or were, in some way, prevented from doing so, which set up a pattern of self-sabotaging their intellectual abilities. If the combination is working well, or if they have learned something about their own unconscious processes, these people may contribute to the collective by using their painstaking intellectual capacities to understand how power circulates between people and in society. They are, then, in more of a position to communicate the knowledge with great depths of compassion for others treading the same path.

MERCURY – URANUS

Those people who express this combination positively are likely to be intuitive thinkers who can use their mental processes flexibly. Though there is no connection in mythology between Hermes and Uranus, in astrological work Uranus is often known as the higher octave of Mercury. This is due to the incredible quickness of the uranian mind, which can seem to make a faster-than-thought connection in understanding. Uranus was, in Greek mythology, the original creator-god, himself created by earthy Gaia. He saw his children by Gaia as imperfect and attempted to shut them up in Tartaros, from where they were rescued by Cronos. He was the primordial father-god who set in train the history of divine fathers destroying their progeny, though, like his son Cronos, he did not succeed.

His destructive capacities were because he thought that his children were less than perfect. Father of Cronos, grandfather of Zeus and great-grandfather of Hermes, he has something of the Mercury-ruled Virgoan about him, needing the perfection of thought-forms to be manifest without error on the earthly plane. The struggle for Mercury and Uranus is to retain compassion for their imperfect creations, not to attempt control by destroying or denigrating their initial chances for an independent life.

Where the combination works well, Mercury/Uranus people have fast and energetic minds. They are able to solve problems by making the necessary mental connections in lightning-quick time. Their speedy mental reflexes are associated with clear forms of speech and expression. They often have original thoughts and can be excited by ideas which seem far ahead of their time. Uranus was the first god to father children; not all children need be earthly ones. At times, the concentration of people with aspects between the two planets is so great and so speedy that they almost seem like human computers. Intellectually honest and independent-minded, they may be found supporting free speech and liberal, if not radical, thought and forms of expression. They are usually direct in speech and can be counted on to speak up in defence of new ideas, whether written or verbal, though these are likely to be ideas which affect the collective rather than individuals. More comfortable with mass communication and innovative learning techniques, they are often seen by other people to be at the forefront of any new thinking.

When these traits are underdeveloped, they may be known for their eccentric opinions and extreme ideas, which they can express in a tactless manner. Being far too outspoken, they often have problems communicating with people at an acceptable level. This happens when there is an unconscious need to shock other people or to rebel against conventional thought – the uranian principle works against Mercury here. They may also have a barely concealed contempt for the more common ways of thought and expression and often have a need to stand out from the crowd by introducing shockingly new ideas. The tragedy is that this process separates them from people who operate at a much more mundane level, leaving them isolated and in pain – much as Uranus was after his separation from Gaia. An immature Mercury goes through a similar process, though, in this case, Mercury, according to mythology, is more prone to ignore his children than actively seek to destroy them.

As a result, people with this combination of planets active in their charts may become inconsistent thinkers who are unable to concentrate on developing their mental faculties or on expressing themselves in a consistent way. They might rely, instead, on making snap judgements which may or may not be right. This is uranian intuition run riot. Unable to connect ideas in a meaningful way, they may be seen as impractical and out of step with other people. Often having restless minds which jump around from one unconnected thought to another, they sometimes run out of mental energy and concentration, which makes it difficult for them to finish work in hand.

People with birthcharts which contain Mercury opposition Uranus, where Mercury trines the Ascendant, as an instance, are likely to come across to others as being forthright in speech to the point of rudeness. It is possibly one of their most obvious characteristics. They may have a conscious need to express themselves in an extreme way, stubbornly holding on to seemingly eccentric ideas, but unknowingly alienating the very people with whom they most need to communicate because they do not explain what they are doing in a clearly understandable way. This was very much what Uranus did when he fled into the heavens to escape from the imperfection of matter on earth, and is not too dissimilar from the way in which immature Hermes relates to women. Family traits have a habit of being passed down the generations, even among the gods. Mercury/Uranus people may develop a habit of becoming impatient, assuming that everybody should be able to make sense of what they are saying. Other people are unlikely to accept what they are trying to express because they dislike the abrupt and sometimes tyrannical manner in which it is being said. So this combination is likely to cause much frustration and nervous tension between people. Where this combination operates in the chart, people may need a more relaxed and slower way of explanation and a greater understanding that other people may not think as quickly as they do.

MERCURY – NEPTUNE

There are no tales told in mythology of Hermes' connection with Poseidon, so astrologers are left with the task of integrating the two principles they represent without any help from the source stories. However, in the *Mutus Liber*, an alchemical work from the seventeenth century, the alchemist, represented by Jacob, falls asleep at the bottom of a ladder ascending to heaven. He is sunk into the sea of dreams while sleeping on a rocky seashore. Even if Greek mythology cannot point us to the connection between Hermes and Poseidon, alchemy may.

The overwhelming neptunian nature of sleep and dreams and the imagination is available to the most mercurial of people. In reverie or dream, meanings may be revealed which are not apparent in waking life; we have seen previously the connections between sleep temples and the early healer gods. Mercury's connective function may help with the daytime, conscious interpretation of these neptunian images. Dream interpretation is strongly emphasized in Jungian circles and, in the ancient world, dream temples were known to be associated with Asklepios and played a large part in the healing arts. So Mercury and Neptune are connected, if indirectly.

When the Mercury/Neptune combination is strong in the chart it can indicate people with sensitive minds who unconsciously tune in to other people's thought processes. This facility can give such persons a considerable insight into others' ways of expression because of the ease with which they can step into another person's shoes. Mental and visual mimicry of this type is strong where the combination works well. People with it have a non-rational, impressionistic manner of thinking which is not obviously communicated to others, nor are others always aware when they have changed their minds and opinions. They often learn best through having their imaginations stimulated and may idealize any learning process which allows them to develop imaginative ideas. These are people who think in terms of images which take a collective as well as a personal form, and they are able to make good use of collective symbols. This impulse towards lyrical and imagistic expression may need to find some outlet in the creative arts. Poets, musicians, photographers and, sometimes, professional mimics can benefit from this combination.

The negative side of Mercury/Neptune often indicates people who are too impressionable and are unused to thinking for themselves. They can unthinkingly imitate other people, or be influenced by those who seem to be more mentally muscular than they are themselves. Where boundaries between themselves and others are not clear, they may be unfocused in their thinking, having confused thoughts and being unable to express themselves verbally or in a straightforward way. So they become secretive, or blank out and retreat into their inner worlds, where they feel safer and more in control of themselves.

They may also fear being swamped by the chaos of their own thought processes. The wool-gathering and daydreaming that are observable with this combination are often a defence against the harshness of the outer world, and other people often see them as more than a little vague and incompetent. Their oversensitivity can produce distorted or deluded thinking which is out of touch with reality, and they may feel that their minds are highly coloured by images which they seem to conjure out of nowhere – a very neptunian way of being. Inability to control the imagination leads, in some people, to deceptive behaviour or to lying, or they may be at the mercy of others who show these traits.

When Mercury sextiles Neptune which is itself in square to the Moon, for example, the combination indicates people who have the aptitude to connect their conscious thoughts with unconscious images, but may not do so because they act in an emotionally self-indulgent manner or are too emotionally confused to realize that they have any creative abilities. This most often happens when Neptune square Moon is the stronger aspect in the combination. These people may be drawn instead to others who are creative, or allow themselves to be invaded by others, unaware that they themselves have the potential to develop artistic and lyrical skills. These planets can produce people who can become addicted to other people's creativity; they may become artistic groupies. Often this is because they have not developed any autonomy of thought and expression and find themselves unable to act on their own judgements; again, this is a neptunian boundary issue and one which may have repercussions in the world of everyday reality. They need the world to think well of them because they do not enjoy suffering, and so they often shrink from taking on activities which leave them exposed to criticism. People with this combination need to develop their own creative skills and the faith in their own abilities, which will, in turn, allow them to judge the worth of other people's influences.

MERCURY – PLUTO

Often people with this combination active in their charts will have penetrating and analytical minds. They take nothing at face value and have the kind of resourceful will-power which takes them to the heart of any matter they have under scrutiny, much like Hermes' ability to penetrate into the plutonian underworld. There is an intensity about their mental processes which enables them to perceive motives, solve mysteries and be in touch with the darker undertow of human nature. Mercury helps to bring some of Pluto's hidden intensity and inexorability to the surface, much as happened in the myths where Hermes acts as the psychopomp between the worlds of the living and the dead.

Mercury/Pluto people are often able to plumb psychological depths which remain out of the reach of others. Infernal Hermes was the only Olympian god who was allowed to make the journey into Hades' realms. The combination deepens the mind and increases the powers of observation, leading other people to see them as possessors of an investigative or research-orientated turn of mind. They may be people whose speech is full of penetrating questions and insights. Sometimes they develop a sense of black humour, which indicates one way of coming to terms with, or warding off, the less easily acceptable sides of life.

When the combination is undeveloped and primitively applied, they might be ruthlessly judgemental and intolerant, perhaps forcing their opinions on others. They may be suspicious of other people's motives, often projecting their seething thoughts on to people around them and then defending themselves by using the kind of poisonous verbal expression which kills any real communication. Often unsatisfied with superficial levels of communication, their very intensity can prevent people from opening up and trusting them freely. An intellect closed to allowing some freedom of speech and action will have difficulty in opening up the way between the lands of the living and the dead. All stifles underground if it cannot germinate.

When Hades abducted his queen, Persephone, to the underworld by force, it was not a trusting start to a marriage. It was only after Zeus took into account both Demeter's and Persephone's needs to be active in the upper world for part of the year that Hermes could act. Given the necessity of doing so, he was able to guide Persephone on her way between the living and the dead, the conscious and the unconscious, in order to ensure that the upper world continued to flourish and exist. If he had not done so, Hades' deathly inexorability would have meant the eventual cessation of the upper world. Inevitably, it would have meant destruction for his realms, too. Unless the living world exists, it cannot supply souls to the underworld – Hades' functions would soon have been redundant.

Sometimes Mercury/Pluto people may become too uncommunicative, developing into secret holders of information which they find difficult to share with others, or else using it to attack when they are in one of their black moods. Still waters often run deep with them, as the four runers did in the Greek underworld, but, once let loose, the power and intensity with which they then express themselves can be fthghtening and destructive to experience. These people often need to explore the depths of their own motives and judgement and to come to some realization of the force with which they express themselves so that they can offset the worst effects of the combination. Here is where

Hermes can help to connect conscious and unconscious processes, alleviating some of the stresses which build up in the psyche, by bringing what is unknown and feared into the light of day. This is why he often accompanies Sun-heroes like Theseus and Herakles into and out of Hades. What is brought out into the open is often less feared.

How Mercury/Pluto works when combined with other planets sometimes makes this clearer. Where Mercury conjuncts Pluto, which itself trines Venus, the effect can be to understand the connective power of love and to bring that insight to all communication processes. If this does not happen, then even love can brew and seethe and grow stale underground. Venus in this combination may mitigate Pluto's need to control and repress all forms of communication between people, but if the conjunction is the stronger aspect, then there may be a love of relentless analysis and intellectual ruthlessness for their own sakes. Then the love of power contained in the Venus/Pluto aspect may be used by people with this combination to manipulate the conditions under which other people are allowed to express themselves, setting rigid limits on the contents of any discussion or communication. Difficult to argue against, because they seem so deeply logical and understanding, they can be as impenetrable as a brick wall when their own perceptions are challenged. The dark realms of Hades are not easily entered unless those wishing to do so have been given permission by the gods. People with these aspects in their natal charts may need to learn that others also need freedom to express themselves. Mercury/Pluto people might learn that this adds to their own understanding of human nature. Learning that other people's views of reality are as valid as their own is the task to be undertaken here.

MERCURY – ASCENDANT/DESCENDANT

Wherever Mercury aspects the Ascendant, it will also have an impact on the Descendant. The Ascendant/Descendant axis indicates our sense of our own identity and where this interacts with our relationships with other people. With this placement,

Mercury's need to show itself to the world through the Ascendant is bound up with the way in which communication is
established with other people; it is linked, also, to the kinds of
people it attracts to itself through the Descendant.

Where Mercury strongly aspects the axis and is used positively,
people often come across with the ability to express themselves
in a fluent manner, to be talkative and quick-moving, with
intelligent, quick and perceptive minds to match. They are likely
to think before they feel or act and to have a mentally flexible
approach to people, adopting different verbal and conversational
techniques to fit different situations.

Physically, they may have slim, lithe bodies and quick responses.
Their curiosity is concerned with learning about themselves and
others and they, anyway, come over as receivers and transmitters of
ideas who are always seeking harmonious communication between
people, sometimes at an individual level and occasionally in a more
public way. These are people with a facility for communication
skills which they need to demonstrate; writing, education and
verbal exchanges with others can be important to them. They often
have an understanding of the movement of ideas through society
and feel most comfortable when they know those ideas are flowing
smoothly and that other people have understood them. Where
they are not so consciously aware of these qualities in themselves,
they could find themselves looking for partners, or being attracted
to partners, who embody some of these characteristics.

Where Mercury's aspects to the Ascendant/Descendant axis do
not work so well, people sometimes find they have difficulties in
communication and self-expression. There are times when they
feel they do not express themselves as intelligently as they would
like to. At odds with their unconscious need to connect ideas
about themselves and their place in the world in a fluent manner,
they can be awkward in speech and movement, finding themselves frequently misunderstood, or themselves misunderstanding
other people's attempts to make contact.

In outward appearance their bodies can communicate much
nervous tension and seem fragile, perhaps unable to withstand
much energetic movement without feeling drained and tired.
Sometimes they feel drained by other people's more robust energy

levels and they can have difficulty with sustaining an adequate level of physical and emotional stamina. Shorter periods of work interspersed with times to relax and recuperate can often help here. They may not be particularly talkative, preferring to leave that to others, and this is often a sign of a tendency to be overadaptable and to lose themselves in other people. Easily hurt by other people's words and abrupt gestures, they withdraw from communication which, itself, can indicate a hidden envy of people who are more openly verbal and who communicate with others more easily.

Mercury in aspect to other planets as well as to the Ascendant/ Descendant axis may indicate a greater variation of responsiveness to Mercury's meaning. People who have Mercury trining the Ascendant, where the angle also quincunxes the Sun, project themselves, on some occasions, as fluent and intelligent speakers or teachers, able to establish with great vitality easily flowing lines of communication with others. They put great emphasis on the need to exchange ideas at an intellectual level. At times, though, where the quincunx with the Sun irritates and subtly subverts, these people can be scratchy and short with others, unable to communicate their real needs, or finding that their ideas are misinterpreted or misrepresented by others.

They may find that, the more tension builds up, the less they are able to discover about how communications broke down. At this point these people can become very volatile, preferring to escape from the current situation rather than stay in it to settle differences. They may be, in fact, the kinds of people who leave the room when an argument cannot be settled at a verbal level. An initial way of trying to work constructively with this characteristic is for these people to agree to come back to talk about the difficulty after a short break to determine what their real feelings are.

MERCURY – MID-HEAVEN/IMUM COELI

The MC/IC axis is concerned with finding our place in the world according to the foundations we have built deep inside us. Where Mercury strongly aspects the MC, people like to be seen as intellectual achievers, presenting a mask to the world which indicates that they have the resources to be effective in this area of work. This may or may not be genuine, depending on the extent to which the IC point, which is also being aspected by the planet, offers a firm basis for subsequent intellectual growth and development in the world.

When Mercury's aspects to this axis are used constructively, people are likely to want to show that they communicate effectively both in the world and privately, having considerable skills in linking ideas and lines of thought with the ways in which society's institutions operate. They need to manifest their intellectual skills publicly and privately, so it is no surprise that, while work and the need to achieve are often concerned with education, the media or literary pursuits, the home also reflects these interests. One or both parents may share these characteristics or may have valued the education process and passed on its values to their children. Work is often seen as a mental discipline and these people need private as well as public recognition that they are making a thoughtful contribution to worldly responsibilities. They may take work home, which, for them to feel at ease, often has to be a place for books, discussion, intellectual pursuits and much lively chatter about what is happening in the world. Work and home are never dull places for people with this aspect.

Where the aspect is underdeveloped, communication is likely to fail in two ways. First, people may give away their powers of communication to those they see as having more authority in the world. So parents or employers are often the authority figures seen to have special powers of communication and the home becomes a place where lively debate and the exchange of ideas do not take place on an equal footing. A strained silence can often be noticed in such surroundings. Conversely, there may be plenty of inconsequential talk with no real meaning or depth. Communication is kept at a superficial level as a defence against any exploration of relationships at home or at work. Polite conversation is sometimes a characteristic here.

Secondly, these people are often afraid of the power of their own intellects. As a result, they are likely to have a deeply buried resentment against those whose intelligence and mental adaptability are securely shown to the world. Any verbal or written communication breaks down and they are often afraid to put forward their views and opinions, secretly believing that all they will achieve is misunderstanding between themselves and people they see as authority figures, both at work and at home. One or both of the parents of these people may be uncommunicative or unable to explain themselves at a verbal level. Alternatively, people with the aspect may not have been given the chances of education which their intelligence deserves. The lack of confidence they feel so deeply often manifests as an unwillingness to attempt any task that involves mentally demanding effort, or where they might have to stand by any actions stemming from what they really think.

Where Mercury sextiles the MC and trines Saturn, for instance, people are likely to want to be regarded as practical thinkers who can put their carefully thought-out plans easily into positive action in the world and in work. Often hard thought takes place in the home, and these can be people who like to know that each thought and action is in its well-regulated place. They often aspire to be good planners and strategists and are happiest and most secure when they can see the concrete results of all their hard work. Where the easiness of the aspect is taken for granted, these people may set more store by their plans of action than by the people who carry them out. Care needs to be taken against assuming that co-workers and family members think and act exactly as they do.

MERCURY – NODES

When the nodal axis is aspected by Mercury, there is an expectation that the flow of ideas is strongly attuned to life's purposes. The North Node is the point at which we need to work and make efforts to fulfil our own potential for growth and awareness. The South Node more adequately describes where we can slip back too easily into old patterns and habits, where we feel most comfortable. Attention needs to be paid to the houses and signs which the Nodes occupy because these will help to round out the Nodes' meanings.

Where Mercury's aspects to this axis are working well, people are likely to use their intellectual faculties to become more aware of the direction in which they are moving; they may be more willing, too, to work at thinking through and forming their own personal path through life. These can be people who have the ability to bring their decisions into line with their understanding of the meaning of life. They may use their mental abilities to work out that falling back into past patterns does not lead to future development. Additionally, they may develop the awareness that, on occasions, they can rest their minds easily and consciously at the South Node point before making the next effort to fulfil the North Node potential of expanding on their intellectual, verbal and, perhaps, literary communication skills.

Where Mercury's aspects to the Nodes work negatively, or are at a more primitive stage of development, people are likely to make little effort to move from where they feel intellectually most comfortable. These can be people who in old age hold similar views to the ones they held in youth. They may unconsciously fear the work involved in taking on responsibility for their own life choices. They may also vacillate between the two positions without conscious awareness or thought of what is happening to their intellectual development, sometimes realizing their aims, but then thinking they have no further need to work in that particular direction. When this happens, they can feel unconsciously driven to work at the difficult North Node point again, like it or not. This occurrence sometimes gives a fated feel to the nodal axis, and the natural fear of change can lead these people to think that life events or circumstances are unfair and oppose their best, by which they mean their most comfortable, interests.

When other planets are included in the combination, then the feeling of 'fatedness' may be heightened. Where Mercury squares the Nodes, which are themselves in aspect to Jupiter, its manifestation will be different. People with this combination in their charts may seemingly have no difficulty communicating that their life purpose is strongly attuned to beliefs and philosophies; they have a need to expand their understanding of universal laws as well as their own intellectual horizons. They are most likely to overemphasize the uniqueness of their systems of beliefs and ideas, or be complacent about them. They risk alienating others because of the unrealistic scope of their visions of life, or expect others to follow their lead as the only true and right way to fulfilment.

Occasionally, people with this combination have difficulty in consciously choosing the right belief system to enhance their growth. There is a tendency to flit from one to the other and finish by being disappointed and rejecting all. They may also be fearful of their own communication skills, but secretly believe that their own life paths are superior to all others. This can lead them to deny the validity of other people's experiences of their purposes in life. Inflation of all kinds needs to be attended to when this combination operates and care needs to be given to communicate realistic and attainable details of their sometimes grand designs.

9
Mercury in the Houses and Signs

While aspects are concerned with the combination of core energies and the urge for expression of them, they also need channels through which to work, both inwardly and in the world. The twelve houses represent the totality of experience in a life, and a planet occupying a particular house shows where we are likely to learn most about its meaning in our lives. The signs have a different emphasis. Each zodiacal sign gives an indication of the manner in which the occupying planet is expressed, allowing the planet to present itself in a certain way, almost as if it were wearing a certain style of clothing. So, while signs show us the way in which a planet operates, houses are the particular sphere of life in which they function. Mercury operates even at this level, differentiating, recombining and synthesizing the essential meanings of the aspects, houses and signs.

FIRST HOUSE AND ARIES

Mercury in the first house displays a need for self-expression through a questioning and inquiring attitude to life. People with this combination gain a sense of identity by knowing how their own minds work. Sometimes they want it recognized that the intellectual way in which they perceive the world has some validity. They are curious, occasionally impulsively talkative, and can express themselves fluently using logic and reasoning to good effect. If aspects to Mercury support it, there can be an interest in languages. Thinking about the world and their part in it is of great importance to them and they are likely to spend much of their time engaged in mind-orientated activities, needing to gather knowledge and communicate it to the world around them, particularly where Mercury conjuncts the Ascendant.

The sign on the Ascendant will colour the way the planet's functions are displayed. Mercury with Capricorn rising, for instance, may express itself through a steady, careful mind and cautious speech, while Mercury here with Sagittarius rising might mean an identity realized through impulsive thinking on a grand scale. Occasionally, tactless speech is an issue for these people. Close aspects to another planet will also influence the way a first house Mercury operates. Conjunct Neptune, it is likely to show itself as a dreamy, elusive quality of mind with some capacity to distort the thought processes and, perhaps, the truth. As another example, Mercury sextile Mars gives a decisive intellect with the ability to draw up clear plans of action and see them through to a productive conclusion.

There is a myth concerning Hermes which has some bearing on the Mercury-in-first-house need to actualize ideas. When the rather belligerent Herakles was on a visit to Troezen, he stopped at the wayside because he was tired. As he sat to rest, he leaned his club against a statue of Hermes which had been erected by the side of a road. The club took root, put out leaves and grew into a tree. Herakles, it seems, needs to produce, rather than destroy, on this occasion. Even a weapon of war can be made productive if a Mars-inclined person stops for a while to take stock and allows a fertile flow of ideas to develop beyond the present moment – a characteristic not often associated with Herakles. The tale is an indication that the Mercury principle and the Mars principle can combine successfully.

Alternatively, people with this placement, especially if the planet is near the Ascendant and/or in hard aspect to other planets, need to ensure against overemphasizing an intellectual approach to life. On first acquaintance, other people may see them as lacking at some deep level the qualities of warmth and intuitive empathy needed to balance the inquiring mind – nobody in their right minds would have called Herakles deeply empathic, usually. But, through their life experiences, Mercury-in-first-house people may come to an intelligent understanding of how to work on the impulse to act first and think later, though the energy for communication will always be high.

Mercury in Aries can lead to incisive and assertive ways of

thinking and action, but people with this placement may be aggressive on occasions and too impulsive in speech and behaviour. This may happen if they meet up with obstacles and opposition to their ideas. When it happens, they can sometimes be seen as headstrong and too personally attached to the importance of their own ways of thinking, and, like Herakles, too forceful and competitive in the way they impose their views on others.

In the world of ideas, they are people who are likely to have plenty of enthusiasm and creative energy, but could show greater awareness of the importance of finishing tasks they initiate. Impatient of others who think in less decisive ways or who are more fixed in their ideas, they might consider, on reflection, that sometimes their initial thoughts could benefit from holding back on immediate action, as Herakles did when he stopped by the roadside. Cooperation and patience are two qualities which people with Mercury in Aries might attempt to develop.

SECOND HOUSE AND TAURUS

In the second house Mercury indicates a mind concerned with securing personal resources which may be both material and psychological. The possession of clear values and a personal sense of worth are important to people with this placement. At heart, they often feel the need for the security which comes with an intelligent recognition of a sense of values and self-esteem, though they might not always be aware of it. Often the trait takes the form of a pride of ownership. Attachment to physical objects, people or inner desires and ways of thinking is characteristic. So people with this placement may need to learn very consciously how to appreciate their worth without being either possessive or smothering to excess. They are capable of reaching a realization of the worth of their inner system of values and the way in which they use these in their dealings with others. At the same time, it is possible for them to combine this inner awareness with a desire for material and intellectual security and resources. Coming to a satisfying appreciation of their possessions without feeling that they themselves are owned by them, or by their own attitudes of mind, may help them considerably.

Choice-making between things of value might be a function which would benefit people with Mercury in the second house. Where there is little discrimination between values, it is often because people are afraid to let go of what they once possessed, even when it becomes redundant. Fear of the consequences of making the wrong choice is a factor involved here. But, sometimes in life, this cannot be avoided, and people with a second house Mercury may find it a painful process. Hermes was party to this dilemma when he gave the golden apple to Paris, asking him to judge who was the most beautiful goddess, Hera, Aphrodite or Athene. Paris attempted to wriggle out of making the choice, but Hermes, on orders from Zeus, would not let him. Possession and repossession was a constant theme in the Trojan War, whether it was of Helen herself, or the city of Troy. Holding on to redundant values for too long can mean that the psyche rigidifies and can develop no further; so keeping a constant eye on the meaning of values may be one of the tasks facing people with Mercury in the first house.

Aphrodite was skilled in drawing her many lovers to her, Hermes among them. So, too, people with Mercury placed in the second house may be skilled, or not, in drawing to themselves the resources they need, depending on the strength and type of the aspects made with other planets in the chart and how aware they are of the qualities of the placement. Mercury here square Jupiter, for example, may cause other people to see them as boastful because they may have an excessive belief in the importance of their own ideas, however well-intentioned they feel they are towards others. Mercury conjunct Venus people may draw towards them the kinds of people who could help develop their artistic and literary talents. The sign on the second house cusp and the planet ruling it will affect Mercury's placement, too. People with Virgo here might develop practical and analytical qualities of mind which could enhance their confidence and self-worth. By contrast, Pluto ruling the second house can indicate those people who have an intense drive to surround themselves with people and possessions which reflect their literary or business pursuits.

Where Mercury is in Taurus, there may be much common sense and many practical ways of thinking. People's minds are likely to be fixed on a materially secure and worry-free environment and they can be stubborn and inflexible in achieving this goal. Aphrodite herself always knew what she wanted, and frequently got it. When this tendency is carried to extremes, others may see these people as grasping and narrowly focused, unable easily to let go of ideas they have taken so long to formulate. We know that throughout the exchange between Hermes and Apollo and Zeus over the stolen cattle, Hermes never let go of the fundamental idea that he wanted divine status on Olympus. Bargaining about the ownership of Apollo's cattle is a significant symbol for Mercury in Taurus people.

They often have an appreciation of well-structured and harmonious patterns of thinking and the placement can indicate an ability in written and verbal forms of expression. Once their minds are made up, their powers of concentration are great, but they may need to be aware of a tendency towards intellectual obstinacy and fixed patterns of mental expression. Flexibility of thought and a continuing curiosity about the world may help to offset these inclinations, as it did Hermes when he made concessions to Apollo and bartered some of his own possessions after the theft. He was able to let go of some of what he most valued in order to have the one thing he really desired — divinity and recognition from his father.

THIRD HOUSE AND GEMINI

When Mercury is in the third house, people are likely to spend much of their time involved with learning experiences of various kinds. These will not necessarily be the kinds of learning which come with a more mature consideration, but can occur where it is necessary to make an initial and energetic push at the beginning of a learning process. People with the placement may be actively involved with their environment and immediate families, particularly with siblings who stimulate their ever-questing minds.

We saw this with Hermes. His first act which involved other

people, on the day he was born, was to steal his half-brother's cattle; his next act was to try to avoid Apollo's anger. Whatever the results, Hermes was a good, if devious, initiator at this stage. The act also set up some interaction, even if it was of a negative kind, with his older sibling. It only later proved to be a beneficial one after Hermes had been introduced to the healing arts which Apollo and Asklepios favoured. So these short-term excursions which Hermes made earlier in life laid some of the groundwork for his later development. To an extent, mistakes and deviousness are part of the early learning process; it is only where they persist as a life-long pattern which takes no account of other people's needs that there are problems.

So people with this placement tend to engage easily with short-term activities and journeys. They are at home with initiating communications and new learning situations. They are often seen as rational and curious, but restless and easily bored, unless other chart factors mitigate the effects of Mercury here. Again, Hermes' myths help. We see from the tales how versatile and inventive he was; alphabets, musical instruments, cattle-rustling, playing the merchant or the thief were all grist to his mill. He seemed to have few fears about initiating any activity which involved his mind rather than his feelings. The danger is that some third house Mercury people may occasionally feel themselves to be eternal students and forever on the move mentally; at times, it can pall.

The cusp sign of Mercury in the third house may show, for example, something of the way people with this placement initially approach their surroundings and the beginnings of relationships with others. Mercury in Pisces people have minds which can easily pick up on the moods and attitudes of the people around them; those with Mercury in Leo may have much self-confidence in their own mental abilities and be strong-willed enough to express these well. Planetary aspects, too, might help to develop or prevent certain characteristics of mind when this placement is prominent. Moon square Mercury can give a whimsical mind to a person who incessantly chatters about trivialities and superficial emotions; Mercury sextile Uranus can indicate someone who is a quick and independent thinker whose new ideas suddenly come to them, seemingly out of nowhere.

People with this placement are able to assimilate concepts and ideas with ease, but may find difficulty with concentration and so need to guard against scattering their mental energies. Hermes' many talents can operate against him if he is not careful. So people with Mercury here may benefit from making sure of strong and viable connections between their many activities and areas of interest by choosing carefully the priorities they wish to develop further. Deepening their interests and staying with the process is helpful to the mercurially minded as they move on their way to self-knowledge; hopping from one area of activity to another without making connections between them may prove frustrating in the end. Even Mercury submits himself to the alchemical transformation when he can take his old skills no further.

Mercury rules Gemini, and people with the planet placed in this sign can be good communicators, eloquent and with quick, versatile minds. They may place much value on the power of logic and be unaware that emotions and intuition also constitute part of mental expression. We have seen this reflected in the many myths of Hermes' treatment of women. Logic and great curiosity may lead them to an awareness of many facts, but they don't necessarily help to discern the truth, be decisive or become aware of other people's emotional needs. Some people with this placement may become confused because their minds are overstimulated by too many options. Attempts to keep all the balls in the air is as much an issue of control as of fear.

Living with much nervous tension can cause them to be irritable and intense, and to tire easily. Their need for original intellectual expression in many areas of involvement may indicate much superficial knowledge, but with little depth of understanding. They may benefit from a commitment to developing their understanding of the interconnectedness of human nature and quietening their minds by focusing on fewer, carefully selected areas of interest and activity.

FOURTH HOUSE AND CANCER

A fourth house Mercury indicates people whose mental activities may include an awareness of their roots and the foundations on which they build their lives. In many cases, this is reflected in perhaps unconscious, predisposed emotions and attitudes to the home and family. At a day old, Hermes was very aware that he and his mother were living in a cave on Mount Kyllene, far from Hera's wrath on Olympus, but also isolated from the other Olympians. For people with this placement, sometimes what is deeply buried within needs to be brought to the surface, but it may take them many years to do so, especially where Maia is more active than Hermes in the placement. Though Maia herself expressed no desire to go to Olympus, it was among Hermes' first thoughts. But if Mercury makes his presence felt early, then people with this placement could experience changeable home conditions while they are children. They may also project many of their intellectual faculties on to their fathers or the less dominant parent. Often there is a desire to make the home a safe hive of intellectual activity or a place of work. These tendencies are likely to be enhanced where Mercury is in strong aspect to, or conjuncts, the IC, but, equally, as life progresses, there may be an increasing urge to uncover what is essential to the self, risking some of the safety that the environment provides.

Most of us like at least one place where we can feel safe, but a fourth house Mercury needs intellectual stimulation there, too. If it isn't provided, then the person with Mercury here may decide to look elsewhere, as Hermes did when he left Mount Kyllene to reside with his father on Olympus – when he wasn't travelling, that is. There is more than a suggestion in the myths that Hermes, unconsciously, took the action he did over Apollo's cattle in order to obtain some of the variety and wider experience of life he needed, having to move away from home in order to do so. Mercury in the fourth house can sometimes feel closed in, even if home is a safe environment.

Cusp signs will affect the strength of such feelings. Mercury with Gemini here may increase the intellectual restlessness to be found in the home, but it can also give the curiosity necessary to discover if the father, for instance, is really as critical as the person seemed to experience. On the other hand, Mercury with Aries on the cusp of the fourth could give an overforceful and impatient expression in any matters which might lead to uncovering the origins of behaviour.

Aspects, too, particularly where the IC is also involved, will influence this placement. For example, Mercury on the IC opposition Saturn can indicate people who, through fear of moving out of the home environment, may seek to control their families in a rather narrow-minded and suspicious way. They may, perhaps, be given to nagging, or might experience these qualities displayed by the less dominant parent. Mercury in the fourth house trine Pluto, by contrast, may give the ability to research deeply into the affairs of the fourth house with seemingly limitless concentration. People with this aspect may be capable of thinking at a very deep level about the conditioning they received from the home and to reflect this in homes which they themselves set up. Once they are aware of it, they often discover that delving into their roots and origins can help to shed light on how they perceive their own families and their own intellectual needs.

Much emotional intensity is given to the thoughts when Mercury is placed in Cancer. People with the placement have highly sensitive minds and are likely to be protective and defensive of the way in which they think, rarely showing how they arrive at the conclusions they reach. While they have the ability to register information at an emotional level, they can also use this characteristic to withdraw into hurt and moody silence if they have been wounded by words. This happens because their thought patterns are influenced at an unconscious level by the impressions and people they become attached to; they can become cranky and stubborn if these are unharmonious or unsettled in any way.

Often others see them as difficult to know and hard to understand, liable to bias and prejudice if upset. Bias towards her son was evident in Maia's protection of Hermes in the face of

Apollo's anger – even though she knew that her son was concealing the truth. To help themselves balance such tendencies, people with Mercury in Cancer may benefit from cultivating some objectivity and detachment concerning their deeply emotional thinking patterns. If this does not happen, then they may, at an early stage in life, develop ways of defending their real thoughts from the people closest to them, much as Hermes did when he deceived his mother by hiding under the bedclothes, pretending to be asleep, after stealing the cattle.

FIFTH HOUSE AND LEO

In the fifth house, Mercury can lead to the development of a mind interested in open, perhaps dramatic and creative forms of expression, particularly where there is a capacity for literary pursuits or activities of skill and strategy. There is often an interest in children or in the abilities of the young for people with this placement. Recreational activities are also seen as creative, and so is the possibility of romance. These people may be fast and precise thinkers in any artistic, literary or recreational endeavours they undertake. The apollonian qualities of a bright vitality are added to the intellectual abilities of Mercury when the two gods meet in myth. The exchange between them is, by turn, angry, witty, conciliatory, creative and interesting.

Aspects to Mercury in this house may influence the ability to think flexibly and creatively. The Sun conjunct Mercury here may lead these people to identify strongly with any abilities they may have, perhaps to the extent of being blind to the effect their forceful minds might have on others. Mercury trine the South Node might incline people to rely too heavily on their own intellectual faculties when entering a new romance, so, perhaps, missing both people's emotional needs. The sextile the planet makes to the North Node may, however, help to balance this tendency with some purposeful activity and interest in the direction the relationship takes. Signs on the cusp of the fifth, too, can also affect the way Mercury works here. Mercury with Taurus may slow down the mind's ability to make creative connections quickly, but could enhance the capacity to produce something worthwhile in tangible form. Mercury with Aquarius would indicate an intuitive, original mind which might need to direct its creativity towards some humanitarian goal.

People with this placement are most often driven to produce at the creative level, as Hermes was when he made the lyre from a tortoise's shell. The difficulty is that people who are as inventive may find that they are engaging in separate activities which seem to have little connection between them; perhaps there is also an overemphasis in one area to the detriment of others. The interconnectedness of fifth house activities is important for these people because it enhances their mental perceptions. They easily identify with a need for continual and enthusiastic creation and recognition.

The myth of Amphion shows something of the fifth house attributes of creativity. He had connections with both Hermes and Apollo. Hermes had given him a lyre because he was devoted to the god's worship, but Amphion was often teased for playing it by Zethus, his brother, because it distracted him from work. But after the brothers had captured Thebes and dethroned the king, Amphion built the lower city by playing his lyre. The power of the sound shifted the stones into place, one on top of the other, so that the city was built in record time. Faith in the gift bestowed by the god meant that Amphion was in a good position to profit from his creativity, provided that the gods were continually honoured.

Those people who have Mercury placed in the sign of Leo are likely to have a strong-willed and authoritative form of mental expression. Like Apollo, they may be frank and outspoken, assertive when solving problems, wanting others to think well of their efforts. Sometimes they overstep limits when displaying this trait, becoming obstinate and impatient, and are then seen as arrogant and overly dramatic in speech and action. Usually self-confident and intuitively aware of the generosity of their thoughts, these people can sometimes overlook the need for detailed planning, content to concentrate on broad, general issues. They can become self-involved with their own mental processes and excessively proud of their achievements in the world of ideas. Humility and tact are two qualities which would help to balance some of the negative traits of this placement.

We see something of this, yet again, in Hermes' relationship with the leonine hero of Greek mythology, Herakles. He was renowned for putting himself through adventures which required all the personal resources he could muster. Sometimes, though, his foresight failed him. When he descended into Tartaros to capture the dog, Cerberos, his nerves were shattered by the ghosts of Meleager and Medusa; he aimed an arrow at Meleager and drew his sword on Medusa. It was Hermes who had to reassure him that they were only ghosts. Heroes find it very difficult to deal with the world of shadows with anything but their usual blunt self-confidence. In the lands of the dead, Hermes' rationality usefully came to Herakles' aid; the laws there are different from the ones above ground and neither Meleager nor Medusa could die a second time. It meant that Herakles had to accept the underworld reality of their ghosts and had to find other ways past the terrors of the dark places. He fairly quickly let Hermes take the lead for the next part of the journey, learning, it seems, some humility in the process.

SIXTH HOUSE AND VIRGO

Those people with Mercury in the sixth house may be concerned with the refinement and perfection of routine skills. They may be very aware of the relationship between mind and body, particularly in the areas of day-to-day work and the people they then come into contact with. They are often observant and thoughtful about the details of routine work and how it may best be put into practice, conscious of the need to reduce tensions in daily life and work routines. One way for people with this placement to ensure a healthy interaction between mind and body is to pay some attention to diet and fitness regimes.

There is a deeper meaning to this placement. Often the care and concern with bodily functions reflect the mature mercurial nature of connecting all of existence through an understanding of the spiritual, psychological and physical needs of human nature. Alchemical Hermes is often at work in Virgo. Work at the level of the physical body and immediate environment helps to prepare a vessel through which the psychological and spiritual functions can best operate. What is above then stands a better chance of integrating with what is below, so the sixth house principle of the concern with everyday needs is an important step in preparation for later alchemical transformation.

We see this step being taken in any preparation for a religious rite. The meeting-place is prepared, the ritual objects and vessels are set out, ablutions may be performed and priestly garments put on. The rite is set so that the minds and hearts of those taking part are purified and are at one with the rituals that are next undergone. These are the ones which, it is hoped, will effect some spiritual transformation. There is analogy here with healing rituals; the preparations for an operation have a similar significance, but at the material level. Mercury, at least in the sixth house, can be as at home with the practical as he is with the spiritual, provided that there is a continual awareness of the meanings which lie behind the practical.

But aspects with other planets will give more indications of how Mercury operates here and sometimes these may be at odds with the underlying Virgoan meaning of preparation and puri-fication. Mercury here square Mars can give an irritable and tactless way of behaving with other people, perhaps co-workers, as well as a capacity for jumping to conclusions. This is not the best way to carry out routine work or make necessary adjustments to work-mates' needs. Conversely, Mercury sextile Jupiter may give honesty and integrity in interactions at work; it generally indicates much goodwill and emotional empathy with people. Signs on the cusp may broaden the scope of Mercury placed in the sixth. Mercury with Cancer on the cusp of the sixth house may indicate people who are aware of how intensely emotional their mental processes are when involved with everyday work; Mercury with Libra may objectively note that they are always trying to achieve a balance between their work and health needs.

People with this placement may develop their capabilities in a way which gives them satisfaction in daily life. Observance of the minutiae of routine work, their connections with colleagues and how their bodies and minds respond to the stresses and tensions they encounter during the working day, will help them consciously plan a way of life. Some relaxation is necessary before they feel they can best serve others. They have a need to remain fit and emotionally at ease with their own work. This way they can best purify themselves before they offer themselves for service.

Mercury rules Virgo and a placement of the planet in this sign indicates a form of mental operation which is practical, precise and analytical. These people have meticulous minds, paying great attention to ordering their thinking, speech and writing, logically and efficiently, much as Thoth is required to do when recording the actions of the dead in the Halls of Judgement. Requiring purity in all forms of intelligence and mental expression, they may become carping and critical towards others if their standards are not met, and we know that Thoth in his early form could be a destructive god if his standards were not attained. The placement may ensure good practices of discrimination and there is often a feeling of satisfaction about the control of thought processes. Where people feel that they are not in control, they may become overly worried and fretful. Though they can express themselves eloquently and clearly, too many anxieties can impede their work. To offset the stress caused by a sometimes exacting mind, relaxation and less nervous attention to detail are a requirement and a necessity for these people, otherwise the essential meaning of the routines may be lost.

SEVENTH HOUSE AND LIBRA

When Mercury is in the seventh house it can indicate how a person develops an awareness of others, much as Hermes began to do in his relationship with Aphrodite. With this placement, a person may need intellectual stimulation in marriage or close partnerships. Much depends on the aspects to Mercury and whether it conjuncts the Descendant. Time may be spent in analysing or discussing the relationship and these people may be unconsciously restless and critical in marriage themselves, or they choose partners who openly display these characteristics. They may display great understanding of other people's intellectual needs, or feel bored and frustrated if these are not forthcoming.

This was certainly Hermes' way with women on his travels

through Greek mythology. One of the bachelor gods of the pantheon, his adventures with women, even with Aphrodite, were short-lived. The sedate, house-husband role was not for Zeus' messenger. It meant that he missed out on the opportunities to form long-lasting relationships and to watch them change over time. Though this is sometimes a painful process, it is not always so, but immature Hermes has none of the judicious staying power of Libra, which knows that perseverance supplies the conditions for the proper assessment of a process. Hermes was often too eager to be on his way.

The sign on the house cusp of the seventh will affect the operation of Mercury. With Pisces on the cusp, the planet may allow people the capacity to talk through emotional difficulties with a partner, though not without some vacillation between conflicting emotions. Mercury with Gemini here can lead to underestimating emotional needs. These people may delude themselves by thinking that all difficulties can be worked out rationally, or they may pick partners who show these traits.

Aspects of Mercury to any seventh house planets will also affect the quality of the relationship. For instance, people with Mercury conjunct Pluto in the seventh may choose partners who have penetrating and incisive minds or, having the same kinds of minds themselves, may see their partners as they truly are, perhaps uncomfortably so. Sometimes people with this double placement in the seventh may marry first the partner who displays mercurial qualities, find the partner unacceptable, and then choose another who has a strong plutonian image. A soft aspect may change the way in which Mercury works. Those with Mercury trine Jupiter may choose a partner, perhaps a foreigner, who is broad-minded and tolerant, or be so themselves. Whatever the aspect, there would still be a need for communication and intellectual stimulation in partnerships.

Over time, people with this placement may discover an urge to become more conscious of the manner in which they co-operate or collude with significant partners, bearing in mind that the underlying meaning is a desire to achieve balance between their own needs and those of their partners. They have the ability to develop an understanding of the nature of their projections and the qualities for which they choose partners. This could help them to appreciate the emotional content of partnerships, developing the detachment and the intimacy necessary to maintain a long-standing involvement. It is where the spirit of Mercury may be profitably active in the alchemical *coniunctio*. Only at this stage of the work on the psyche can the sacred marriage take place, a complete relationship between two opposing principles which allows for future progeny. In the seventh house, Mercury may help with the conscious recognition of both partners' needs, emotional and intellectual.

Mercury in Libra denotes a mental orientation which seeks intellectual harmony and balance with others. This placement can lead to much curiosity about the workings of the human mind and relationships; people with Mercury in Libra often show a great interest in what others think. They can be too concerned about seeing the relevance of all arguments and issues; this characteristic may lead to an inability to be decisive, particularly in crises. They may be good communicators with a wish to appear upright and just in all forms of mental expression. Sometimes, though, their wish to please others, their concern with what others think of them, can lead to prevarication in speech and thought, if not outright dishonesty. Occasionally defensive of their carefully thought-out honesty, they can be unbending if they think their principles are being challenged, though they often have trouble making up their minds about relationships. The tendency is reminiscent of Persephone's part in the judgement processes of the underworld, and of her initial reactions to Hades. People with this placement may need to cultivate the ability to act humanely and mercifully when circumstances require it.

EIGHTH HOUSE AND SCORPIO

Where Mercury is in the eighth house, the house of long-term relationships, there may be a tendency to collude with or submit to partners at an intellectual level. The eighth house issues of death, sex and the inheritance of resources can cause people with this placement to be acutely aware of unconscious interchanges between people. Often they look for the moments of change and transformation in relationships which they can use to best advantage. These people may be penetratingly aware of the nature and motives behind sexuality and hidden agendas; in dealing with these issues, they may need to keep in bounds tendencies to be tricky, controlling and secretive.

It was a sexual issue that led to the eventual downfall of Pelops and his house. Pelops love Hippodameia, the daughter of Oenomaus, king of Pisa, but her father wouldn't let her marry, because with the marriage of the daughter went the kingship. Pelops and Hippodameia bribed Myrtilus, the king's charioteer and Hermes' son, to help kill the old king. After Myrtilus had done so, he was killed by Pelops. His dying curse was that Pelops and his house were doomed. Though Pelops then built a temple to Hermes to propitiate the god's wrath and was purified of the murder by Hephaistos, Myrtilus' curse came to pass. Pelops was the ancestor of Helen, and through her actions his descendants perished at Troy or soon after.

Mercury's dealings in the eighth house sometimes have far-reaching consequences. No matter how tricky and controlling Pelops was in arranging Oenomaus' and Myrtilus' deaths in order to secure the throne of Pisa and a wife, he was unable to control the fates of the kin who came after him. We see something of the interrelationship of Mercury and Pluto in Pelops' tale; more so, since the eighth house is governed by Pluto in the natural zodiac and the story concerns a mortal. Exacting retribution by killing is a divine function, not a mortal one, and Pelops had usurped both Hades' and Hermes' functions by killing Myrtilus by trickery.

Canniness and an intense drive will work in tandem with the sign on the eighth house cusp when Mercury is placed here. Mercury with Sagittarius on the cusp may actively seek out lasting resources and arrangements which will give them the intellectual freedom to pursue their visions; others might regard them as self-seeking and uncaring. Mercury with Taurus could ensure that complicated legacies are dealt with practically and with great determination of mind, perhaps unaware how much other people might be upset by such a seemingly cold approach to death or periods of great transformation.

Aspects with other planets will also influence how these people deal with eighth house issues. For example, Mercury here square Uranus can cause these people to be impatient and impractical and be unwilling to put in the groundwork necessary to develop lasting resources. There may be a tendency to escape from dealing with the realities of death and separation; there may be, also, great fears of being tied to long-standing partnerships of any kind. Mercury conjunct the Moon in the eighth may indicate someone who is perceptive and aware of the emotional responses of other people, particularly within the family, when dealing with joint resources. Dexterity and flexibility in handling financial issues which have long-term consequences are indicated for this placement.

People with the placement might need to develop an awareness of a tendency to control others intellectually by coming to a better understanding of the nature of the darker, plutonic forces underlying their behaviour. A rational examination of destructive issues in long-standing relationships may counterbalance the tendency to lash out verbally when thwarted by partners. These people need greater consciousness of the benefits of self-mastery to release them from the stifling effects of repressed emotional energy.

The placement of Mercury in Scorpio can give incisive thinking and a penetrating mind capable of deep insights into the motives which underlie human behaviour. Often mistrustful of their own and others' feelings, people with this combination can, if aroused or hurt, inflict severe wounds on others with their sharp and sarcastic tongues. Much of their thinking is conducted in secret, and, like Hades, they have the mental resourcefulness to lay careful plans before they act. They perhaps need to be aware of a tendency to scheme and plot destructively when their ideas and thoughts, to which they are emotionally and often subjectively attached, are challenged. Often acutely perceptive and thoughtful in a silent way of others' unexpressed needs, these people can be profoundly charitable as long as they are not emotionally threatened themselves. Gentleness and consideration are two characteristics they may need to acquire to offset the negative inclinations of the placement.

NINTH HOUSE AND SAGITTARIUS

When Mercury is placed in the ninth house it can indicate an intelligent use of a broad jupiterian mind which seeks to make connections between philosophical, religious and moral issues. Discovering the meaning of the underlying laws of life is important to these people. This placement can give great depth to study and higher education and can give an indication of the principles to be met as a result of widening mental perspectives or taking long journeys. People with this placement may have some intuition about needing to submit their egos to a broader form of wisdom which has the effect of being a divine law, often inspired by a jupiterian recognition of order and regulation. At a concrete level, the study of the laws governing wider social structures can be of some appeal, but these people may need to become aware of the tendency always to take the long perspective and to ignore issues closer to hand. At another level, Mercury aids the capacity to understand, in some cases transmute, the laws of conventional life when he is placed in his father's house.

In myth, the effect is miraculous on occasions. The birth of Orion indicates one such translation. Hermes and Zeus visited Hyrieus, a farmer and beekeeper who lived in poverty. He entertained the gods to the best of his ability and was then asked what he most wanted. He said he would like a son, but it was impossible because his wife had died. The gods told him to sacrifice a bull, soak its hide in his own urine and bury it in his wife's grave. He did so, and in due time Orion was born.

Unfortunately, when he grew, Orion had a tendency to seduce goddesses – not an unusual tendency where Zeus and Hermes were involved in conception and birth. He had slept with Eos, the goddess of the dawn, and Apollo, fearing for his sister, Artemis, had her shoot him unknowingly. There was no rescue. Orion died and was placed in the constellation of the hunter. Where the ninth house impulse is too strong, and where Mercury here might rise too high and risk offending the gods, then there is, inevitably, a fall. It seems as though Orion had not the humility to propitiate his gods, but in his pride had usurped their privileges. It was not an act the gods forgave.

The sign on the house cusp may rule the way in which wider perspectives are reached. Mercury with Virgo here may indicate the powers of a discriminating mind which can meaningfully distinguish between important and less important philosophical issues; the fall would be into criticism and denigration of others if the wider perspective were lost. Mercury with Aquarius in this position may concentrate on developing a mind detached enough to examine new and unconventional ideas which may benefit humanity; too much Aquarian detachment could lead to the tyranny of ideas over emotions – a further example of the fall.

Aspects to other planets may also influence the way Mercury operates in the ninth. Mercury here opposite Jupiter may cause a person to pursue grand ideas but be unable to make connections between them or to determine their practicality, much as Ixion did in his failed attempt to seduce Hera. Mercury sextile Neptune indicates that an imaginative form of written work may be the outcome of any studies undertaken in the field of higher education, or, perhaps, religious knowledge; the fear might come from being swamped by too much information.

The acquisition of greater knowledge is important to people with a ninth house Mercury placement, but they may need to guard against developing dogmatic intellectual attitudes or an over-insistence on their need to be the best-qualified interpreters of moral law. There may be an intuitive approach to systems of belief and a tendency to ignore any facts that are not consistent with strongly held opinions. These people may have a visionary and prophetic quality of mind and this can be enhanced by ensuring that their views are based on strong ethical foundations, or, like Orion, they may fall.

Mercury in Sagittarius can indicate a mind which engages in an eternal quest for universal knowledge and general moral truths underpinning social formations. People with this placement can sometimes be accused of hypocrisy and cant when their acceptance of more popular and socially agreed philosophical insights and norms leads them to forget about the need for some moral guidelines in personal interactions and relationships. Zeus himself was not above making mistakes, or playing the hypocrite in his constant unfaithfulness to Hera, sometimes with Hermes' aid, as we have seen in the myth of Argos. The far-sighted and intuitive minds of Mercury in Sagittarius people are often found resenting the restrictions imposed by a need to examine what is directly in front of them. Any limitation to their freedom of thought could lead these people to be harsh and direct in speech and action, while, at the same time, they want to be recognized as intellectual leaders and to achieve some moral or philosophical authority. More at home with abstract concepts and ideas, people with this placement could cultivate a rigorous honesty with themselves and pay greater attention to concrete reality and the more mundane details of their lives.

TENTH HOUSE AND CAPRICORN

When Mercury is in the tenth house it may cause people to try to actualize their beliefs through a contribution to worldly responsibility. Those people with this placement may then choose a profession which exercises their intellectual faculties and brings them recognition. If Mercury is conjunct the MC then these people may well use their mental capacities to project on to the world an idealized image of themselves. They may want to be seen as intelligent, lively minded and well educated and to place themselves in the type of work where others might appreciate and admire these qualities. Sometimes they may experience their mothers or the dominant parent as intellectually curious, mentally flexible, perhaps overly rational, somewhat elusive and not so much concerned with their emotional well-being as with their education, sense of duty and community. They may also display the same qualities themselves.

The effect of Mercury in the saturnian house is shown well in the alchemical text *The Book of Lambspring*. Here there is an illustration of the old king devouring his young son, much as Cronos did his children. For sprightly and immature Mercury to take on the responsibilities and duties of governing, he must first understand and accept those principles from the authority figure who enacts them. All early learning takes place by mimicry or identification, and the old king has a way of ensuring that his son identifies with his values. The old king then brings forth a new son, one who is capable of reigning with him. So the meaning of Saturn devouring his son is to ensure, positively, that responsibility is understood. But there is also a danger, as with any alchemical work, that Mercury is ingested for the wrong reasons — fear of relinquishing what has already been gained, which is a negative development of the saturnian principle. In this case, the Great Work may be spoiled and future progress halted.

The positive and negative effects of the tenth house operation of Mercury can be judged by the aspects to the planet and by the sign ruling it. People with Leo on the cusp, or on the MC, may take some time to make up their minds about executing plans in a professional capacity, but once they do they are likely to carry them through with considerable will-power and dramatic flair. Where Libra is on the cusp, these people may view their mothers, or themselves, as capable of seeing all sides of an argument. Perhaps they may also see them as indecisive and unable to find points of harmony between conflicting ideas.

Planetary aspects to Mercury in this placement may incline people to express their modes of thinking with difficulty or ease, depending on whether the aspects are hard or soft. Mercury here trine Saturn can lead people to think hard and precisely about how best to organize their work at a practical level; or they may be so overcome with fear of responsibility that they might not be able to act at all. People with the Sun conjunct Mercury here may develop the capacity for independent thought in any work they do which is of an educative or communicative nature. Alternatively, they may find themselves curiously mute in public, unable to find the right expression to fit the occasion.

Where this placement is strong, people may have a tendency to idealize the capable, intellectual image they adopt in business and professional life. They may unconsciously take on the mercurial qualities of the mother, or the more dominant parent, not seeing how they can use their own considerable intellect to help decide on the most satisfying way of achieving some status or professional standing for themselves. There may be, also, an emphasis on gathering any kind of knowledge other than the type of self-knowledge which would lead to a sound recognition of their intellectual status and professional attainments.

Ambitious and practical organizers, people with Mercury placed in Capricorn tend to a realistic mode of thought and may be wary of any ideas which seem nebulous or unconcerned with achieving some materially secure status. Hard-working and with patient if somewhat plodding minds, these people think conventionally and methodically, one step at a time, often dismissing the joys of speculative thought as unproductive time-wasting. They value a disciplined and serious form of mental expression and can seem to be of a humourless turn of mind as they struggle to achieve professional and material goals – there was nothing very humorous about Saturn devouring his own children through fear of being usurped. Steady and logical, though perhaps unoriginal thinkers, people with this placement incline to a thorough knowledge of practical affairs and established institutions. Some practical idealism and an acceptance of human inconsistency would help to counterbalance the depressing effects of the more negative qualities of this combination.

ELEVENTH HOUSE AND AQUARIUS

Mercury's placement in the eleventh house can indicate the type of person who needs to exercise his intellect as part of the larger human family. This house is often where people look for intellectual friendship and companionship. It indicates the kinds of associations they join and where they find or reject group identity. People with this placement may develop an interest in gathering knowledge by promoting groups with a common purpose. They may or may not be vociferous in their interests, depending on how they use the aspects made to natal Mercury. Often they can be intellectually engaged in formulating ideas of their ideal society, which may reflect both their hopes and their social objectives.

Mercury is anyway known for his friendliness, so he is likely to feel at home in the eleventh house. Aquarius has the ability to strengthen the bonds of humanity between people, and Mercury's connective principle helps that process. We see the more realistic extension of this principle in the myth of Prometheus. When the gods sent Pandora and her jar of evils down to earth as punishment for Prometheus giving the gift of fire to mankind, they were unaware that Hope had been enclosed in the jar. Prometheus had included her so that humanity should not feel eternally afflicted. It was Hermes who conducted Pandora, the 'all-giving', to Epimetheus, so Hermes had a certain responsibility for introducing both good and evil to mankind. Prometheus, the light-bringer, was not to be entirely divorced from his shadow side; Hermes, the god of duality, sees to that.

Aspects made by Mercury in this house to other planets will indicate how socially skilful people with this placement are. Mercury here trine Mars could incline people to become the spokesmen of any associations they join because they often have much mental vigour and a charismatic way of speaking which helps them to be good communicators. The aspect's shadow, though, could display itself in the dissent which may erupt either within the association or in response to its aims. Mercury in the eleventh house may feel surprised by this, because its conscious aim is fraternity not disruption. Moon opposition Mercury here could, by contrast, produce much emotional irritability and sensitivity, which can lead people with this aspect to the need to talk constantly about their emotional difficulties. Such behaviour is not always well received in groups which may have other priorities in mind. But its positive shadow side might be to make the group aware that it has concentrated on the rational needs of the group and has forgotten to incorporate its emotional needs.

The sign on the house cusp will also influence the way in which the thinking qualities of this Mercury placement are expressed in group or friendly activities. Mercury with Scorpio on the cusp may have a tendency to keep its thoughts to itself unless it can be sure it will be really effective in any joint activities undertaken. Mercury with Aries on the cusp may produce many original ideas in groups, but dislike the slowness of the decision-making process. Mercury's real function in any group activities is to recognize what has been left aside and to attempt to incorporate it, where possible.

People with an eleventh house Mercury may come to a realization that their effectiveness in groups and friendly activities is based on their own ability to communicate well. They then see that they need not project these qualities on to other people. There may be a desire to be open to the ideas put forward in groups which have a common and humanitarian purpose, but they may have to learn to integrate individual thought with feeling and action, otherwise there could be a tendency to emphasize group ideas only. Prometheus himself seemed more concerned that fire should reach mankind. He does not concern himself with the immorality of the act of stealing it from the gods. He was punished because he did not take the gods' requirements into consideration, and Hermes ensured that humankind shared in that punishment.

Mercury in Aquarius inclines the mind to give importance to humanitarian values and encourages a detached and objective, if sometimes impersonal, mental expression. Again, both the archetype and the shadow are apparent here. People with this combination can be original thinkers with unconventional minds, though perhaps rather rebellious and eccentric at times, like Prometheus himself. This tendency could put them at odds with more conservative types. If they feel misunderstood, they can become annoyed and excessively determined, bringing in some uranian tyranny to prove a point. This often works against their best interests, particularly because they also seek cooperation and friendship with others at a mental and intellectual level.

If prevented from expressing themselves intellectually, or otherwise being unable to do so, these people can be badly wounded in the area of creative thought. As a result, they could become biased in speech, nervously tense and apprehensive or, in their frustration, disruptive of others' thought processes. Like Prometheus, they need some freedom of thought to pursue their own truths, the beneficial and original results of which they can then offer to humanity, but this needs to be balanced by a concern for other people's feelings. Tranquillity and emotional warmth are qualities they could learn to develop to help them offset an overemphasis on intellectual capacities.

TWELFTH HOUSE AND PISCES

If Mercury has this placement it can lead people to some intellectual understanding of the unity of all life. Able to use their considerable mental powers to tap into the collective, these people may develop an awareness of the archetypal and mythic roots of being. Mercury here can be at its most alchemical, trying to connect the worlds of the conscious and unconscious minds, both for their own and for others' understanding, successfully or not according to the aspects made by other planets. The placement can lead to introspection and, occasionally, to obsessive thoughts, and there may be an occasional need to retire from society in order to think difficulties through clearly. Often, Mercury in this position is in touch with collective forces which may not be consciously felt by other people, but are experienced at the feeling level. It indicates people who sometimes may not find it easy to distinguish their own thought processes from those of others; boundaries around thinking are clearly an issue here.

There is a description by Eireaeus Philalethes in *An Exposition upon Sir George Ripley's Vision*, another seventeenth-century alchemical work, which explains something of the way Mercury operates in the twelfth house. He speaks of one of the changes of 'the Toad', a synonym for the base substance which transmutes during the alchemical process:

> . . . once the true body is Impasted with its true Leven, it doth calcine it self, and dissolve it self for the dissolution of the Body into a black and changeable coloured Water, which is the sign of egression of the Tincture, is the Congelation of the Spirits into this lowest Period of Obscurity . . .

So part of the process of change Mercury has to submit himself to in the twelfth house is the neptunian dissolution. The black and changeable water breaks down all that has gone before, becomes formless and uncertain before it is transformed into the dark substance which eventually becomes the philosophical stone. Purification in the chaotic waters of the unconscious is a necessary and feared part of change, before the separation from unconscious identification can occur. Those who take the risk of fishing in Neptune's waters must face being swamped by what they find there, if only in imagination. If Mercury is to rise again in purified form, he must first submit to the death of old ideas and associations, allow his old boundaries to be penetrated and to dissolve.

House cusp signs can reveal the way in which this sometimes impressionistic Mercury works. Mercury with Cancer may prevent objective thinking and encourage a clinging attitude to sometimes outworn ideas and emotions. Becoming aware of the appropriateness of a response to difficult circumstances is often a problem for these people. Mercury with Capricorn on the cusp of the twelfth house can incline people to overemphasize or repress the practicality of their thinking when they feel threatened by structures imposed on them by others; it may impede the process of necessary dissolution. But aspects from other planets to Mercury here will often indicate in more complexity just what it is that Mercury picks up from the collective at an unconscious level. Where the twelfth house is involved, dissolution may take place whether the person is aware of it or not. Mercury trine Uranus would need to feel free to develop the intuitive side of its mental faculties and abilities, though people with this aspect may not be conscious of the depth of their intuitions. People with Mercury conjunct the North Node in the twelfth may need to work at developing a more compassionate and wiser way of communicating with others by first clearly understanding their own deeply buried emotional needs.

People with Mercury placed in this house may come to develop their potential as way-guides between the everyday world and the world of a universal and archetypal imagination. Thinking and speaking in images to the collective would be of some importance to them, or they may draw on the collective for the kinds of symbolic language they need in order to communicate their knowledge of deep levels of the psyche. In any case, they may find a periodic need to be sunk in the collective, neptunian waters of the unconscious. But they may also need to guard against the effects of obsessive thinking, and to protect themselves from the invasive thoughts of others.

Those people with Mercury in Pisces may be intuitive thinkers with impressionable imaginations. Highly receptive to the thoughts and feelings of others, their mental processes may reflect, not logical thought of their own, but almost visual perceptions which they have unconsciously received from others. Sometimes they have difficulty recognizing quite where their knowledge comes from. Their minds operate with a sensitivity so great that they can misinterpret reality, particularly when the contents of the unconscious are stirred up by present emotional experiences. They can vacillate between two modes of thought, often expressing themselves as optimistic at one moment and pessimistic the next, communicating these states of mind in a very subjective way. Others may interpret this tendency as wool-gathering and indecision, being unable to see the enormous empathy and compassion of which these people are capable. Recognizing the occasional need to draw boundaries between themselves and others and to trust their own mental processes would help those with Mercury in Pisces to connect with unconscious personal and collective emotional influences in a more realistic manner.

PART THREE

MERCURY IN ACTION

Mercury at Work

Mercury can be seen at his most alchemical when we examine his place in a chart in the light of a whole life. Often what we see is not the steady, linear progress of Mercury from *puer* to *senex*, but partial development in some areas and underdevelopment in others. The charts below give an indication of how this comes about. Sylvia Townsend Warner (see p. 224) was a writer, poet and musician active between the world wars, whose Mercury in Scorpio in the first house conjunct the Ascendant clearly shows both a conscious and unconscious use of the attributes and deficiencies of the intellectual process. Frida Kahlo (see p. 238), a Mexican painter, also active in the same period, had an unaspected Mercury in Leo in the twelfth house square the MC, which indicates her strong, sometimes obsessional drive to communicate her sense of life and death through her paintings.

SYLVIA TOWNSEND WARNER

A short biography

She was born at 6 a.m. on 6 December 1893 at Harrow near London, where her father, George Townsend Warner, was an assistant master at Harrow School. He was a cultured man who, as well as teaching, wrote history books and one on the use of English, still standard in schools in the 1930s. Her mother, Nora, eccentric and domineering, was the daughter of a retired colonel in the Indian army.

Sylvia was their only child and she showed in her early days a bright intelligence which delighted her father. Favoured by her father and resented by her mother because she was not the son she had wanted, Sylvia developed into an attention-seeking child who was something of a mimic. Precocious and a strain on her teachers, she was withdrawn from kindergarten at the age of six and was afterwards taught by her mother.

A lively minded child, early to read and write, not particularly beautiful, as her mother continually reminded her, she learned to compensate for her looks by her erudition, encouraged by her father and other masters at Harrow. She was very musical, but rather lonely as a teenager, making no friendships among the boys at the school. As she grew older, George extended her education in literature. By 1911 she was composing music regularly and at sixteen she had started the serious study of music with Percy Buck, who was at that time teaching at Harrow. An affair between them began in 1913; he was married and twenty-two years older than she, but she remained his mistress for seventeen years.

At the outbreak of the First World War Sylvia began some war work, though there was no pressure on her as the daughter of a middle-class household to work for her living. That changed when, in September 1916, George died suddenly. Nora's devouring grief was bitter. Sylvia found living with her disapproving and grief-stricken mother claustrophobic, but she kept the household together and in 1917 began work, with others, on editing the first collection of *Tudor Church Music*, having been recommended for one of the editorships by Percy Buck. It took five people twelve years to finish the task and Sylvia was among the hardest working and some of her work was extremely original. As a result she was asked to contribute a chapter on sixteenth-century notation to the *Oxford History of Music*.

Her salary and a small allowance gave her much-needed independence from her all-consuming mother, allowing her to rent a small flat in Bayswater. A rather solitary life ensued, initially, with visits to and from a few close friends. Her life was, in some areas, necessarily secretive, to accommodate Buck's visits, but during this period, she had other affairs, some with older, married men. By 1920, she was leading an active social life, was known for her rather arch, clever speech and became a listening ear to those of her friends who had troubles. In this year, too, she fell in love with Stephen Tomlin, an artist, but though he remained friendly, he did not reciprocate – a situation which was to cause her some pain over the next four years.

The first volume of *Tudor Church Music* appeared in 1922. She was still writing poetry and in 1923 started a novel on the theme of witchcraft, a theme that was to recur throughout her life in her poetry and prose. Often fey and romantic in her work, she eventually learned to combine these qualities with a good deal of earthy realism, though this first novel was never published. During the period 1922–5 she had mostly given up composing, retaining her musicality in the lyricism of her language, though the content and structure of her work was often deliberately at odds with the language she used. By 1923 David Garnett had read some of her poems and they were accepted for publication in 1925 under the title of *The Espalier*. The reviews of her first book were encouraging. The poems are crafted reasonably well and recapitulate something of her feeling about her relationship with Buck, yet somehow many of them grate. There are rhymes which are gratuitous and some of the language is archaic; at other times it is tortured and twisted out of shape. She was a promising and imaginative poet, but by no means always a master of her craft at this stage of her development.

Her novel *Lolly Willowes*, submitted at the same time as *The Espalier*, was published in 1926. It tells the tale of a conventionally brought-up, dependent, middle-class woman, who, after the deaths of her parents, lived with her brothers' families for twenty years. She then broke away to live in the country, becoming a witch, but eventually choosing to live undisturbed. The story is about a break-away to freedom and privacy of a sort, a constant theme of women writers in the years after the First World War. The novel was a success and she began to write reviews, articles and short stories. This was the same year in which she first met Molly Turpin and the same year in which her friendship with Stephen Tomlin came to a close. He had hurt her very deeply by breaking with her and then marrying.

By 1927 she was ready to publish her second novel, *Mr Fortune's Maggot*, about a missionary who finds only one convert to Christianity on a South Sea island. By the end of the book the missionary is disillusioned and has lost his faith in God. Odd, whimsical and fantastic, but again with a core of reality, the book shows a man who has failed to manifest his dream of faith. Again she received good reviews. By this year, too, Sylvia had a full working and social life, and had once more met Molly Turpin, now called Valentine Ackland. The meeting was not successful and Sylvia was dismissive and rude towards the younger woman. The last volumes of *Tudor Church Music* were moving towards publication, but her musical colleagues, even Buck, seemed uninterested in her literary career. In 1928 her second book of poetry, *Time Importuned*, was published.

The year 1929 saw the publication of another novel, *The True Heart*. Sales were better in the United States than in Britain; a trend that was to remain constant for most of her writing life. It is a weak book and in effect a fairy-tale with a fairy-tale ending. It was still acclaimed a success, but her personal life was less so. The affair with Buck was staggering on to its unhappy finale, and the embryonic one with her publisher, Charles Prentice, was not taking off; Charles was, like Stephen Tomlin, diffident. Her work on Tudor church music was more or less finished and she began to feel seriously depressed.

Sylvia lived through her books, but in situations where she felt herself to be emotionally exposed she was easily embarrassed, with little sense of self-worth. When her lack of self-confidence was displaced in favour of her work and work persona, she could see herself as witty and intellectually clever, though occasionally nervous and abrasive.

> Suddenly I do something clumsy or idiotic and Sylvia is in torment. But I soon forget her again, she is no more to me than the woman reflected in the mirror opposite. [Diary entry, 20 January 1928]

Early in 1930 she again met Valentine Ackland and by the summer of 1931 they were living together. Valentine was Sylvia's great love and her greatest trial. She was alcoholic, without self-confidence, had been bisexual from adolescence and continually suffered from hysterical illnesses and migraine. During the 1930s Sylvia published yearly, poetry, novels and short stories, producing in 1934, jointly with Valentine, a book of poetry entitled *Whether a Dove or a Seagull*. Reviews were mixed. Although Valentine had some talent, she was no professional poet and her pieces are slight. Sylvia's are more solidly crafted, but still retain the forms of archaized language which make her seem arch, precious and rather outdated today. But in these years she was also showing her skills as a homemaker and practical worker. She hand-sewed her own clothes, gardened, made pickles and jams, decorated their shared home and helped care for their many animals. During the same years, she and Valentine became increasingly concerned with political developments in Europe and in 1935 both joined the Communist Party, in which they became very active, visiting Barcelona in 1936, at the beginning of the Spanish Civil War.

The next year saw them again in Spain, and the result was another book, *After the Death of Don Juan*, which continues the story of Don Juan where Mozart's opera *Don Giovanni* stops. It is a political novel; she takes the village of Tenorio Viejo and its inhabitants as an allegory of the political dissension in the Spain of her time. Her political work has less of an impact than that of, for instance, George Orwell, because she is more of a storyteller, always mixing fact with fantasy, and less of a clear polemicist.

About the same time, Valentine had taken another lover, with Sylvia's permission. While this affair was not at that point a threat to their relationship, Valentine had always made it clear that she intended to take other lovers. Sylvia acquiesced and even encouraged her, with one important exception. In 1939 they visited Valentine's lover in America, which was an unhappy experience for both of them. They returned to England just after the outbreak of the Second World War. Valentine spent the war years engaged in war work and Sylvia continued to write. Her novel *The Corner That Held Them*, which she started during these years, took six years to write and was not published until 1948.

It is an epic novel about life in a convent in the Fens and is dominated by a need to present a Marxist explanation of medieval financing arrangements. Reviews were good, the work showing an emotional depth of understanding of medieval religious life while retaining a careful intellectual structure. Sylvia had published no books of poetry since her joint effort with Valentine and her and Valentine's interests began to diverge sharply from 1948 onwards. In 1949, Valentine revived her affair with the American woman and Sylvia prepared to move out of the cottage so that the couple could live together when she came to England. Separated from Valentine, Sylvia was miserable and depressed at this time. They were together again within a short while, but Valentine's affair continued to drift on until its close in the early 1950s.

The years of the 1950s were busy. Valentine opened an antique shop and became a Catholic; Sylvia wrote, but less successfully than previously, though she published more poems, *Boxwood*, in 1957. She came to spend more time with friends other than Valentine and was devoted to her garden, growing herbs, vegetables and flowers. By the early 1960s she and Valentine had grown apart even farther. It was at this time that Sylvia extended her writing skills by completing a biography of T. H. White, another writer in the fantasy idiom, which was published in 1967. By the following year Valentine was diagnosed as having cancer, which rapidly spread. In November 1969 she was dead and Sylvia was distraught. By now she was seventy-seven years of age and, apart from a book of poems published in 1968, *King Duffus and Other Poems*, her best writing years were over.

King Duffus presents some of Sylvia's maturest poetic work in which many of the earlier mannerisms are smoothed away. It is also a book which is concerned with death and despair, written at the end of an emotionally testing life, as the title poem indicates. This poem, together with 'Gloriana Dying', is among her best and shows starkly her understanding of suffering and longing for peace at the end of her life.

She was desolated by Valentine's death, mourning her deeply, and these last poems indicate her own move towards death and her own acceptance of it, however unconscious she had been of its operation throughout her life. She spent her remaining years revising her own and Valentine's work and had a brief flurry of writing short stories about elves and Elfhame, her fairy kingdom, in the mid 1970s. In the main, these were highly satirical and sometimes bawdy, but were well received, for a time, in American journals. Thereafter her creative work dried up and she died in her eighty-fourth year on the morning of 1 May 1978 at East Chaldon.

Though not a great woman writer when compared with George Eliot or Iris Murdoch, Sylvia Townsend Warner is important because she was one of the few women writers to span the period of the two world wars and to record changes in social attitudes. Politics, women's emancipation, the loss of faith, the descent to despair, the juxtaposition of fantasy and reality and the need for seclusion are her most constant themes. The themes are large ones, but, more often, she trivializes them by her self-conscious cleverness and the sometimes overmanipulated interweaving of the fey and the real. In contrast, those books and poems which openly reveal the depth of her emotional reactions to people and life are the ones most likely to last.

Astrological interpretation

When we look at her chart, we can see how closely Sylvia's life fits the horoscope. Mercury rules her MC and the tenth house; it also rules the eighth house. Mercury is especially important because it is placed in first house Scorpio, conjunct the Ascendant and the Moon, both opposing Jupiter in the seventh house. It also sextiles Venus in Aquarius in the second house and quintiles the MC. A person with this combination may have an emotional need to communicate and dramatize partnerships and close relationships in a comical or whimsical way, usually to gain some response from others. There is also a tendency to be drawn to partners who are idealized and expected to be deeply transformative, but who, in reality, may find it difficult to commit themselves. The Sun opposing Neptune/Pluto in Gemini indicates as much.

Unconsciously, Sylvia was pulled between the desire to maintain relationships and the need to escape from them. In her life she was the one who remained faithful to Valentine, aware at the rational level only of her own need for freedom. Her intensely

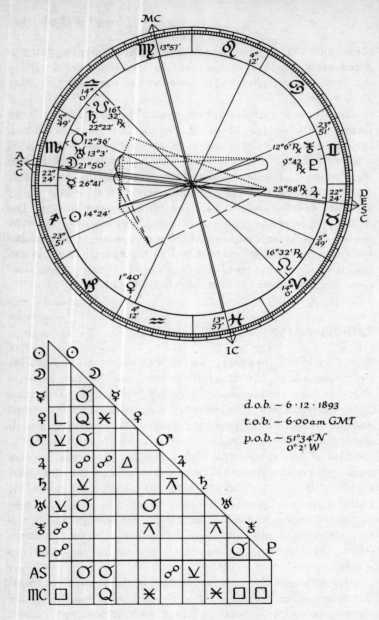

Birthchart for Sylvia Townsend Warner.[1]

loyal and fixed first house Mercury would want to keep close
relationships safe, but we know what happens when Mercury
stays in the plutonic underworld. He stifles; he cannot move
easily. His function is to make transitions, to move between
Hades and the Zeus-ruled upper world. Though Sylvia lived out
that Mercury/Jupiter opposition in her written works, her close
relationships were another matter. Power of movement and a
sense of moral freedom were given away to partners, to the
extent that Sylvia colluded with Valentine's behaviour when she
took a lover, much as she had accepted that Percy Buck would
never leave his wife. It was left up to Valentine to make the
choice about whether she wanted to go or not; even Sylvia's
short separation from her seemed to happen more in response to
the pressure of Valentine's affair, not because she wanted the
relationship to break up. Mercury's tricksterish way of rationalizing scorpionic emotions seemed to win out here.

Yet, as a child, Sylvia had been quite mercurial. She was
known for her mimicry and her early teachers found her rather
difficult to contain. As she grew older, she became adept at both
hiding and using her feelings in her work, something which a
twelfth house Scorpio Moon would need to do in order to hide
the painful feelings aroused by people and partners who were
not committed to her beliefs and values in relationships. Sylvia's
nigredo was always in the area of relationships. She came back to
this point many times in her life, but mostly with Valentine, and
the issue was never resolved or healed.

Mercury conjunct the Moon on the Ascendant would indicate
the strategies she used to cover over her woundedness – a bright,
witty exterior hiding the powerful feelings which planets in
Scorpio represent. Her first novel, *Lolly Willowes*, describes what
happens when the mask cracks. There we see the pain of a
woman forced to live until middle age under the patriarchal,
spirit-crushing domination of her Victorian family, until she
could bear it no longer and escaped into rural solitude, which is
one way of living out Jupiter in Taurus.

Sylvia had experienced something of the same dominating
manipulation from her mother after her father's death. While
she escaped from this situation into her own flat and work, she

did not escape its effect on all her relationships. Buck's early, exploitative relationship with her indicates as much. He was, essentially, jupiterian – an unobtainable, magisterial father-figure who, though helpful to her in her earlier career, was not about to besmirch his increasingly public reputation as a musicologist by leaving his wife for Sylvia. Their relationship was a secretive one and, when it ended, Sylvia's twelfth house Moon ensured that she neither wrote nor spoke about the extent of their relationship in public, though she recorded her pain in her diary, perhaps knowing, as a literary figure, that this was likely to be quoted by biographers after her death. A twelfth house Moon in Scorpio sometimes adopts devious ways of taking its revenge, especially when it conjuncts shape-shifting Mercury in the first house.

The relationship did, however, set the pattern for her subsequent affairs and eventual partnership with Valentine Ackland. The men she fell in love with were, like her dead father and Percy Buck, unobtainable. Stephen Tomlin married someone else; Charles Prentice was simply not interested enough. In her hurt she seems to have sought something of Jupiter's adventurousness and lack of committedness in the lesbian Valentine, put it outside herself, let Valentine carry the projections of her own escapism.

Unable to come to terms with her own unconscious conflict between freedom and emotional expression in close partnerships, this was projected on to Valentine, who was, in the long term, limited in her emotional range, as well as unfaithful. The combination of the Moon, Mercury and Venus in Sylvia's chart, together with Mercury's aspects to the Ascendant and MC, and its rulership of the MC, would long for an open expression of affection from partners and recognition from the world. The Moon's conjunction with Uranus and Venus in the twelfth house indicates that any anger she felt at the lack of recognition was probably deeply buried or visited on to the collective.

Mercury's opposition to Jupiter, though, would ensure a particular type of response to that unacknowledged dilemma. Any partner she had might feel intellectually inferior in the light of Sylvia's public literary achievements and aspirations. Unconscious resentment and lack of confidence may have underpinned Valentine's gradual withdrawal from Sylvia, and they did grow apart intellectually in their later years. Sylvia was seemingly unaware that Valentine's behaviour was a reflection of the repressed fears inherent in her Sun opposition. In the years before Valentine's death, she was seen, by friends who knew them both, as the faithful partner who was badly hurt and burdened by the unfeeling and unachieving Valentine. After Valentine's death, she was more apt to recall their love and her own despair, not the pain and misery of their relationship – a very one-sided, though mercurial response. The lack of a real *heiros gamos* indicates her pain at Valentine's loss, but not the reality of their relationship.

It was different in the early days of their partnership. They worked together on a book of joint poems and the book that Sylvia produced on Spain was a result of their joint allegiance to the Communist Party and visits to the war zone. At this point in their relationship literary Mercury and belief-orientated Jupiter worked well together, Mercury heralding Jupiter's need for recognition, much as he did in mythology. Neither this, nor their initially close physical relationship, was enough to bind them together over a lifetime.

We can see why from Sylvia's chart: Moon opposite Jupiter has a tendency to be extravagantly generous, or to expect this from partners. There is an emotional arrogance here, exacerbated by the Moon's conjunction to Mercury, which states that, 'As I am, so you must be,' an expectation that partners must fulfil her deepest, hungry emotional needs in the way in which she most desires them – a theme backed up by Mercury's rulership of the eighth house. But even classical Zeus could not find this satisfaction among his many women; still less could the mortal Sylvia. No partner of Valentine's fragile emotional disposition could bear the brunt of such voracious needs. Valentine did, of course, bear some responsibility for the deterioration of the relationship, but Sylvia's unconscious drives also affected her partnership and helped to pull them apart emotionally, though they shared the same house until Valentine's death. Her own unacknowledged needs allowed disillusion with Valentine to set in. In an inward sense, she also was party to cracking the *alembic* of their relationship; Valentine's unfaithfulness wasn't the whole of the story, just the most obvious part.

The same aspect between Mercury and Jupiter indicates that some of Sylvia's need for love and recognition was transferred to her literary life. She had a faithful reading public, particularly in the United States, and retained, in her short stories, her idiosyncratic style of writing with its strange mixture of fact and fantasy for many years. She was not a writer of deep psychological insight, but chose to set and explore her characters against a system of prevailing beliefs, so that they are seen to be engaging in a heroic war between beliefs and their own sense of reality – a very jupiterian theme, but one that does not engage the issues of power and betrayal reflected by her Moon/Mercury in Scorpio, or Pluto in the seventh house. There is never a struggle for resolution of the conflict between social systems and individual reality; one or the other has to win.

This is apparent in *Mr Fortune's Maggot*, where the central character eventually doubts and discards the religiosity taught him by the established church. What makes Sylvia's work seem artificial, in some respects, is that she chose to set the scene for this book on a remote island, almost as though it would have been impossible for her to examine the same theme in the heart of her own culture. This is where her Mercury opposition to Jupiter and the sagittarian Sun opposition to Neptune and Pluto do not act in her best interests; there is the need to fantasize, remove, escape and surround the theme with an air of missionary zeal and failure, isolating the character from any influence but the one under scrutiny. It is a trait that permeates most of her books and stories, so that, at best, her characters seem simplified and, at worst, contrived, always unaware, until the end, of the betrayals that are involved in any loss.

Though it is not mentioned in her biography, there is a question about the extent to which Valentine may have been, or was unwittingly set up to be, the living embodiment of Sylvia's unconscious dilemma between betrayal and conversion. They both went through a conversion experience to Communism, though Valentine was the first to show interest in the ideology;

Valentine also became a Catholic in later life, and Sylvia disapproved. Sylvia might recognize the themes enough to write about them, but living them in a conscious way through the alchemical fires of her relationship with Valentine was a different art altogether.

Mercury conjunct Moon in Scorpio has more than one way of disguising the seamier sides of human nature. The artificiality she sometimes assumed could upset friends. She was known to be clever and cutting in speech and occasionally adopted a rather self-conscious manner of talking, arch, light-hearted and rather fey, which could grate on the ears of her listeners. It seems that she felt a need to hide, at least early on, the raunchier, more earthy aspects of her personality. This was partly in response to the literary conventions of her time, partly as a cover for her then unconventional lifestyle. Later in life, her stories of fairies and Elfhame contained ribald humour and description, almost as though she needed the licence of old age to admit to this part of herself in writing. Even then it was disguised: the common-sensical descriptions of scorpionic sexuality are relegated to the fairy kingdom and her poetry; they do not appear in her novels. She perhaps needed to have the darker aspects of her sexuality and power drives where she could keep them safe – away from her relationship with Valentine and in the realms of unreality which she herself created and controlled, much as she created and controlled the more taurean parts of her home environment.

She was proud of, and known for, her domestic skills – cooking, gardening, dress-making and interior decoration. They were a genuine expression of Moon/Mercury opposite Jupiter in Taurus, and indicate something of the alchemical need to bring together separate talents to make a life, but how Valentine felt about Sylvia always playing queen in their joint kitchen we do not know. What we do know is that she opened an antique shop and that the business ran down as her cancer took hold. How far this was a response to Sylvia's power on the domestic, artistic and literary front we cannot say with certainty, but we do know that Moon/Mercury in Scorpio is very likely to manipulate domestic situations and use them as a battleground for power issues in relationships – all under the loving cover of the detached Venus in Aquarius sextile to the conjunction.

But both Sylvia and Valentine were well-bred, polite women of their time, and there is no evidence that they fought over these issues, so this may be yet another instance of the battle being waged underground, in Pluto's kingdom, the unconscious. Pluto in the seventh house would ensure that the sphere of action would be relationships. Friends sensitive to atmospheres must have caught the occasional tremor signalling the destructive forces lurking beneath the façade of the Ackland/Warner partnership before they drifted apart. Whether they suspected that this was Sylvia's issue we do not know.

On the whole, Sylvia found her literary work a safer container than her partnership with Valentine in which to explore her feelings, and her escape was into the literary world, as we can see from her Mercury ruled MC. If we look at her poetry, we see that the aspects to Mercury and their house and sign placements are starkly apparent in the themes she explored. Sexuality, world-weariness and loss are the major points of focus, but there are others. The jupiterian expression of freedom in conflict with seventh house commitment is shown in poems inspired by her early love for Valentine. In the middle of the Second World War, she wrote about the themes of war and death in some very plutonic poems which indicate the uncertainty of a resurrection of the world she had known. There are poems of love and mourning written after Valentine's death, and those which contain a bleak acceptance of her own death reveal to us the jupiterian without hope which Sylvia had become once Valentine was gone.

In the end, Sylvia seemed to will herself to die, succumbing finally to cancer, as Valentine had. Even her mercurially hopeful spirit seemed to desert her in her last poems; they are about loss of meaning and communication. The heartachingly loyal Scorpio Moon had given up on Valentine, on literature and, finally, on life itself. Alchemical Mercury was, for Sylvia at the time of her death, still at a stage of very uneven development. We hear an echo of pain in the childlike puzzlement of her own last words to a friend of her closing years: 'What *is* the meaning of all this, Antonia? They assure me there is one.'[2]

FRIDA KAHLO

Biographical details

She was born at 8.30 in the morning, on 6 July 1907, in Coyoacan, a suburb of Mexico City. Her father, Guillermo, a German-Jewish immigrant who had arrived in Mexico with few possessions, was a highly regarded professional photographer with a well-established reputation. Her mother, Mathilde, Guillermo's second wife, was of Spanish-Indian descent and a strong-minded, intelligent, capable housewife. Frida was the third daughter of four sisters and she had two half-sisters by her father's first marriage.

Her father's favourite daughter, she was talkative and mischievous as a small child, well able to hold her own against her older sisters, but at the age of six she caught polio and was confined to home for nine months. At the end of the illness the muscles in her right leg had withered and she turned into a taciturn, introverted child who invented imaginary playmates. Her mother was determined that Frida would return to an active, physical life, and encouraged her to take part in some unusual sports. Football, wrestling and boxing, as well as the more conventional swimming, became part of her life and she was known as something of a tomboy with a fierce determination and a fiery temper to match.

Once she started school her father seemed to increase his interest in her. He encouraged her curiosity in nature and natural objects, and she built up collections of her finds. He took her with him on painting and photographic expeditions into the Mexican countryside and local parks. She caught from him an interest in Mexican art and archaeology. As she grew older, she was often by his side when his attacks of epilepsy started, learning how to ease the seizure and often rescuing the cameras and other equipment he carried with him. Pity, tenderness and respect are the emotions Frida expressed about her father. With her mother it was different. Both she and Frida were strong-willed, and though she loved her mother, Frida resisted her conventional religious attitudes and accent on the proper way for middle-class daughters to behave; they openly disagreed throughout Frida's teenage years.

At fourteen Frida was sent to the best school in Mexico City, her father seeing in her the promise he would have hoped for in a son. She was an intelligent student, though not particularly hard-working, involved with a group of students who read and debated widely in the arts, politics and literature. She drew and painted avidly and made herself known to Diego Rivera, the Mexican Communist painter, who was at that time working on some murals on a site near Frida's school. Like most passionate teenagers, she developed a relationship with a schoolboy friend which lasted for some years, though there are indications that towards the end of her school life she had a lesbian affair with an older woman and a brief affair with an older man. All her life Frida would be drawn to women as well as men.

At eighteen, on a bus ride home from school, she met with an accident, the results of which were to affect the rest of her life, both professionally and personally. A street-car ploughed into the bus and an iron hand-rail pierced her pelvis. Her spinal column and pelvis were broken. So were her collarbone and some ribs. Her right leg was fractured and her right foot crushed. She sustained the first of many operations she was to have throughout her life. She feared the boredom of being confined to hospital, home and plaster corsets for months, but three months later was well enough to go to Mexico City, and though she did not attend school again, she painted. This marked the beginning of her working life and her many self-portraits, both those that depicted her physical state and those that showed the decorated, icon-like mask she adopted in public in order to hide her constant pain.

In 1928, she joined the Communist Party and renewed her acquaintance with the womanizing Diego Rivera. Years earlier, Frida had told school friends that she intended to bear Rivera's child. Rivera was attracted by her open sensuality and her unconventional, lively mind, and by the end of the year they were lovers, though he was still married to his second wife. She worked hard at her painting throughout the next year, and though Rivera advised her, he refrained from teaching her or consciously influencing her style. In 1929, after Rivera's divorce, they were married in a civil ceremony, but of all her family only Frida's father attended the wedding; her mother disapproved of the match.

Though she did little painting in the months after her marriage, by 1930 she was working again. In the intervening months Frida had fallen pregnant, but had an abortion because her doctors advised her that she was unlikely to carry a child to full term as a result of her injuries; it was also rumoured that Rivera had the first affair of their married lives around this time. Her first self-portrait of that year shows a woman who is both self-contained and sad, and Frida herself acknowledged that it was a result of the realities of marriage to Rivera. Their marriage seemed to be one of Titans, stormy, battling, loving, sometimes supportive, more often not, and full of suffering and infidelity. While Frida seemingly adored Diego, even through the years of their later divorce and remarriage, Diego became dependent on her, but continued to be unfaithful to her. She was to remain something of an indulgent mother-figure for him, until her last years, when their roles reversed.

In these years, too, she began to spend more time on her appearance, deliberately adopting a style of dress and hair that was distinctly Mexican – long, flounced dresses, unusual footwear, heavy, pre-Columbian jewellery and ribbons, braids and bows in her carefully chignoned and plaited hair. Her appearance took hours of preparation and she became a somewhat stylized work of art in herself, which grew more bizarre and outmoded as the years progressed. Many of her later self-portraits show the formality and colourfulness of the clothes she wore in everyday life. They were at once a display and a mask. They both concealed her bodily disfigurements and her increasing emotional fragility and revealed the flamboyant determination to overcome and make good use of her handicaps in her life and in her art.

In the years prior to the Second World War, she underwent many operations on her back and foot, grew used to and fought against Rivera's womanizing, including his affair with her younger sister, visited America with him and France on her own, had a miscarriage and at least one more abortion, drank and swore heavily, took lovers, both men and women, among them Trotsky, kept a journal, wrote many letters to her friends – and painted. All her life was grist to her painterly mill, and she herself was the centre of it. Her work developed into a synthesis of styles, Mexican-Indian and Mexican-Catholic, which indicated the gruesome and the visceral along with the beautiful. Death in the midst of sex and life was a constant theme; above all, the narcissistic, primitive and stylized self-portraits reigned supreme. In 1937 she met the surrealist poet, André Breton, who praised her work, and in the following year she mounted her first exhibition in New York. The show was a success and her paintings began to be collectable. The year 1939 saw her with an exhibition in Paris, arranged under André Breton's guidance. Again, it was a success.

In late 1939 Frida and Rivera separated and divorced as a result of infidelity on both their parts, and of the strain of constant battles. Rivera declared he could take no more. Unconventional as ever, they met often and their lives, in the small Mexican art community, constantly overlapped. They appeared together in public and entertained jointly. They lived apart for two years, both pursuing other affairs and both continuing to paint. Frida's drinking increased and the pain from her many wounds grew worse. She was on constant medication, often in traction to help relieve the pain in her back, and was concerned not to be dependent on Rivera financially, increasing her workload to ensure her independence.

Her health continued to worsen. She suffered from various skin and kidney infections and, in 1941, spent three months in bed strapped into a corset to help relieve the pain in her back. Her spine had degenerated and the doctors thought it tubercular; later in life, she was diagnosed as having degenerative osteomyelitis. Trotsky was assassinated in the same year and she was arrested on suspicion because she had known his murderer. Rivera, increasingly worried about her health, arranged for her to enter hospital in San Francisco, where she was also ordered to stop drinking. On her recovery and after another brief affair in

New York, Frida remarried Rivera, but she stipulated that there would be no physical relationship and that they would share household expenses while continuing to inhabit their joint house, though in separate apartments. This time Frida was determined to live life more on her own terms, though she still continued to care for and order Rivera's domestic needs as far as she was able.

Her father's death in the same year and her continued ill-health depressed her, and her state of mind is reflected in the paintings she finished some months after her remarriage. Melancholy and sombre, they suggest mourning. She continued to paint throughout the 1940s and began to have some success in the international art world. Exhibitions were held abroad and at home, her output increased and she began to teach both children and older students.

By 1945 she was wearing a steel corset permanently, syphilis had been diagnosed and treated, but poor medical treatment left her with constant headaches. She was confined to bed on occasions and made to wear a succession of plaster corsets in order to relieve the pressure on her spine. She found it increasingly difficult to sit up and paint. Though she put a brave face on her illnesses in public, in private she was obsessed by her ill-health. Her temper worsened, she constantly consulted a retinue of doctors, medical books and articles, and there is more than a suggestion that she used her physical deterioration to bind Rivera more closely to her. At the same time she was able to use her wounding in a narcissistic manner in her paintings. She had mirrors fixed above her bed so that she could paint the corsets that she wore, and when she could sit up she continued to use herself as the subject of her paintings. Wounding, death, sexuality and her relationship with Rivera, together with some still lifes, were the subjects of her paintings in her last years.

By 1950 Frida was confined to hospital for a year. Her spine was operated on again and the wound was slow to heal. She says of herself:

> I never lost my spirit. I always spent my time painting because they kept me going with Demerol, and this animated me and it made me feel happy. I painted my plaster corsets

and paintings, I joked around, I wrote, they brought me
movies . . . I cannot complain.

When she returned home she became increasingly desperate
and, at times, suicidal. She would paint in bed and, less and less
often, in her studio. She took larger doses of drugs and started to
drink again, and as she worsened she became more compulsively
attached to Rivera and her friends. Her formerly meticulous
painting broadened and simplified and some critics have said that
she became hasty and clumsy in her work. Certainly her style
changed.

She attempted suicide on several occasions as a result of her
pain and Rivera's continued affairs, and her temper with her
nurses and her friends was unpredictable. When she was up, she
was mostly confined to a wheelchair. In 1953, most friends
around her knew she would not recover. A one-woman exhibition of her work was arranged in Mexico City and she managed
to attend the opening on a stretcher. A photograph taken of her
attendance shows her haggard, immobile and decorated, almost
a living corpse, reminiscent of the painted sugar skeletons made
and distributed at the celebrations for the Mexican Day of the
Dead.

A few months later gangrene had set in her damaged leg and
the doctors decided on amputation. For Frida, it was a death-
knell, and for what remained of her life she never accepted the
brutal reality of its removal. She clung to hope and sank into
bitterness and agony, recording her feelings in drawings and
writing in the journal she had kept almost constantly since 1944.
There were further suicide attempts, her drug intake increased
and there were times when she was almost deranged with anger
and need and pain. Yet she painted up to the last months of her
life. She survived her forty-seventh birthday in 1954 by a week.
The night before she died, she gave Rivera the gift she had
bought him for their wedding anniversary and he asked her why
she was giving it to him so early. She replied, 'Because I feel I
am going to leave you very soon.' She was found dead in bed by
her nurse the following morning, 13 July 1954; suicide was
rumoured, but it was never confirmed.

Astrological interpretation

When we look at Mercury in Frida Kahlo's chart, we see that it is in Leo in the twelfth house and unaspected, though it does square the MC axis. It also rules the empty second house, the Sun/Neptune conjunction in Cancer in the eleventh, and the Venus/Pluto conjunction in Gemini in the same house. The Sun is also conjunct her twelfth house Jupiter in Cancer, which, in turn, is conjunct the North Node. Mercury, then, even though it is unaspected, is significant by house placement and rulership.

An unaspected Mercury in Leo in the twelfth house is likely to show itself in people who have fixed opinions and are strong-willed, though this may not be apparent at first meeting. We know that Frida was seen, in her childhood and early adulthood, as lively minded and given to dramatic speech and action, though she was often forced into twelfth house seclusion through illness. This tendency to open and artistic expression, often a feature of Mercury in Leo, was encouraged by her father, especially after her educational opportunities were blocked by polio at the age of six and by her accident at eighteen. The square to her MC/IC axis is shown to be active by the number of times her artistic work and her personal life were interrupted by operations and physical ailments. It was only towards the end of her life that she was recognized as an important artist in her own right. Her struggle was always against physical illness – or so it seems, on the surface.

But Mercury in the twelfth house can adopt the role of shape-shifter quite easily. Unaspected, and likely to show itself in an undeveloped manner, it is in the Piscean house of martyrdom and suffering. There is more than a hint that Frida suffered through her relationship with Rivera. But victims may also victimize, and though her illnesses were real, she may also have used them to hold Rivera to her. Their co-dependency was suffocating. Many times, both he and she tried to escape from the bonds of their relationship through affairs and, after their divorce and remarriage, by inhabiting separate apartments in

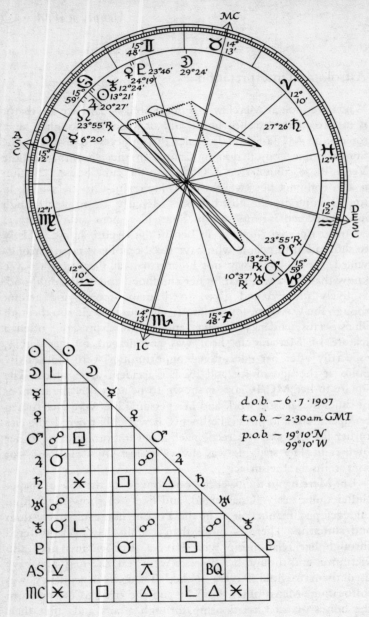

Birthchart for Frida Kahlo.[3]

their joint house. Ever-flexible Mercury in the twelfth has more than one way of keeping communications going while retaining some essential privacy, though the way to attain both was never an easy one for Frida.

Strongly home- and work-centred, with Venus and Pluto ruling the MC/IC axis, she struggled with the need to keep both going. At times it was difficult because her Mercury-ruled Venus/Pluto conjunction in the eleventh house corresponded to her need for a powerful emotional expression outside the home, needing recognition from her peer group. Friends always played a large part in Frida's life. Her art was the positive expression of the conjunction; her affairs were, perhaps, its negative manifestation, but neither prevented her from paying attention to her home. She was always concerned with domestic arrangements, a feature of a strong Leo, until ill-health finally prevented her from being so. She always stated that it was for Rivera's benefit and that it left her less time for painting. The ability to give herself away, sacrifice herself to others' needs, is signified by Mercury ruling her Cancer Sun. Somehow one gets the impression that Frida colluded in this less than happy relationship, partly through addiction to pain and suffering and partly because she was unable to tap fully the intense physical capricornian energy of her Mars/Uranus placement; her South Node was, after all, in the sixth house. Holding steady was never Frida's way, nor, with this opposition, or an unaspected Mercury, would she have found it easy to try.

The benefit from this collusion was considerable. She was the wife of a world-famous painter, and through him, even though he did not directly interfere with her work, her own artistic work became known. But there is an indication in her Mercury-ruled eleventh house that she was capable of manipulative behaviour in relation to men met in artistic groups and associations. Indeed, she met the artist Rivera through her political association with the Communist Party, which itself is signified by the Sun/Neptune opposition to Mars/Uranus in fifth house Capricorn. Years earlier, before she met him officially, she had expressed an interest in Rivera as the father of her children. Again, whether through illness or an unconscious fear, that desire never came to fruition – except in one sense. She married Rivera, she could not bear his children, but she could treat him as her child. At least one of her paintings depicts him as her baby; it may have been a way of cutting what she experienced to be his monstrous behaviour down to size. If so, then the painting shows more mercurial wit, if of a savage and denigrating kind, than we usually associate with her paintings. It also indicates how incomplete the *coniunctio* was between her and Rivera and how much she felt the pain of that disunity.

For Frida, Mercury's association with children was not to have concrete expression in the external world. Her wounded and enclosed Mercury in the twelfth house has a very poignant message here. What she did instead was to paint her inability to have children. There is a painting, 'My Birth', depicting her lying, like a sacrificial lamb on an altar, legs apart, on a blood-drenched bed, undergoing the throes of giving birth to herself. Shocking in its day, it shows something of the rawness of Frida's emotions at the time, particularly as she had recently had a miscarriage. The message seems to be that, if she couldn't give birth to live children, she would certainly give birth to herself through her painting, and receive public recognition for it in the manner her taurean tenth house Moon demanded.

The needs of her unaspected Mercury in Leo are revealed in the painful confusion of life with death in this work. Frida was always aware of polarities in her life and she was determined to have her pain and illness recorded in some way. There is a certain narcissistic ruthlessness about this painting which would certainly upset the squeamish; at the same time, there is a haunting sadness that she can display so openly the cruelties life brought her. Mercury-governed Venus/Pluto square Saturn in the eighth house signifies as much; the legacy her love brought her was death of her child and a brave, though doomed, attempt at self-love. Displacement activities do not necessarily mean self-healing and her buried Mercury seems unable to help her with the transition. She was depressed at this time, but it could not be said to be a true *nigredo* experience; her wounds were displayed, not healed, and similar themes are repeated in too many of her paintings. It seems that she was often stuck in the same negative *congelatio* phase.

Yet, throughout her paintings, Frida displays a brave defiance in the face of death, though this was something of a mask. We see this in her many self-portraits. Whether she appears as a latter-day Virgin of Guadaloupe, a Mexican sun goddess or surrounded by exotic flora and fauna, her face appears impassive. Frida copes; her pain is never shown in these icons. Her Leo Mercury translates the apollonian mask she puts on for the world to see. There is an attempt to show us in these self-portraits that the *alembic* never cracked. The reality was rather different and even a twelfth house Mercury can be full of contradictions.

She paints both the hidden and the primitive, often using the seemingly naive technique discernible in Mexican popular painting. She also paints the highly decorative which borders on the vulgar. Both are an expression of her Mercury placement. Obsessed with death and the disguise and revelation of pain and mutilation, longing for unity in her relationship with Rivera, her painting is a conscious reflection of the culture around her. It is both a displacement of her needs and a celebration of them and is the way in which her dualistic Mercury rawly displays itself. Mexican culture celebrates the interrelation of life and death in a way that Europeans often find garish and gruesome. By highlighting its acknowledgement of the transitory nature of life in her work, another indication of elusive Mercury in the twelfth house, Frida both wove herself into her culture and could not disentangle from its effects.

Dualistic Mercury in Leo in the twelfth works both ways in this aspect of her life and the contradictions inherent in her Mercury-ruled eleventh house planets are apparent in other aspects of her life. She was an avowed Communist in public, yet kept a houseful of servants. She and Diego lived in relatively comfortable surroundings, building their own house, but they were often pushed for the immediate penny. She was generous with gifts, but mean to people who did not treat her to the full attention she felt was her due, particularly in her last years. There is no evidence that she was disturbed by the contradictions, which indicates how split she was between her need to be seen and her need to hide. No amount of cultural and colourful camouflage could hide her pain and need for ever – and there were times when she didn't want that. She seemed to both fight and submit to death and decay. Mercury, it seems, crippled in the twelfth house, could not help her transcend her dilemmas; the best it could do was to help her record them in her paintings. There are strong indications of a very stuck Infernal Hermes at work here.

What made Frida feel momentarily safe, and is a reflection of her Mercury-ruled second house, was that she could, in her painting, show both her bravery and her wounds. There are memorable ones where she attempts to bring her woundedness and courage together. One, called 'The Tree of Hope', shows two Fridas, one lying with her back towards us on a hospital trolley, displaying the open wounds made by her most recent operation on her back; by her side sits a statuesque Frida dressed in a blood-red Mexican peasant costume. The pressure pads of the spinal corset she is wearing are visible above her breasts. She is carrying her latest spinal support in one hand and, in the other, a flag with a legend which translates as, 'Tree of hope stay firm'. They are painted against a Mexican desert landscape which is parched and fissured under the light of both Sun and Moon. A powerful self-portrait, it shows her need to integrate pain and strength. Yet she remains separated from herself. Painted in 1946, when transiting Pluto had completed its final conjunction with her Mercury, it reveals something of her unconscious inner torment, the internal pressure to accept her woundedness. The sadness is that she was never able to do so, but that would have been an almost superhuman task for somebody who was so physically mutilated, and had been so from adolescence. So the two Fridas eternally sit and lie back to back on the same uncomfortable trolley, never fully able to recognize each other.

In a letter to a friend she said about this painting:

> The landscape is day and night, and there is a skeleton (or death) that flees terrified in the face of my will to live. You can imagine it, more or less, since my description is clumsy.

Later the skeleton was painted out: there is an ambiguity about the will to live.

She did not wholly give up trying for the next few years, but her paintings from this time on portend death in some way. Time and life seem to be running out in a very mercurial way. A later painting from 1946 shows Frida's head, painted above the body of a running deer shot full of arrows. Frida turns a sad face towards us and the deer shows no signs of dying as it runs through the clearing of a forest, about to enter the shadows between the trees. There is a path down to some water, but Frida has her back to it as she runs. No branches are visible on the trees; we see only their trunks, but the wounded deer tramples a falling branch underfoot. Living leaves are still visible on it. Frida ignores the water and the living branch, yet still she keeps on running, a dead thing still alive. The feeling that reoccurs throughout her work is that she can have neither a whole life nor a complete death.

Similar hopes and fears are visible in her painting of the following year, 'Sun and Life', which shows a dully glowing, three-eyed Sun, held against a background of fleshy vegetation. In one of the womb-like hollows in the vegetation we can see a foetus. Unlike many of her previous paintings, this one shows the use of muted and sombre tones of colour. The Sun does not seem very vibrant or leonine; we are unsure whether it is rising or falling; we are unsure whether we are being shown life or death. Frida's descent into terminal ill-health was about to begin, but the painting reflects her cancerian uncertainty about the outcome. Here, Mercury governing her Sun indicates her unconscious vacillation between the will to live and the will to die.

Physical illness was not the only agony she underwent; suffering was a conscious part of her life with Diego. Publicly, Frida put on a brave face:

> I will not speak of Diego as 'my husband' because it would be ridiculous, Diego has never been anyone's 'husband'. Nor will I speak of him as a lover, because to me he transcends the domain of sex, and if I speak of him as a son I will have done nothing but describe or paint my own emotions . . .

But friends remembered her differently. She would say how sad her life was with Diego; that she never became used to his loves.

Each time the wound seemed new and she went on suffering till the day she died. Diego never cared and couldn't understand why people took it so seriously. Frida, it seems, used her strong will and twelfth house transcendent qualities to keep her marriage going, but the face of the mercurial myth which she chose to present was at odds with the difficulties of being married to Diego.

Her sense of martyrdom in relation to Diego was almost complete and her Mercury-ruled Sun stellium explains why. Yet it is in opposition to the angry Mars/Uranus conjunction in the fifth house. Though she was able to use the combination of a strong will and suffering to such good effect in her painting, there is more than enough evidence that her relationship with Diego constantly undermined her fortitude, if not her faith in him. She paid a terrible price. She was by turns angry with Diego and turned the anger with Diego against herself in her suicide attempts in the last years of her life; people around her constantly suffered from her explosions of fury and frustration. The Sun/Neptune martyr couldn't, at times, prevent herself from turning into Medusa – and she was in constant physical pain from her degenerating spine and many, sometimes botched, operations. One wonders how often her doctors unconsciously colluded with Frida in her desperate need to be cured or die.

Her Jupiter in Leo wilfulness often won out, but in these last years she alternated openly between despair and hope, rage and submission, fury and gentleness. The painting of 1951, 'Self-portrait with the Portrait of Dr Farrill', shows her in her wheelchair before her easel. The corner of her studio, where she has stopped painting the doctor's portrait for a moment to look at us, is bare and bleak in colour. She is dressed in simple black and white, with a pair of deflated lungs – a very mercurial symbol – painted on the front of her smock. Her face is mask-like and impenetrable. The only living thing in the room, it seems, is the doctor's painted face – and his expression, though more mobile, resembles Frida's own. Her diary describes her feelings:

> I do not have pains. Only a weariness . . . and as is natural, often desperation. A desperation no words can describe. Never-

theless, I want to live. I already have begun the little painting I am going to give to Dr Farrill and that I am doing with all my affection for him.[4]

Frida could sometimes express herself very movingly through her unaspected Mercury.

Frida continued to vacillate between desperation and strength of will in her final years and throughout the time of the amputation, never able to accept what she experienced to be the ultimate contradiction between life and death. It would have been next to impossible for anyone in her physical condition and with her world-view to do so. To the end, she remained as fascinated by death as she was by life, unable to transcend either consciously. Her twelfth house Mercury was ungraspable even at this stage of her life. In the year of her death, 1954, one of her final still lifes, 'Viva la Vida', which translates as 'Long Live Life', shows a vibrant use of simple reds and greens in the painting of an arrangement of cut and whole water-melons. Wanton and lusciously displayed, they are both available and closed. Set on a bare brown table, they are seen against a vivid blue sky. She was still translating between life and death, light and shadows, openness and secrecy in her work to the day she died, yet her exhausted Mercury could not fully combine the contradictions. Years later one of her friends said of her that she had spent all her life dying. Frida had struggled to make it an art.

II

Mercury and Necessity

Throughout the previous chapters of the book there has been a continuing thread – the historical and psychological appearance and disappearance of the mercurial archetype. Mostly it is assumed that archetypes remain constant; all we see or experience are different facets of their operation. When we are dealing with the archetype of choice, liminality and change itself, we are on much less certain ground because the core of the archetype is concerned with changeability. We can see this in the way that Mercury the god developed through the ages. The early erotic, tricksterish and shape-shifting facets of the archetype are still in operation, but it took the development of the gnostic and alchemical Mercury from Alexandrine up to medieval times to reveal the deeper meaning of his transformative and connective roles. These were implied in the myths of the classical period, but their meanings were submerged over time. Each age, though, has had to rediscover Mercury in one form or another. How far this is to do with the actual and perceived evolution and development of man's consciousness in relation to changing social conditions, or to what extent man, even rational man, always needs his gods, is conjectural and worthy of a study of its own.

What can be said is that individuals have the capacity to develop consciously along the lines of alchemical Mercury; whether they do so is a matter of awareness and choice. People are part of a wider collective and may fear that personal development will put them at odds with social norms and values. Often, though, they have something of worth to offer which has to be tested in the fires of experience and opposition before the world gives any recognition. We have seen that certain people have been able to offer the products of their own development to the collective. If we take note of the trials of Assagioli, Frida Kahlo, Sylvia Townsend Warner and Elizabeth Kubler-Ross, then we also note that much personal pain had to be endured before worthwhile values and behaviour were added to their individual stocks of experience and accepted by the cultures within which they worked. But although the function of Mercury is obvious in their lives, we know nothing about how they viewed the archetypal image itself – if they did.

This leaves us with questions about whether the archetype of Mercury is a construct which we as astrologers and psychologists choose to use because it helps us to explain people's lives, or whether the archetype resides in all of us. All we have to go by is whether or not the archetype resonates with our clients when they come for a reading. Most times, it seems, it does, but there will always be some clients who, initially, may find it difficult to connect with the archetype's meaning. What ebbs and flows at the individual level also does so at the collective level. There are sure signs that it has done just that, at least so far as the West is concerned. We know of the decline of gnostic and esoteric studies, astrology among them, in the seventeenth and eighteenth centuries, and we know some of the reasons why – the growth of rationalism and enlightenment, the split between science and religion in the post-Newtonian era, the age of revolution as the breaking-point between modern and feudal societies in the West.

Since the Industrial Revolution there has been an increasing emphasis placed on the importance of public and universal social and welfare provisions. The educational meritocracy which has developed as a result is as divisive in social terms as the ancient split between educated Greek freemen and illiterate slaves. The Oxbridge educated still have rather more life chances than those who do not make it beyond secondary education, though there are individual exceptions. What is not often discussed is how the narrow specialization that is a product of present education systems affects the individual. Often, people are squashed to fit preformed and specialist expectations which result from collective economic, political and social needs and pressures – even where the result is unemployment and very few life-enhancing expectations at all for a good proportion of people. In these conditions Mercury is likely to turn very sour, tricky and destructive if he is repressed for too long.

248 Mercury in Action

In the twentieth century, people are not required, on the whole, to be polymaths. This trend tends to result in the splitting of the modern mercurial function into distinct areas of knowledge. It is a separation of functions known mostly to the modern world. In classical Greece, priestly activities were not necessarily distinct from the activities of war or rulership. There were close social contacts and some overlap of functions because populations were that much smaller, and so more intimately connected. Huge population explosions in the twentieth century have ensured that the old intimacies and networks are in the process of breaking down and may be re-forming into new social formations and institutions, as we have seen in Eastern Europe over the past few years. We are not yet, perhaps, in a position to understand fully what is happening, but we can be sure that Mercury is still disconnecting and reconnecting. It seems that in complex modern societies his functions have become increasingly complex and difficult to discern.

We can see similar developments in the twentieth-century expansion of the communications industry, the professionalization of politics and the development of economic prophecy, all of which are commented on and tracked in the academic and cultural worlds. So we have a parallel growth of academic research into sociological, economic and political developments. We see it again in current developments in the arts, literature and music. All these are reflections and shadows in the current movements of the mercurial archetype. For us to add to our knowledge that this process is actually happening and is not a figment of imagination, we need to know if they add anything to his role as the translator between Hades' inexorable transformation and Zeus' conscious law-giving; if they add anything to his alchemical role of continuing change, choice and purification. When we can see it clearly, then we may be on more certain ground.

Though the core of the mercurial archetype seems to remain constant, Mercury does add more to his role as he passes through successive ages. Perhaps he can add even more to the further development of human consciousness, if only in individual terms. It may be too much to expect whole societies to undergo such radical change voluntarily and at the same time. If we do expect that, then we are in danger of over-idealization and the use of coercion in attempting to realize the mercurial ideal.

Though we may not yet see the core archetype developing, we do see the conditions for myths clearly arising in the collective with the development of world and continental organizations – UNO, world banks, world money markets, world trade agreements, the development of multinational companies and the EC. Many of these have stated aspirations about bringing the world closer together – more peace, greater harmony, the beneficial developments of trade. More often we have seen the shadow side of Mercury take over – the Wall Street crash of 1929, the rise and fall of money markets in the 1980s, the increasing bureaucracy of the cumbersome EC, the UN's inability to keep peace in Bosnia, the exploitation of the developing world, the increasing likelihood of political and economic destabilization in parts of Eastern Europe. In this process all the nations of the world are affected; where one brick cracks, the rest shiver. Mercury may have translated his actions to a more interconnected, global level, or, at least, his effects have become more apparent. If this is a true reflection of how Mercury is operating in the collective now, then it would certainly have repercussions for his role in mundane astrology as much as for the heroes of the political collectives.

At the cultural level, we see more immediate mythic images develop, sometimes deliberately hyped, but often, again, a reflection of what is happening in the collective, brought to us on mercurial wings through the communications industry. So we are swamped by the quick rise and fall of pop groups, Madonna's launching of the explicitly raunchy and supposedly liberated female, Jack Nicholson's version of the psychopathic Joker in the Batman films, the implications of genetic engineering in *Jurassic Park*. Whether the individual stars can sustain the mythic images thrust upon them is another matter; we have seen what happened to Marilyn Monroe and Jimi Hendrix. Literature and art are also affected, from the tortured figurative painting of Francis Bacon to the dark fairy-tales of Angela Carter, from the stark questioning of faith in the poetry of R. S. Thomas to explorations of the limits of free-will in the work of Marguerite Yourcenar. We have seen the rise of mass culture and how it has become split off from ethnic and élitist cultures. The shadow side of the collective Mercury seems to predominate here; again, such splits would need to inform our astrological work, both at the mundane and personal levels. Where Mercury divides, he can also be used to reconnect.

It seems as though Mercury connects us with what we have to change at the individual level and how we have to live with the results of our choice at the collective level. There is always an interaction between the individual and society, even where alternative ways of living operate. This process is now pressurizing – speeded up, constantly changing and ever more relative. We react to change in different ways, whether we are driven to it, avoid it, are cajoled into it or go willingly. We have to make choices about where and how we operate in society and these invariably affect our individual growth. We make choices about how we are with ourselves and with significant people in our lives, whether we know it or not. All choices involve pain and necessary loss, even if that pain is unconscious and unrealized. By sharpening the splits in the collective and in the individual psyche, Mercury aligns himself, as he did in myth, with the Fates and Ananke, that spindle-bearing goddess who is none other than necessity itself. But those ancient and anarchic goddesses will have no other choices made than the ones which lead to understanding and acceptance of the basic laws of life and death inherent in the innermost Self, and these may oppose individual and ego-driven desire and will. They may also oppose stated collective needs. If their rites are not honoured they are capable of inducing alienation, madness and death, as the myth of Orestes shows.

So Mercury will act as the saboteur, the harbinger of both escapism and conscious choice, personally and socially, until we can understand the choices we have made and integrate them with a much wider perception which gives us a meaning for our necessary pain. We can individuate beyond society's demands on us, whether they come at us through partners, parents or organizations we work for, but not without an aching sense of loss and separation for what we have left behind, even when it proves to be redundant and too innocent. Then we need to reintegrate what we have learned about ourselves in a way that takes account of other people's lives and society's process; sometimes, necessary acceptance is accompanied by anger and suffering. This is not a paean in praise of pain; nobody desires to go through it; most of us are humanly imperfect enough to try to find ways of avoiding it. The conscious mercurial journey is not for the faint-hearted. In itself this can help astrologers to feel more compassion for their clients. But it seems as though an aware acceptance of pain and choice as a means of individual growth may be a necessary development for the current archetype of astrological Mercury.

Let us see how this process develops in the final chart, that of a woman born in a coastal town in north-western Scotland towards the end of the 1940s. Claire's father was the district public health officer and her mother was a telephonist. She is the eldest of three children, her sister being born when she was seven and her brother when she was fifteen. She now works freelance as a psychotherapist, writer and astrologer, is married and has two stepchildren. Her life path has been very mercurial and she is constantly aware of how the archetype continues to operate in her life. Her mercurial journey has been one of discovery and considerable pain, but she feels that she understands as much of the archetype as will allow her to manage her life consciously and with a good deal more ease than formerly. Mercury, for her, has brought many gifts and considerable hard work.

When we look at her chart (see p. 252) we see how mercurial it is. Her Ascendant is in Virgo and Virgo is also on the cusp of the second house. Mercury itself is in eleventh house Leo in a close stellium with Venus, Saturn and Pluto; the latter three planets are in the twelfth, where they complete the stellium with the Sun and Moon. Mercury is also semi-square Uranus in Gemini in the tenth and sextile Neptune in second house Libra. As well, it forms a semi-sextile with the Ascendant and a quintile with her Taurean mid-heaven and her North Node in the ninth house; the tenth house itself contains the intercepted sign of Gemini where Uranus is placed.

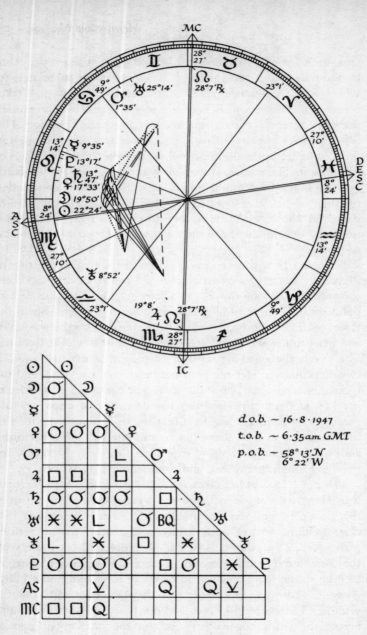

Birthchart for 'Claire'.[1]

Her earliest memories are, as for most of us, patchy, but are interestingly mercurial. According to family stories, she was a curious, bright child with a strong will of her own and she was an only child for the first seven years of her life. She vaguely recalls moving house for a while when she was about two, when her father undertook a course of technical study. She also remembers her grandfather, who used to look after her on frequent occasions, saying to her mother that he was amazed at the depth of some of the questions Claire asked him while she was still under the age of ten. More clearly she remembers her father taking her to join the local library when she was six, which is indicated by the conjunction of Mercury and Saturn. He loved reading – his own chart had a Virgo Ascendant and a Gemini MC – and she did, too, becoming a voracious reader from that time onwards. She quite vividly recalls reading her father's books by torchlight after she had gone to bed, though she read her own rather more openly.

Reading was a subversive activity in childhood. She read what she liked, when she liked and nothing discouraged her. At the age of seven, she can remember the local librarian disapproving of her choice of *Uncle Tom's Cabin*, announcing that it wasn't suitable for a child of her age. By ten or eleven she was reading widely outside the school curriculum, anthropology, archaeology, quests and travel books being the main fascination. No doubt the Mercury, Saturn and Pluto conjunction was operative here, echoing her twelfth house need to be in touch with the wider collective culture, if only through reading.

At the same time, Saturn and Pluto's square to third house Jupiter in Scorpio ensured that she learned as much about the death process as she was able to absorb at this age. She can remember reading most of Mortimer Wheeler's accounts of his digs and asking a friend of her parents what might happen if an Egyptian mummy were unwrapped. Knowing, in theory, how to shrink a head by the age of twelve, she longed to acquire the practical skill – as well as the head itself! In this way, she put herself in touch with the wider world and educated herself beyond her parents' ken. In these early years, they neither actively encouraged nor discouraged her activities, and in many ways she discovered her own world, both by exploring the countryside around her and by reading. She was not yet in a position to explore the larger world beyond her immediate environment, and in many ways, as she grew older, she was prevented from doing so, as we shall see later. The issue of Mercury breaking the grip of Saturn and Pluto was to be a theme in her life for many years until she consciously began to hold the tensions between the functions of the three planets.

Her leisure activities were many. At five, she was constantly in her father's workshop, making constructions with considerable dexterity from the bits and pieces to be found there, a very mercural activity. Her imaginative faculties were already clearly at work and she proceeded to call these constructions 'fibilisses'. She can remember whittling wood, making wooden knives and making telephones with cocoa tins, trying to improve on their quality by introducing gravel into the earpieces. Games were a constant source of entertainment – playing at 'armies' with toy soldiers and destroying them with marbles, taking part in rounders and cricket with children from the neighbourhood and the cousin nearest to her in age.

She liked being with boys better than girls, finding them more active and stimulating, though she always had one best girl-friend. With this friend she formed a gang, appropriately called, in view of her later astrological activities, the 'Star Gang', which eventually shrank to two members. The name seems to relate to the tension between the Mercury/Saturn/Pluto conjunction and its sextile to Neptune in the first house. There was little ambiguity about the gang's behaviour; the irritating semi-square aspect between eleventh house Mercury and tenth house Uranus indicates some of its more outrageous activities. It seemed to spend a good deal of its time firing lighted paper arrows under the doors of the school lavatories and throwing other children's balls over the school wall into the provost's garden. But there was a come-back to these activities from those in authority. For this she was made to stand in front of the class holding a picture of a caveman, because, the teacher said, 'That's just what you're like.' She can remember feeling deeply humiliated by this incident – an emotion that anyone with such a stellium in Leo would feel, particularly when the square to third house Jupiter was lived out by her teacher.

Though she loved primary school and did well, she can remember being belted for getting sums wrong. She can also remember being needled by a classmate, losing her temper, and being found sitting on his chest, banging his head against the floor. She seems to have found the Mercury, Saturn and Pluto conjunction helpful when it came to holding her own, though she now acknowledges that there was a certain cruelty to it, too.

With a stellium of six planets in Leo, five of them in the twelfth house, her fantasy life was bound to be rich. She tapped her own inner collective experience as well as the worldly one. When her parents were out, she used to imagine that she was a child abandoned by settlers and was being brought up by Red Indians. Sitting in the empty bath wearing a loincloth, imagining that she was a Viking, was another activity. She also had a tribe of six-inch-high slaves, always chained together, who used to shuffle along behind her on her way to school and sleep under her bed at night like a pack of dogs. These had to do exactly what she told them – including drowning in the bath if she ordered it. One time, when she was about nine, and just becoming curious about sex, she had them get into the bath in pairs, then leaned over the bath to see what happened. Nothing ever did because Claire didn't know what it was they were supposed to do! Her twelfth house collective experience of sex was rather lacking at this stage of her life.

It seems that these activities and abilities to make a relationship with herself were some compensation for the loneliness and powerlessness she often felt as a small child. Twelfth house activities were always likely to be of great importance to her. She was both fascinated by death and terrified by it. For years she had a fantasy about the dead Dutch explorer from *King Solomon's Mines*; his body inhabited her wardrobe and she had a number of rituals and incantations to keep him at bay when she went to bed. She could not talk to her parents about this, but she was frightened of the dark and her mother had to see her upstairs to bed until she was in her mid-teens. The reality of death frightened her, too. At eleven, her father tried to drag her into the dark room where the dead body of her grandfather lay waiting for burial. Claire remembers kicking and screaming, refusing to enter the room. If she was to learn about underworld and death experiences, she preferred to do it in her own way, through books. Saturn/Pluto, sometimes lived out by her father, had a way of trying to force the unwelcome reality on to her.

Her relationship with her parents was variable and fraught with tension and sadness. She was devoted to her father and was his companion for years, which is shown by her Mercury/Saturn/Pluto conjunction. She can remember playing Scrabble with him in games where they invented new rules; he also used to get very upset when she beat him. He was a larger-than-life character, bright, good-looking, arrogant and domineering. Though he worked in an official capacity, he was a known hunter and poacher, always in trouble with officialdom.

Two family stories show something of his dual nature. As public health officer, he campaigned for better-quality milk to be delivered. Once, when the consignment of milk was off, he invited the local press to meet the delivery and then proceeded to tip the contents of the churns into the local harbour. He won the campaign. The other story concerns his poaching activities. He often received letters from the local estate's lawyers threatening to tell his employers about what he was doing. He had them all framed and hung on his office wall. The people he worked for respected him and ordinary people thought well of him because he was straight-talking and had no time for repressive or overconventional authority. Claire's perception of him is very much in line with her Jupiter square the Leo stellium, as these stories show; they also shared a Virgo Ascendant, and both identified with a conscious, public purity of motive.

Yet Claire remembers another, more hidden, plutonic side to his nature. She clearly recalls the rows between him and her mother and his occasional, drunken violence towards herself as well as towards her mother. One Christmas he had arrived home drunk and asked Claire for one of her chocolates. She was angry because he was drunk and refused to give him one. He then threw all her Christmas presents at her and she spent the day hidden under her bed crying. There were many times that he took her out with him, only to leave her sitting in the car outside the pub while he got drunk inside. Her sharpest memories of this are the grief, sadness and fear that she felt, but could express to neither of her parents. Mercurial expression was often blocked by their lack of awareness of her innermost fears.

Her father, she feels, was a *puer* type, interested in hunting, fishing and shooting, which reflects his Moon in Sagittarius. He found the confinement and limitations of family responsibility restrictive and Claire sensed that her mother acted out the victim to that. Her Virgo/Pisces Ascendant/Descendant axis would ensure that Claire was sensitive to that dynamic, wherever it occurred in the family. There was always tension in the house and many rows about money. Claire can remember walking a tightrope of virgoan anxiety in case she said anything that caused a further explosion. She could not understand how her parents could be rowing so violently one day and, the next day, be seen arm-in-arm, walking around the local golf-course. The paradoxes of human nature are not something that a child with a strong Leo stellium would find easy to understand, particularly where Mercury is involved.

Her mother, like her father and herself, had a Virgo Ascendant. She was an attractive woman with conventional values, kind, compassionate, with a sense of humour, and highly regarded in the community. She was musical, but never had the opportunities to develop her talents or express her potential. Life, it seemed, had stopped for her at fifteen; she remembered an idyllic childhood and after that little else that was pleasurable. Claire has said that, though she could read her father like a book, she felt that she never knew her mother, who remains something of a mystery to her to this day. Yet, Claire felt, she also showed a repressed, dark, plutonic side at home. She was irrational and would reinterpret the world to suit herself, preferring her own fantasies of events, disregarding other people's viewpoints and reality. Claire experienced her as controlled, manipulative and depressive, but with a strong instinct for survival. Claire remembered one row between her parents when she was eight. Her mother yelled at her father that she would commit suicide and take the children with her. It is an incident that Claire has never forgotten; her journey into the underworld started early, with fear and without safe guidance on occasions.

Her mother constantly criticized their father to the children, driving him wild with her irrationality, and manipulating them to take sides. The obverse of the mercurial archetype is apparent in Claire's experience of her mother. While she felt her father to be upfront in his actions, her mother seemed to live out the slippery and untruthful side of Mercury's nature. Often this happens in partnerships and marriage; one partner displays the characteristics openly, the other covertly. This seems to have been the case with Claire's experience of her parents.

Her parents, she feels, were of incompatible temperaments. Though she has no conscious recollection of it and only found out in her twenties, they separated for some time when she was three. She was told that she screamed and clung to her father's legs, crying out for him not to leave. It was the main reason why he returned. This was at the time when transitting Uranus was making its first semi-sextile to natal Mercury. Though her father was a restless spirit, in those early days Claire identified with him, but for years she was angry with both of them. She bottled up her feelings and didn't trust anyone enough to be able to talk to them about it. She certainly couldn't talk to her parents about how she felt, nor to any members of her extended family; children's feelings simply weren't regarded as all that important. But Mercury, as we know from the myths of his childhood, has ways of compensating for that. While Mercury stole Apollo's cattle in order to gain his birthright from his father, Claire became, in some intellectual senses, her father's companion. It was as though she felt that the only way in which she could survive was to display her interest and learning when she was with him; at the same time, she loved him deeply and loved his attention.

Though there were many difficult times with her parents, Claire said that she always felt loved by them and in some ways her father was quite proud of her. He saw her as a good companion and recognized her bright humour. He, too, was quick-witted, with something of a graveyard humour, and the verbal repartee and sparring which took place between them sharpened her wits. Mercury conjunct Pluto is often the indicator of such wit and Claire enjoyed the connections with her father at this level. This is not surprising in view of the conjunction's place in the Leo stellium which squares Jupiter. One part of Claire's experience of her father was that he could be extremely jupiterian if the right occasion arose. Though her father never attended university, Claire sensed that he had the capacity, enjoying her intelligence because it stimulated him – at least, in her early years, when she was no intellectual threat to him.

At seven, Claire remembers that she began to apply her mind quite consciously to her schoolwork. This was the time of the first square of transitting Saturn to natal Mercury. Just after its passage, she ceased to be an only child when her sister was born. The two events are not unconnected; in later life Claire was to see how stages of her intellectual development often coincided with issues which arose in her family. She had no overt feelings of jealousy or resentment before her sister's birth, but they surfaced afterwards and the sisters did not get on until the youngest was about fourteen.

When transitting Uranus conjuncted Claire's Mercury, her sister nearly died at three years of age. Afterwards, her behaviour was never checked by her parents; unlike Claire, who felt herself subjected to too much parental authority. So feelings of rivalry between them were engendered early, though Claire never faced this in herself until much later in her life. Mercury in Leo may not take too kindly to siblings, particularly if they happen to be younger, thus usurping the pride of place which the oldest child has held up to the time of their births. This was also the period when Claire was occasionally in trouble at school; but there were compensations. She remembers spending much time with her extended family at that period of her growth. A boy cousin was a favourite playmate and both sets of grandparents kept open house, so Claire was often to be found there among cousins, aunts and uncles. These experiences somewhat offset the more fraught conditions in her own home and the occasional aggression she showed and experienced at school.

By eleven, Claire had passed her qualifying exams for senior school and was doing well academically. Her relationship with her father deteriorated because she now began to identify with her mother and her mother's description of events. Perhaps, unconsciously, her father was beginning to sense her to be an intellectual rival. Whatever the real reasons, she began to experience at first hand her father's more controlling, domineering nature. She realizes now that his more saturnine side is a reflection of part of her own nature. As a child and young teenager, she thought she was without the power to resist both the projection and the actuality of his oppressive behaviour. He could be repressive, unsupportive and rude when she was studying for important exams and needed to absent herself from the family. She was often afraid that his anger would result in him assaulting her. She can remember the incident when she first confronted him at the age of fifteen or sixteen. He was drunk and had been shouting at her. As he towered over her on the stairs, she turned to face him, raging beyond the fear she felt, and dared him to hit her. He dropped his eyes and turned away.

Yet there were good moments, too; the Saturn/Pluto/Mercury conjunction meant that Claire could experience her father humorously. He was something of a marauder and anything free or for the taking usually ended up in their larder or fridge. Claire can remember once taking an evening stroll with him around the harbour when they came across a huge pile of fish. Checking that there was nobody around, the pile disappeared into the boot of his car. They were gutted, filleted and in the freezer within an hour. Two days later a headline appeared in the local paper to the effect that a person or persons unknown had stolen the entire catch of the local sea-angling competition. From that day to this nobody knows who did it. He also had his own peculiar standards of honesty. The local procurator fiscal had charged him for poaching and it had been revealed that he had accidentally shot a hind out of season. He was so mortified by what this would do to his reputation that he went to the fiscal and begged him to change the animal's sex from a hind to a stag. These more humorous moments offset, for Claire, some of his cruelty towards her.

The square from transitting Neptune in the third house to natal Mercury was the time when Claire found herself spending more time on her schoolwork. She was also reading and writing creatively and extensively. At the end of this transit, which coincided with transitting Pluto's semi-sextile to Mercury, life at home continued to be unpredictable and tense. During this period, Claire also had her first Saturn opposition, following on from its opposition to Mercury and her second Uranus semi-sextile to Mercury.

When she was fifteen, during the Pluto semi-sextile, her brother was born. Her mother had been pregnant throughout the time of her Saturn opposition to Mercury. This time she can remember feeling angry and resentful before the event. It centred around having been promised her own bedroom, but she knew now that it wouldn't happen. The Leo stellium in the twelfth house would ensure that she looked forward to her own space – and resent an intruder who took it away. She can recall spending hours in the local library, reading up on the development of the foetus, seething with anger and feeling fairly murderous. Yet, when her mother was confined, Claire took over the running of the household, doing it efficiently, but still feeling resentful. It brought her and her father closer for a time. She took one look at her new brother, however, and all the resentful feelings vanished; she fell in love with him then and has got on well with him ever since.

By this time, Claire was well into her schoolwork. She was clever, but could have done better than she did if it hadn't been for the disruptive atmosphere at home. She was a good all-rounder, excelling at games, gym, English, history and languages. She used education as an escape route from home, and once she got a university place, when Uranus was making its second semi-sextile, from the first house, to her Mercury, she left home at seventeen. The event which precipitated her leaving home was her father assaulting her, knocking her down twice and being verbally abusive on getting her into the house. This came about after he had followed her and a boyfriend home, during which walk the young couple held hands.

She had had as much as she could take and applied for a university place the next day. During the vacation preceding her first university term, she also worked at her first temporary job.

Transitting Uranus in the first house aspecting Mercury, and the progressed Sun conjuncting her natal Ascendant in Virgo, ensured that she put into operation her plans to leave home, precipitating herself into the more responsible world of adulthood. Unfortunately, she had not received good models at home for responsible behaviour towards herself, let alone towards her work and other people. While parental pressure was relatively less, she found herself without clear guidelines to support herself through early adulthood. It was a time of much trauma and depression for her.

Her teachers had wanted her to take an honours degree, but she managed to get a four-year ordinary degree, only, she feels, with the support of her friends and tutors. As she says, 'That degree was one of the minor miracles of the Scottish education system, because I was hardly ever there.' Depression and confusion dogged her steps and she lost confidence in her own abilities, fearful of putting them to the test. Mercury was indeed in the underworld. She had left home full of resentment, anger, pain and desperation for experience. Her parents tried to interrupt her university career by informing the vice-chancellor that she wasn't emotionally stable enough to continue and should be at home. That was because she hadn't phoned home, as promised, for a week. She was summoned before the university authorities and convinced them that her parents were more disturbed than she was. Even then, her parents would not let go. Her father refused to sign her passport application, so she couldn't travel abroad for holidays as other students did.

Life was not easy at university. A year before she took her final exams, she became profoundly depressed because her boyfriend had been killed in a car accident. At that point she realized that she didn't believe in anybody or anything, would make no commitment to anyone, and felt shattered by the whole experience. She feels that it was sheer mercurial brains and panache that got her through her final exams. Before this, her tutor had wanted her to transfer to an honours course and had set up an interview with the relevant professor. Claire spent the interview convincing him that she shouldn't do it because she was in too much of an emotional mess. Then she started to drink, gambled for the whole of one term, and had awful relationships with men. Her emotional life was tempestuous and turbulent and she now feels she was living out anger towards her father and recapitulating his own experience of emotional failure in relationships. She feels she used her sexual power to get involved with men and to walk all over them. No matter what, she knew she had to pass the exams; she would never have lived down the taunts at home otherwise. She passed and, conventionally, there was a family party when her results came through.

She then needed to decide on a career and applied for a personnel management course. She soon realized that it was a mistake – and so did the course trainers. Like her father, she was worker- rather than management-orientated, and she was asked not to complete the course. She then used the mercurial side of her nature to decide her fate on the toss of a coin. The choice was between teaching liberal studies in a college of higher education or joining the RAF Education Department. Liberal studies won.

Claire then found that teaching gave her the opportunity to discipline herself. Though she had previously let herself down all the time, she found she could not let her students down. At the age of twenty-two, she caught up on the work she hadn't completed at university, spending a good deal of time in the college library, encouraged by her teaching colleagues and her growing interest in her work. It felt as though she had discovered a point to her university studies; it was the beginning of commitment to her own and other people's processes. She felt her responsibilities towards her students keenly and worked hard at the preparation and presentation of her courses. Her Mercury quintile her Taurus MC seemed to come into its own in these years.

During these years of teaching she had her first introduction to astrology, reflecting something of natal Mercury's semi-square to Uranus which conjuncts Mars in the tenth house, though she was not yet ready to study it for professional purposes. Though initially a sceptic, Claire came to change her beliefs. While living in Bath, she met and made friends with a child whose father was an astrologer. She agreed to let him read her chart and was astonished that he was able to read the hidden parts of her character so well. He also said that in her early thirties she would have opportunities to become an astrologer or something like it. During the period 1971–4 she had some psychic experiences and another astrologer told her that she was likely to be restless for some years. All these experiences piqued her curiosity in the more hidden side of life which had remained dormant since childhood.

True to maturing Mercury, she started to become conscious, in her twenties, of how she was living her life. She now realizes that she was living out her father's irresponsibility, loneliness and pain. This showed itself in her treatment of men close to her. She had one relationship, off and on, for eight years, and though this ended, the process deepened her and made her more aware of the effect she had on other people. Previously, she had found herself not caring about other people's feelings, unless they were close friends and not lovers. Recurrent depressions from the age of seventeen plagued her, though she could talk herself in and out of any situation with a great deal of charm, as only Mercury can. Her world was divided into those she saw as her friends and the rest; she kept contact with a few good friends for many years.

Gradually her choices were narrowed down through a process of reflection which began around the age of twenty-two. By the time that transiting Saturn squared her natal Mercury for the second time, from the ninth house, she began to realize that teaching and relationships focused her, and she came to know that the core issue for her was about taking responsibility for her own life – a state of being that mercurial people often come to by recognizing where they lack responsibility. As she became more professionally adept and caring, she began to enjoy what she was doing, learning to confront her ego in writing; she wrote, off and on, for various magazines and papers throughout her twenties. She began to come to terms with her use and abuse of men. She also learned to consolidate and value her friendships.

In the latter part of her twenties, after various jobs in education, she left teaching. She was still restless, and was driven by a desire for adventure, still holding, as she puts it, a grandiosity about not fitting into conventional structures. This had been fuelled by occasional serious clashes on points of principle with college authorities throughout her teaching career, though her teaching skills were respected. Mercury could still operate from both sides of his own door in these years. At twenty-six, at the time of transitting Saturn's semi-sextile to Mercury, she went back to her home town. Her father had just taken early retirement and had not been happy in his last few years of work. She felt she could offer him some support and embark on a writing career. Instead, she took herself to the edge of despair. Though she had a talent for writing, she found that she did not have at that time the personality to continue with it and sustain herself throughout the long periods of isolation that writing entails. She now feels that she was forced to face her own grandiosity and to recognize the limits of her mercurial possibilities. Fear of failure was her biggest fear and she felt she needed to confront this in interactions with other people; she hadn't yet the resources to do it on her own. She also realized that her father was experiencing himself as a failure. Both his behaviour towards her mother and his control over drinking deteriorated; Claire could not help him, or stay at home. So, in October 1974, just before transitting Neptune trined Mercury, she left.

After two years combining part-time teaching and writing, during which she became quite depressed, she made another major shift in her life, seemingly by accident. She decided that she wanted to be a social worker and, on impulse, phoned the local social services department. She was sent an application form for the post of an unqualified social worker, was accepted, and started on the next stage of her career. She realized within a short time that she loved her work and had found her vocation. The feeling never left her, and her work after that, including astrology, served only to deepen that feeling. Under transitting Uranus' square to Mercury she applied for and was accepted on to a one-year qualifying course for social work, again, seemingly, by accident. She had thought that she would only be accepted for two-year courses and filled out four application forms. Unknown to her at the time, she had mistakenly entered a one-year course on the form. This was, of course, the one for which she was accepted.

She had also made another shift in her personal life. At the age of twenty-nine she and her then partner finally parted. Claire finished her course and started work as a social worker. She worked with needy children and gradually gained more self-confidence. She was able to use various of her gifts — fighting for the rights of the underprivileged, powerful report writing, skills in tapping appropriate resources — all now underpinned with a strong feeling of solidity of purpose which had not been hers previously. Her powerful, driven Mercury was beginning to accept maturity. She also found that she had to face the fear of failure in this job, and her dislike of structure and authority, just as she had previously. The difference was that this time she stayed and worked with it. In time, she graduated to teaching social-work skills and took on counselling as part of her professional work.

Claire then progressed to psychiatric social work and stayed for five years, consolidating her counselling and therapeutic skills, before she was ready to make a further move. She had spent the years since she was twenty-two in coming to terms with the mercurial archetype and felt, by her early thirties, that she had made significant progress. She had recognized her own slipperiness and dishonesty and was, by then, increasingly honest with herself and, by conscious extension, with other people.

In her thirties, there were other significant shifts in her life. She met her husband in 1980 and married him in 1982, helping to share care of his two children by his previous marriage. During transitting Saturn's sextile to Mercury she took up the study of astrology, qualifying in 1983. At the same time, her sister's first marriage broke up and Claire's relationship with her started to deteriorate. Between autumn 1983 and spring 1984, under transitting Saturn's square to natal Mercury, she held her first class in astrology. In 1985, making good use of her qualification in astrology, she decided to set up in private practice as an astrologer and counsellor; it was the same year that her father died. At this time, also, she began to teach assertiveness courses at a local university. Happenings in the family again coincided with a shift in Mercury's influence.

By the time transitting Pluto squared her natal Mercury, she felt she had made many gains from her early, painful beginnings. She felt a deepening interest in astrology and withdrew from public groups in order to get on with her own work. She stopped smoking. She felt she had come to terms with being married and being a part-time parent; her sense of success also grew as her possibilities for self-employment increased. Since that time, she has extended both her counselling and astrological work, running classes and courses in astrology, writing on astrology, and supervising counselling students. When transitting Uranus quincunxed her Mercury, she had a sense that she was consolidating her astrological work and that, as well as offering it to other people, she was able to use its insights to underpin her experiences in her own life.

She saw more of this when Saturn made its second opposition to Mercury. Around that time, her sister had a child, her stepson left home and her mother died. It was a time of both pain and an increasing sense of her own direction in life. She feels that she has had to work hard, deeply and with much pain, to achieve what she values today, and that a major part of that work has been understanding how the mercurial archetype operates in her life. Becoming conscious of its shadow side has, she has said, played a large part in her redemption.

Though the mercurial journey cannot account for all the events in Claire's life, it has been a continuing thread in her development. Even in her twenties, before she gained any knowledge of the mercurial archetype, she saw that she was beginning to repeat her family pattern of emotional failure. She was able to benefit from the strength offered by her powerful Leo stellium, rather than continually fall under its negative influence – cruelty and a power-driven egotism and sense of control. She feels that only by recognizing the darker aspects of her nature has she been able to transmute them into qualities which can benefit herself, her family and the collective. This is not to say that all her struggles are over.

There are still times when she battles to prevent herself falling into negative mercurial drives and she realizes that the path of understanding that she has consciously decided to take is hers for life. But she would be the first to say that her life is now full and satisfying: a major contrast with the early part of it. Despite being a serious person, she has a well-developed sense of humour and refuses to take herself and her life too seriously. She values her family and her friends, and is valued by them in return. Her work continues to be fulfilling. She is more clearly able to see her individual strengths in relation to family and collective expectations and needs and is able to act, for the most part, accordingly and awarely.

The mercurial archetype, then, can be used awarely to deepen our sense of purpose and responsibility without crushing its curious and connective nature. Claire's story indicates how Mercury can transcend socialized behaviour and conventional collective values where they are detrimental to individuation, though not without pain and a deep awareness of the emotions involved. That soul-connection is what is developed and refined by experience. It gives the mature and transmuted Mercury the capacity to return to earth and offer his hard-won wisdom and compassion not only to others who may yet decide to make the journey, but also to the person who has undertaken, as consciously as he or she is able, to walk the path of deeper self- knowledge.

EPILOGUE

There is a question about whether the core archetype of a god or a planet changes or not. Much of the work in archetypal psychology indicates that the core does not change, particularly as we receive and understand it now. But, historically, it did change. At first, Hermes was a fertility and agricultural divinity and his origins are shrouded in mystery on account of the lack of historical records. Only later did he take on the characteristics of trickiness, youthfulness and changeability and the connections with Zeus, Apollo and Hades as recorded in the myths of Homer and later writers. It was not until the Alexandrine period that his attributes were seen to mirror those of Thoth and Anubis, and it was at that time that the seeds for the development of alchemical Hermes Trismegistos were sown. The full flowering of the alchemical archetype did not develop in European thought until the Middle Ages and the Renaissance. From then until now there has been a gap. Belief in the old gods and their functions slipped into obscurity as the split between the age of rationality and the age of belief widened.

Today, it seems, there is in some sections of Western society a recognition that rationality cannot give us all we require, and interest in the numinous and less easily accessible parts of the psyche has revived. With it has come an interest in the meaning of the old deities' functions, Mercury among them. We are still in the process of seeing just how relevant his known functions are to people in the modern world, but it is uncertain quite how our knowledge of the archetype will evolve further. We have a grasp of the core archetype as it is now, and we have seen in Chapter 11 the areas in which it might be functioning during the current era. These are difficult to fix upon with any degree of certainty and may not become clear until much time has passed, perhaps beyond the span of our own lives. Whether it will add anything to the core of the archetype as we now know it, we cannot say.

What is certain is that knowledge of the archetype must develop. If it does not, then it ceases to live and be meaningful. It cannot help people's understanding of their lives if it becomes inflexible or remains hidden. An archetype stuck mirrors a person stuck, and Mercury is not happy or useful in that condition; pressure and pain both build up. There is, though, enough about Mercury for us to know that he always pushes to find a way through, even if he meets obstacles. Not for nothing was Hermes given Hades' helmet of invisibility so that he could pass round or through any difficulty which might impede him. But people are not gods and they often need more immediate help when they are travelling through unmapped territory.

It is here that psychological astrology can be beneficial. An understanding of how the archetype tracks its way through a person's life and natal chart may indicate some skills which need to be developed or rediscovered in the present situation so that he or she can move on. So archetypal psychology does not stay with the past; it has to be relevant to a client's present life circumstances. As astrologers we are in a position to offer the support and compassion which are needed on the journey of discovery, at the same time ensuring that people are empowered to find their own solutions to life's difficulties. So we tread a fine line between explaining how the archetype works and opening up options which the person who has come for a reading might choose to explore further, or which they may fear. We can neither push a person nor hold him back. We take account of our clients' feelings and resistances in all that we explore. The work is always delicate; we are always on the mercurial threshold, unable to go back because our new knowledge will not let us, yet perhaps fearful of moving forward into the unknown.

Mercury, though, through his roles of psychopomp and alchemist, indicates that his natural function is to make a move. Curiosity, flexibility and the will to travel are some of his core attributes. His journey is also a long one. He begins as the youthful, tricky god, moves through a relationship stage which is fraught with unacknowledged feeling, and learns to relate in the reflective, alchemical stage where his attributes are contained, encouraged and used purposefully. Mercury has the ability to move through the worlds of action and psychological development, if not with the ease with which he is sometimes credited, then, at least, with work and understanding. His connective function is at the core of making sense of people's lives.

How he develops beyond that needs further discussion. Alchemical and cabbalistic literature indicates that he has a spiritual purpose, one that adds a further dimension to the spheres of concrete reality and the less easily grasped psychological inner life. Whether astrology is a suitable vehicle for that journey, and Mercury an appropriate way-finder, remains to be explored. But that is another book.

NOTES AND REFERENCES

INTRODUCTION

1. The original draft of the introduction appeared as an article in *Pulsar*, the journal of the Scottish Astrological Association, issue no. 8, winter 1992/3.

CHAPTER 5

1. Aeschylus, *Choephori*, in *The Oresteia*, trans. Tony Harrison, Rex Collings, 1982.

CHAPTER 7

1. Libellus 1, *Corpus Hermeticum*, in A. G. Gilbert (ed.), *Hermetica*, trans. Walter Scott, Solos Press, 1992.
2. Smaragdine Tablet: Latin original from Julius Ruska, *Tabula Smaragdina*, Heidelburg, 1926. Quoted in Cherry Gilchrist, *Alchemy: The Great Work*, Aquarian Press, 1984.
3. Roberto Assagioli's birth data are from Dane Rudhyar's *Astrology and the Modern Psyche*, CRCS Publications, 1976; date and place corroborated by Jean Hardy in *A Psychology with a Soul*, Routledge & Kegan Paul, 1987.
4. Elizabeth Kubler-Ross's birth data are from Lois Rodden's *Profiles of Women*, American Federation of Astrologers, Arizona, 1979.

CHAPTER 10

1. Sylvia Townsend Warner's birth data are from Claire Harman, *Sylvia Townsend Warner: A Biography*, Minerva Press, 1991.
2. Quotations from Sylvia Townsend Warner's diaries and her own last words are from Claire Harman, ibid.
3. Frida Kahlo's birth data are from Hayden Herrara, *Frida: A Biography of Frida Kahlo*, Harper & Row, 1983.

4. Quotations from Frida Kahlo's diaries and letters are from Hayden Herrara, ibid.

CHAPTER 11

1. 'Claire's' chart provided by 'Claire' herself.

SUGGESTED READING LIST AND
GENERAL BIBLIOGRAPHY

SUGGESTED READING LIST

Alchemy

Albertus, Frater, *Alchemist's Handbook*, Samuel Weiser, 1974.
Burckhardt, Titus, *Alchemy*, Element, 1986 (reissue).
Gilchrist, Cherry, *Alchemy: The Great Work*, Aquarian Press, 1984.
Rola, S. K. de, *Alchemy: The Secret Art*, Thames & Hudson, 1973.

Astrology

Greene, L. and H. Sasportas, *The Development of the Personality*, Routledge & Kegan Paul, 1987.
Greene, L. and H. Sasportas, *Dynamics of the Unconscious*, Arkana, 1988.
Greene, L. and H. Sasportas, *The Inner Planets*, Samuel Weiser, 1993.
Valentine, C., *Images of the Psyche*, Element, 1991.

Biography and works

Frida Kahlo and Tina Modotti, exhibition catalogue, Whitechapel Art Gallery, 1982.
Garnett, Richard (ed.), *Sylvia and David: The Townsend Warner–Garnett Letters*, Sinclair-Stevenson, 1994.
Harman, Claire, *Sylvia Townsend Warner: A Biography*, Minerva Press, 1991.
Harman, Clare (ed.), *The Diaries of Sylvia Townsend Warner*, Chatto & Windus, 1994.
Herrara, Hayden, *Frida: A Biography of Frida Kahlo*, Harper & Row, 1983.
Pinney, S., and W. Maxwell (eds.), *Letters by Sylvia Townsend Warner*, Chatto & Windus, 1982.
Warner, Sylvia Townsend, *Collected Poems*, Carcanet, 1982.

Warner, Sylvia Townsend, *Selected Poems*, Carcanet, 1985.
Wolfe, Bertram D., *The Fabulous Life of Diego Rivera*, Stein & Day, 1963.

Mythology

Bachofen, J. J., *Myth, Religion and Mother Right*, Bollingen, 1967.
Davidson, H. R. Ellis, *The Gods and Myths of Northern Europe*, Penguin Books, 1964.
Graves, Robert, *The Greek Myths*, 2 vols., Cassell, 1958.
Guirand, F. (ed.), *New Larousse Encyclopaedia of Mythology*, Hamlyn, 1969.
Lurker, M., *Gods and Symbols of Ancient Egypt*, Thames & Hudson, 1974.
MacCana, P., *Celtic Mythology*, Hamlyn, 1970.

Patriarchy

Alic, Margaret, *Hypatia's Heritage*, Women's Press, 1986.
Eisler, Riane, *The Chalice and the Blade*, Harper & Row, 1987.
Lerner, G., *The Creation of Patriarchy*, 1986.
Ochshorn, J., *The Female Experience and the Nature of the Divine*, Indiana University Press, 1981.

Psychology

Abrams, J. (ed.), *Reclaiming the Inner Child*, Mandala, 1990.
Berry, P., *Fathers and Mothers*, 2nd edn, Spring Publications, 1990.
Brown, Norman O., *Hermes the Thief: The Evolution of a Myth*, Vintage Books, 1969.
Franz, M. L. von, *Puer Aeternus*, Spring Publications, 1970.
Kerenyi, K., *Hermes: The Guide of Souls*, Spring Books, 1976.
Neumann, E., *The Origins and History of Consciousness*, Princeton University Press, 1970.
Neumann, E., *The Child*, Putnam's, 1973.
Viorst, J., *Necessary Losses*, Ballantine, 1986.

GENERAL BIBLIOGRAPHY

Aeschylus, *The Oresteia*, trans. Tony Harrison, Rex Collings, 1982
Apocrypha, The, Oxford University Press, n.d.

Apuleius, *The Golden Ass*, trans. Robert Graves, Penguin Books, 1950.

Aries, P., *Centuries of Childhood*, Cape, 1962.

Arroyo, S., *Astrology, Karma and Transformation*, CRCS Publications, 1978.

Assagioli, R., *Psychosynthesis*, Turnstone Press, 1975.

Assagioli, R., *Transpersonal Development*, Crucible, 1991.

Astour, M., *Hellenosemitica*, E. J. Brill, 1965.

Bell, H. I., *Cults and Creeds of the Graeco-Roman World*, Liverpool University Press, 1953.

Bernal, M., *Black Athena: The Afroasiatic Roots of Classical Civilization*, 2 vols., Free Association Books, 1987.

Bettelheim, Bruno, *A Good Enough Parent*, Alfred A. Knopf, 1987.

Bowlby, J., *Child Care and the Growth of Love*, Penguin Books, 1965.

Boylan, P., *Thoth, the Hermes of Egypt*, Oxford University Press, 1922.

Budge, E. A. Wallis, *The Egyptian Book of the Dead*, Arkana, 1989 (reprint).

Burt, Kathleen, *Archetypes of the Zodiac*, Llewellyn, 1988.

Butler, E. M., *The Myth of the Magus*, Cambridge University Press, 1979.

Caesar, Julius, *De Bello Gallico*, trans. S. A. Handford, Penguin Books, 1951.

Campbell, J., (ed.), *The Mysteries*, Routledge & Kegan Paul, 1955.

Campbell, J., *Oriental Mythology: Masks of God*, Viking Press, 1962.

Campbell, J., *Occidental Mythology: Masks of God*, Viking Press, 1964.

Campbell, J., *Hero with a Thousand Faces*, Princeton University Press, 1968.

Campbell, J., *The Flight of the Wild Gander*, Viking Press, 1969.

Chadwick, N., *The Celts*, Penguin Books, 1970.

Chodorow, Nancy, *The Reproduction of Mothering*, University of California Press, 1978.

Christie-Murray, D., *A History of Heresy*, New English Library, 1976.

Cobb, Noel, *Prospero's Island*, Coventure, 1984.

Coudert, A., *Alchemy: The Philosopher's Stone*, Wildwood House, 1980.

Covitz, J., *Emotional Child Abuse: The Family Curse*, Sigo Press, 1986.

Crossley-Holland, Kevin, *The Norse Myths*, André Deutsch, 1980.

Davidson, H. R. Ellis, *Myths and Symbols in Pagan Europe*, Manchester University Press, 1988.

Dobbs, B., *The Foundations of Newton's Alchemy*, Cambridge University Press, 1975.

Dodds, E. R., *The Greeks and the Irrational*, Cambridge University Press, 1951.

Doresse, J., *The Secret Books of the Egyptian Gnostics*, Viking Press, 1960.

Edwards, Ruth B., *Kadmos the Phoenician: A Study in Greek Legends and the Mycenaean Age*, A. M. Hakkert, 1979.

Eliade, M., *Shamanism*, Princeton University Press, 1964.

Eliade, M., *The Forge and the Crucible: The Origin and Structure of Alchemy*, Harper & Row, 1971.

Erikson, E., *Childhood and Society*, W. W. Norton, 1950.

Erikson, E., *Insight and Responsibility*, W. W. Norton, 1964.

Erman, Adolf, *The Literature of the Ancient Egyptians*, Methuen, 1927.

Fabricius, Johannes, *Alchemy*, Aquarian Press, 1989.

Ferrucci, P., *What We May Be*, Turnstone Press, 1982.

Franz, M. L. von, *Alchemy*, Inner City Books, 1980.

Frazer, Sir James G., *The Golden Bough*, 12 vols., Macmillan, 1922.

Freud, Sigmund, *The Psychopathology of Everyday Life*, Penguin Books, 1975.

Gimbutas, M., *Goddesses and Gods of Old Europe, 7000–3500 BC*, University of California Press, 1982.

Godwin, J., *Mystery Religions of the Ancient World*, Thames & Hudson, 1981.

Goorick-Clark, N. (ed.), *Paracelsus: Essential Readings*, Aquarian Press, 1990.

Gordon, C., *Common Background of Greek and Hebrew Civilization*, W. W. Norton, 1965.

Graves, Robert, *The White Goddess*, Faber & Faber, 1961.

Graves, Robert, and R. Patai, *Hebrew Myths: The Book of Genesis*, McGraw-Hill, 1966 (reissue).

Guggenbuhl-Craig, A., *Eros on Crutches*, Spring Publications, 1980.

Halliday, W. R., *The Pagan Background of Early Christianity*, Hodder & Stoughton, 1925.

Hamilton, B., *The Albigensian Crusade*, Historical Association, 1974.

Hand, Robert, *Planets in Transit*, Whitford Press, 1976.

Harrison, J., *Prolegomena*, Cambridge University Press, 1903.

Harrison J., *Themis*, Cambridge University Press, 1912.

Hart, G., *A Dictionary of Egyptian Gods and Goddesses*, Routledge & Kegan Paul, 1986.

Hawkes, J., *Dawn of the Gods: Minoan and Mycenaean Origins of Greece*, Random House, 1968.

Hesiod, *Theogony*, in *Hesiod and Theognis*, trans. D. Wender, Penguin Books, 1973.

Hermetic Journal, The, ed. A. McLean, issues 1–2, 1978; 23–6, 1984; 31–4, 1986; 1989; 1990; 1991; Oxford.

Herodotus, *The Histories*, ed. E. V. Rieu, Penguin Books, 1954.

Hesiod, *The Homeric Hymns and Homerica*, trans. H. G. Evelyn-White, Heinemann (Loeb Library), 1914.

Hillman, J., *Puer Papers*, Spring Publications, 1979.

Holmyard, E. J., *Alchemy*, Penguin Books, 1957.

Homer, *The Iliad*, Oxford University Press, 1984.

Hubert, Henri, *The History of the Celtic People*, Bracken Books, 1992 (reissue).

Humphreys, S. C., *The Family, Women and Death: A Comparative Study*, Routledge & Kegan Paul, 1983.

Iamblichus, *On the Mysteries*, trans. T. Taylor, San Diego, 1984.

Jonas, H. (ed.), *The Gnostic Religion*, rev. edn, Beacon Press, 1963.

Jones, G., *A History of the Vikings*, Oxford University Press, 1968.

Jonson, Ben, *The Alchemist*, Methuen, 1958.

Jung, C., *Psychology and Alchemy*, Routledge & Kegan Paul, 1953.

Jung, C., *Aion*, Routledge & Kegan Paul, 1959.

Jung, C., *Alchemical Studies*, Routledge & Kegan Paul, 1968.

Jung, C., *Four Archetypes*, Routledge & Kegan Paul, 1972.

Kerenyi, K., *The Gods of the Greeks*, Thames & Hudson, 1951.

Kerenyi, K., *Asklepios: Archetypal Image of the Physician's Existence*, Pantheon, 1959.

Kerenyi, K., *Apollo: The Wind, the Spirit and the Gods*, Spring Publications, 1983.

Kirk, G. S., *Myth: Its Meaning and Function in Ancient and Other Cultures*, Cambridge University Press, 1970.

Kirk, G. S., *The Nature of Greek Myths*, Penguin Books, 1974.

Kirsteller, P. O., *The Philosophy of Marsilio Ficino*, Columbia University Press, 1943.

Kitto, H. D. F., *The Greeks*, Penguin Books, 1951.

Klein, Melanie, *Envy and Gratitude and Other Works, 1946–1963*, Hogarth Press, 1975.

Lacarrière, J., *The Gnostics*, Peter Owen, 1977.

Lambert, M. D., *Medieval Heresy*, Edward Arnold, 1977.

Lindsay, J., *The Origins of Alchemy in Graeco-Roman Egypt*, Frederick Muller, 1976.

Lopez-Pedraza, R., *Hermes and His Children*, Spring Publications, 1977.

Lowen, A., *Narcissism: Denial of the True Self*, Macmillan, 1983.

Luke, Helen M., *Kaleidoscope*, Parabola Books, 1992.

Mabinogion, The, trans. Lady Charlotte Guest, John Jones, 1977 (reissue).

Markale, J., *Celtic Civilization*, Gordon & Cremonesi, 1978.

Markale, J., *Women of the Celts*, Inner Traditions, 1986.

Matthews, C. and J., *The Western Way*, 2 vols., Arkana, 1986.

Mead, G. R. S., *The Hymns of Hermes*, Theosophical Publishing Society, 1907.

Mead, G. R. S., *Thrice Greatest Hermes*, 2nd edn, Watkins, 1964.

Miller, A., *Drama of the Gifted Child*, Basic Books, 1981.

Milner, M., *The Suppressed Madness of Sane Men*, Tavistock Publications, 1987.

Montessori, M., *The Child in the Family*, Aron Books, 1970.

Needleman, J. (ed.), *Sword of Gnosis*, Penguin Books, 1964.

Nieman, H., and J. Cooper, *Astrology/Psychology*, American Federation of Astrologers, 1986.

Nock, A. D., *Conversion: The Old and New in Religion from Alexander the Great to Augustine of Hippo*, Oxford University Press, 1933.

Onians, R. B., *The Origins of European Thought*, Cambridge University Press, 1954.

Otto, E., *Egyptian Arts and Cults of Osiris and Amon*, Thames & Hudson, 1967.

Otto, W., *The Homeric Gods*, Thames & Hudson, 1979.

Osherson, S. O., *Finding Our Fathers*, Ballantine Books, 1986.

Ovid, *Metamorphoses*, trans. F. J. Miller, Heinemann (Loeb Library), 1916.

Pagels, E., *The Gnostic Gospels*, Random House, 1979.

Paris, G., *Pagan Greece*, Spring Publications, 1990.

Parry-Jones, D., *Welsh Legends and Fairy Lore*, Batsford, 1953.

Pausanius, *Guide to Greece*, trans. P. Levi, 2 vols., Penguin Books, 1954.

Pearce, J. C., *Magical Child*, Bantam Books, 1986.

Piaget, J., *The Construction of Reality in the Child*, Basic Books, 1954.

Pirani, A., *The Absent Father: Crisis and Creativity*, Arkana, 1989.

Plotinus, *The Enneads*, trans. S. McKenna, Penguin Books, 1991.

Pomeroy, S. B., *Goddesses, Whores, Wives and Slaves: Women in Classical Antiquity*, Schocken Books, 1975.

Powell, N., *Alchemy: The Ancient Science*, Aldus Books, 1976.

Quispel, G., *Secret Book of Revelations*, Collins, 1979.

Radin, P., *The Trickster: A Study in American Indian Mythology*, Schocken Books, 1972.

Redgrove, H. S., *Alchemy Ancient and Modern*, Penguin Books, 1973 (reissue).

Rees, A. and B., *Celtic Heritage: Ancient Tradition in Ireland and Wales*, Thames & Hudson, 1961.

Rosenblum, B., *The Astrologer's Guide to Counselling*, CRCS Publications, 1983.

Rubin, T., *Compassion and Self-hate*, Macmillan, 1975.

Runciman, Steven, *The Medieval Manichees*, Cambridge University Press, 1960.

Sakoian, F., and L. S. Acker, *The Astrologer's Handbook*, Penguin Books, 1981.

Samuels, A., *The Religious Quests of the Graeco-Roman World*, John Murray, 1929.

Samuels, A. (ed.), *The Father: Contemporary Jungian Perspectives*, New York University Press, 1985.

Schermer, B., *Astrology Alive*, Aquarian, 1989.

Scott, W., and A. S. Ferguson (eds.) *Hermetica*, 4 vols., Clarendon Press, 1924–36.

Secret of the Golden Flower, The, trans. R. Wilhelm, Arkana, 1984 (reissue).

Seltman, C., *Women in Antiquity*, Thames & Hudson, 1936.

Seltman, C., *The Twelve Olympians*, Pan, 1952.

Singer, J., *Boundaries of the Soul*, Doubleday, 1972.

Singer, J., *Androgyny*, Anchor Books, 1977.

Snorri Sturluson, *The Prose Edda*, trans. J. I. Young, Cambridge University Press, 1954.

Spence, Lewis, *Myths of Ancient Egypt*, Harrap, 1922.

Splendor Solis, notes by 'J. K.', Kegan Paul, Trench, Trübner, n.d.

Squire, C., *Celtic Myth and Legend*, Newcastle Publishing Co., 1975.

Stanford, W. B., *Greek Tragedy and the Emotions*, Routledge & Kegan Paul, 1983.

Tabori, P., *Secret and Forbidden*, New English Library, 1969.

Tacitus, *Germania*, trans. H. Mattingly, Penguin Books, 1948.

Tompkins, S., *Aspects in Astrology*, Element, 1989.

Toynbee, A. J., *Greek Civilization and Character*, Mentor, 1953.

Turville-Petre, E. O. G., *Myth and Religion of the North*, Weidenfeld & Nicolson, 1964.

Versluis, A., *The Egyptian Mysteries*, Arkana, 1986.

Waite, A. E., (ed.), *The Hermetic Museum*, Robinson & Watkins, 1973.

Wakefield, W. L., *Heresy, Crusade and Inquisition in Southern France, 1100–1250*, Allen & Unwin, 1974.

Walker, B., *Gnosticism*, Aquarian Press, 1983.

Wallis, R. T., and J. Bregman, *Neoplatonism and Gnosticism*, State University of New York Press, 1992.

Wehr, G., *The Mystical Marriage*, Aquarian Press, 1990.

Wickes, F. G., *The Inner World of Childhood*, Appleton Century Crofts, 1927.

Winnicott, D. W., *The Child, the Family and the Outside World*, Penguin Books, 1964.

Wood, Michael, *In Search of the Dark Ages*, Ariel, 1981.

Yamauchi, E: M., *Pre-Christian Gnosticism*, Tyndale Press, 1973.

Yates, F., *Giordano Bruno and the Hermetic Tradition*, Routledge & Kegan Paul, 1964.

Yates, F., *The Art of Memory*, Routledge & Kegan Paul, 1966.

Yates, F., *The Rosicrucian Enlightenment*, Routledge & Kegan Paul, 1972.

Yates, F., *Ideas and Ideals in the North European Renaissance*, Routledge & Kegan Paul, 1984.

INDEX

Fir Bolgs, 126
Flamel, Nicolas, 140
Freud, Sigmund, 141, 144
Frigg (Frija), 61

Gaia, 172, 174
garden of Eden, 119
Gemini:
  and child's approach to new
    situations, 7
  indecision, 118
  and knowledge in the metaphysical
    field, 109
  linking mind to body functions and
    awareness, 95
  Mercury rules, xi, 19, 42, 138, 192
  and organizing ability, 38–9
  putting pieces together, 115, 125
  staff and snake attributes, 112
  Sun in, 19
gnosticism, 11, 12, 14, 15–16, 17, 30,
  58, 127, 130–33, 247
go-betweens, 102–4
Gorgons, the, 99–100, 101, 148
Graves, Robert, 11, 15, 115
Great Goddess, 20, 64, 97
Great Work, the, 133, 134–7, 207
Greek Myths, The (Graves), 11
Greene, Liz, ix
growth of a god, 3–18; developmental
  psychology, 4–11; mythology and
  history, 11–15; patriarchy and
  cultural change, 15–18
Gwyn ap Nudd, 126

Hades, 10, 18, 65, 74, 84–90, 97, 98,
  108, 109, 114, 115, 116, 138, 145, 146,
  148, 152, 177, 178, 179, 201, 202, 203,
  225, 248, 269, 270
Hall of the Dead, 95
Halls of Judgement, 199
healer gods, 105–28; boundaries and
  ethics, 108–10; connection and cure,
  105–8; nurturance as well as pain,
  120–23; the threshold of

consciousness, 123–8; a willingness to
  change, 118–20; *see also* healing
healing: attributes of, 110–12; Hermes
  and, 73–4, 83, 109, 110, 112, 113, 114;
  the initiation of the healer, 112–13;
  Mercury and, 17, 18, 105; the paradox
  of, 114–18; and the sixth house, 105;
  and Virgo, 105
healing cults/rights, 122, 127
Hecate, 18, 51, 97, 98, 145, 147
Hector, 102, 117, 163
heiros gamos, 140
Hel, 81
Helen of Troy, 189
Hendrix, Jimi, 249
Hephaistos, 49, 139, 165, 167
Hera, 22, 29, 67, 93, 117, 120, 148, 189,
  193, 205, 206
Heracles, 88, 89, 90, 147, 148, 149, 152,
  187, 188, 197
Herm, the, 64–5
Hermanubis, 95
hermaphroditic state, 53
Hermaphroditos, 52–3, 62, 140, 141, 146,
  165
Hermapolis, 95
Hermes:
  acquisitiveness, 86–7
  and alchemy, 25, 75, 82, 83, 133, 134,
    136–7, 138–9
  androgyny, 64
  and Asklepios, 104, 106, 110, 112, 124
  and astronomy, 39, 75, 78
  birth, 20, 22
  and boxing and gymnastics, 28, 73,
    75
  and Caduceus, 65, 73, 95, 104, 110,
    111
  and the collective, 115, 120
  and conscious/unconscious
    connections, 74
  and death, 97, 102, 110, 114, 152, 220
  deceives himself and others, 23–4
  and denial of pain, 66–7
  and Dionysos, 120